virtual water

virtual water

tackling the threat to our
planet's most precious resource

TONY ALLAN

I.B. TAURIS

Published in 2011 by I.B.Tauris & Co. Ltd
6 Salem Road, London W2 4BU
175 Fifth Avenue, New York NY 10010
www.ibtauris.com

Distributed in the United States and Canada exclusively by Palgrave Macmillan
175 Fifth Avenue, New York NY 10010

ISBN:
978 1 84511 984 3 paperback
978 1 84511 983 6 hardback

A full CIP record for this book is available from the British Library
A full CIP record is available from the Library of Congress

Library of Congress Catalog Card Number: available

Designed and typeset by Angela Morelli, London, UK

Printed and bound in Great Britain by CPI Antony Rowe, Chippenham, Wilts

Contents

I dedicate this book to Murray Watson, in recognition of his inspired contribution to ecological sciences and the monitoring and evaluation of the natural resources of Africa and South-east Asia. And for touching so many with his unforgettable integrity and commitment.

And to Mary – who continues to remind me that people do not like being written about.

Preface

Halfway through the past half century a few wise folk
realised that we could no longer do wrong and stupid
things to the water environment. We needed to start
doing the right things – even if they could only be done a
little badly. Rapid increases in the global population, in
industrialisation, urbanisation and privatisation, together
placed immense strains on local water resources. The
dangerous consequences of farmers being tempted to pull
more and more water out of limited local water environments became painfully evident. The inappropriate
production of crops that love to grow at temperatures
at which we humans need expensive air conditioning
devastated vast tracts of land. We dried up one of the
biggest inland seas in the world in Central Asia, at least
one major river in the US and another one in China.
Capitalism and communism proved to have the same self-
destructive tendencies.

Environmental activists were the first to spot that
societies had been doing too many wrong things spectacularly well. The global atmosphere on which we all depend
had been heated and polluted, so that climate changed.
Surface water resources and groundwater had been over-
pumped and polluted locally. Damaged water-resource
hotspots became evident. Each local crisis reinforced the
paradox that the most water-scarce regions were actually

'exporting' water – in the form of the water embedded in water-intensive crops – to regions that were much better endowed with water.

Between 1800 and the 1970s politicians liked the things that engineers had done for them. Engineers had shown that it was possible to banish discomfort, ill-health and reduce social strife. But by the 1970s water engineers found themselves having to catch up with new ideas on the value of water. Urgent problems associated with massive environmental uncertainties could no longer be automatically remedied by concrete infrastructures. The voice given to the environment changed the discourse.

This book acknowledges the massive contribution of the hydraulic mission. But the main purpose is to draw attention to two of the very important agents who will in future determine whether or not the population of the world will be water secure. The first is the farmer. The second is ourselves – the consumers of food. Farmers, by deploying a lot of inputs wisely – or not – determine whether they get high crop yields that use water effectively. We consumers, and our food choices, at the other end of the supply chain determine how much water is diverted into crop and livestock production. Our food preferences, our tendencies to waste food, our increasing longevity and our other demographic tendencies, determine the demands made on the water environment.

The aim of this book is to get both food consumers and farmers to grasp their role in future global water security. Other agents in the food supply chain – the food commodity traders, the food processing and retailing corporations – are also important target audiences. As are the governments of over-powerful economies that distort global trade.

Currently, and increasingly in future global financial markets, sovereign wealth funds will determine global water and food security and whether it has been achieved by sustainably intensive means.

The concept of virtual-water 'trade' and water footprints will be used to explore the food supply chain and trade relations. It will be shown that global commodity production and trade enable local water security. The concept of virtual water, coined in the early 1990s, has had to live with the anger that its revelations sparked. Governments and societies existing in blissful apparent water security made possible by virtual-water 'trade', easily constructed arguments that resisted its adoption. Two decades on they can still drown the idea if it distresses their citizens. But it is now commonplace for virtual water to have a prominent place in any analysis of water security. And understanding the vital role that virtual water plays in global water security will help consumers, their governments and corporations to make the choices that will secure livelihoods, societies – and the future of our planet.

The water-footprint statistics used in the book should be regarded as first approximations. They have been developed by Arjen Hoekstra and his network of researchers. New approaches, heroic assumptions and reliance on global datasets have been unavoidable. More accurate numbers based on more precise methods are being developed at the national and sub-national levels.

Acknowledgements

Books get written despite. Despite competing time demands. Despite the impossibility of distilling complexity. And especially despite the problem of writing convincing prose that simplifies the distilled complexity that the reader wants. This book exists because a number of good people had faith and wanted to see distilled complexity.

David Stonestreet has been a committed and supportive publisher throughout. He also recruited two wonderful professionals to enhance the project. Michael Flexer fixed the language register and Angela Morelli designed the graphics and the book.

My past two decades of almost five in science have been the best of all. Somehow one has been able to focus on water-resource issues and stop dabbling elsewhere. It has been fun to spot a number of ideas that thousands of other scientists and millions of engineers in the water sector have not. It has been a uniquely pleasant experience to watch the ideas gain currency without them being captured or devalued – yet. One or two are original. Others are the result of the amiability of the water professional community and of the synergies they generate. I feel privileged to have had the chance to engage with great hydrogeologists such as Mike Edmunds, Alan MacDonald, Richard Taylor and Ramon Llamas. And with deeply cerebral hydrologists such as Malin Falkenmark. Also with prominent water engineers, enriched by the ideas of economics, such as Peter Rogers and John Briscoe, and especially Jack Keller. Jack came up after a short presentation to tell me that I had just conceptualised his fifty-year career in water science and policy. Bless him: he also liked the idea of virtual water. Dipak Gywali is another exceptional engineer. In his case, one who has journeyed far and wide in the terrain of social theory to the great benefit of international water science. Munther Haddadin has been a very special friend, engineer and ally in promoting the concept of shadow water, which he coined – also in the early 1990s. Munther has hugely promoted the concepts in the Middle East, where they are especially relevant. I have also greatly profited from the abrasive, sometimes patronising, rigour of economist friends. They are not comfortable that a non-economist identified and developed the idea of virtual water and they concede it only a tiny place in the economics firmament. I thank very warmly Steve Merrett, Jeremy Berkoff, Dennis Wichelns, Alberto Garrido and Chris Perry – who is as much a water scientist as an economist. All have helped tether the idea. I have discovered one cannot speak to enough farmers if one wants to understand the effective consumptive use of water. My access to the importance of the role of farming and farmers and the need to speak to more of them has come from my friends Brian and Lynne Chatterton.

As I have indicated, water-resource scientists are very amiable and helpful people. My most helpful ally in water science has been Arjen Hoekstra. I knew of his capacity to work across science boundaries, and when a decade ago he emailed to ask me where I had first published the concept of virtual water, I realised that he was taking the idea seriously. In the ten years since, it has been a very special experience to observe and occasionally participate in his development of our understanding of virtual-water 'trade' and of water footprints. Modelling requires great courage as well as competence. He has deployed these qualities and nurtured them in his group in IHE Delft and now at Twente University. It included Ashok Chapagain and Maite Aldya and many others. Their contributions have always been internationally significant. I have also appreciated the chance to share and develop ideas with scientists in SIWI, a number of whom spent time in London at key moments in the journey of the virtual-water concept. Jan Lundquist is a wonderful colleague, and it has also been a privilege to share time and ideas with Anders Jakerskog and Anton Earle. The inspiration of Malin Falkenmark has been seminal and enduring. Her concept of green water has been of profound importance and has proved to be entirely compatible with that of virtual water. Ana Cascao has joined SIWI in Stockholm and is one of a number of SIWI researchers who have been based for periods in London. They and many others have all helped to sustain the intellectual energy of the research group. In this connection I would like to thank Steve Brïchieri-Colombi, Mark Zeitoun and Naho Mirumachi and a number of other researchers based at SOAS and King's College London who have made significant contributions to the development of the virtual-water concept in their studies – mainly relating to Middle Eastern political economies. They include Chris Handley, Gerhard Lichtenthaler, Elie Elhadj and Michael Talhami. Other associates of the London Water Research Group, David Phillips and Fuad Buteh, have also made important contributions. I enjoy relating to all the current generation devoting precious years to water science and policy. They are just as original and just as good as those who have gone before.

I am also grateful to some outstanding individuals who have crossed my path in a number of international agencies and NGOs. David Grey has been an important sounding board for over twenty years at the World Bank. More recently, Julia Bucknall, also at the World Bank, has given the concept of virtual water oxygen. I have also appreciated the chance to exchange ideas with Pasquale Steduto at the FAO in Rome. Charlotte de Fraiture and David Molden, scientists at IWMI, have also very usefully critiqued the idea. It has been a special privilege to have the inspired cooperation of Stuart Orr and David Tickner, at WWF, and Joanne Zygmunt at Waterwise. WWF has also been very important in getting the agri-trade corporations to focus on the importance of embedded water. The recent interest of the private-sector corporations has been impressive in opening up the discourse on water

security. It has been a new and unexpected pleasure to listen to the much better dressed from the global corporations, mobilising the concepts of virtual water and water footprints with effortless and persuasive prose. Andy Wales of S.B. Miller makes particularly fluent contributions, while Peter Brabeck Letmathe, CEO of Nestlé, and Paul Polman, CEO of Unilever, have, through their status and commitment, lifted the water-security agenda very significantly. Two other friends in the private sector have been endlessly useful and critical – Jack Moss of Aquafed and Joppe Cramwinckel of the World Business Council for Sustainable Development. The important water, food and trade nexus idea, and the bigger water/energy nexus, have been additionally energised by discussions at the World Economic Forum, where Dominic Waughray, Arjun Thapan and Maggie Catley-Carlsson have been important allies, as have all the members of the WEF Water Advisory Council. I have been fortunate in the quality of my relationship with two London colleges – SOAS and King's College. They have employed and indulged me for nearly four decades. Both have continued to be generous since my retirement. They are great institutions, populated by exceptional people, and I am very grateful that they have allowed me to be around long enough to enhance them a little with my recent work.

Two friends in science stand out. The first is Tony Turton, who joined the London Water Research Group in 1999. For six months he devoted his considerable intellectual energy and his extraordinary emotional reach to helping develop the ideas then in currency. From his numerous professional positions in Pretoria he has remained a priceless source of advice and insight. The second is Murray Watson. Exceptional people cross one's path only a few times in a lifetime. Murray Watson is one. He is a scientist, professional and entrepreneur of exceptional energy. On countless occasions he has passed judgement on one's ideas. When he thought they were good, one felt relieved that they would pass muster in other arenas. He was kidnapped in Somalia on 2 April 2008 and has not been heard from since. The gap is elemental for many of us. I wish so much that I could have his opinion on what follows.

xv

CHAPTER 1

Getting wise about water

This book will shock you into thinking about water in new ways. Put simply, we human beings don't understand the true value of water, and we are at a point in our relationship with nature's vast but limited water resources where we simply cannot afford to stay ignorant. Already, our over-consumption and mismanagement of water has had a very serious impact on our water environments and the essential services they provide.

Our ignorance is immense. Most of us don't have the slightest idea about the sheer volumes of water involved in our daily lives. At the start of the twentieth century, with a global population of one billion, this ignorance simply did not matter. The ratio of water to people was so massive that it was as if our water supply was infinite. But it is not. And now, with a global population pushing seven billion, water scarcity is not just a possibility. It is already a reality for many.

Our imagination allows us to understand water scarcity in far-off places. We can picture the arid desert, the drought-cracked soil and treacherous dirty water supplies reported in news footage and charity appeals. Water scarcity belongs in the world of famine, cholera and five-hour treks to the nearest reliable well. In the industrialised world, where clean water is forever available at the simple turn of the tap or twist of a bottle top, we can't conceive of the possibility of its absence. The hydrological and eco-nomic processes that make this possible are an invisible hand, operating outside the scope of our daily concerns. But this hand is faltering.

How much water do you have for breakfast?

We are addicted to over-consuming water, and we don't know it

It's an easy question: how much water do you have for breakfast? You might think you have none. Then you might remember that, of course, there is water in your tea or cof-fee. And your milk. Isn't there, technically, some water in that? So, you're having at least 300–400 millilitres. Right?

2

Let's look a little closer. Take a normal – if slightly indulgent – breakfast in the US or UK. There is a cup of tea or coffee, a slice or two of toast, perhaps bacon and eggs, maybe a glass of milk, and possibly a little fruit as a nod to health and a leaner waistline. Now, what is that in water terms? Let's start with coffee. Well, you might say, I like my coffee strong. There's barely any water in there at all. Maybe...But what if I told you that in your tiny espresso there is 140 litres of water. Yes – 140 litres. You might think I was slightly deranged. But that is the *virtual water* hidden in the coffee. That is the amount of water used in growing, producing, packaging and shipping the beans that make the coffee. Here is a simple example of what we mean by something's cost in virtual water. It is, I am sure you will agree, rather a lot more water than you first thought. But it is just the tip of your breakfast's virtual-water iceberg.

There's the toast. Forty litres of water are expended to bring that toast to your table. Per slice. That is the cost in water of making, transporting and finally toasting. An apple is 70 litres. The eggs are 120 litres. Throw in a glass of milk at 240 litres. And then there is the bacon, at 480 litres for one portion. In all, this full English breakfast has cost about 1100 litres. That's a little over a cubic metre of water. If you find it hard to imagine a cubic metre of water, imagine a full bathtub. Now imagine three baths. Full. That is the cost of your breakfast in water.

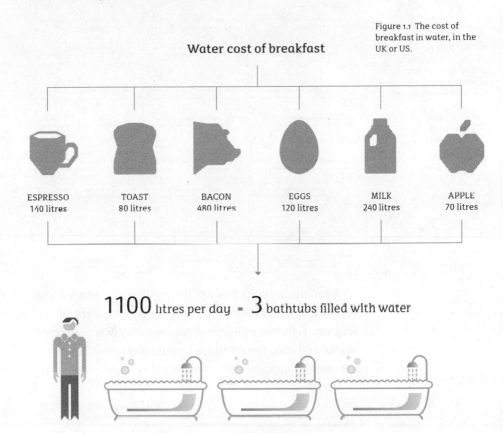

Water cost of breakfast

Figure 1.1 The cost of breakfast in water, in the UK or US.

ESPRESSO	TOAST	BACON	EGGS	MILK	APPLE
140 litres	80 litres	480 litres	120 litres	240 litres	70 litres

1100 litres per day = **3** bathtubs filled with water

Of those three baths, over two-thirds of that water goes towards making the animal products – the milk, the eggs and the bacon. The meat non-vegetarians eat is the biggest single source of water consumption in their life. The average non-vegetarian diet in the US or Europe consumes about 5 cubic metres of water each day. That is 15 bathtubs, each and every day, consumed just to keep one person fed and watered.

Figure 1.2 Daily water consumption of a non-vegetarian diet: 5000 litres of water per day, namely 15 bathtubs filled with water.

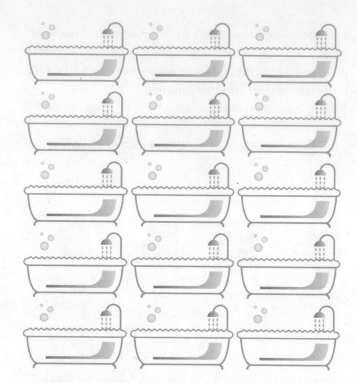

Vegetarians can consider themselves a bit more frugal on water consumption; they only need eight bathtubs per day. Consider the millions of people living in the Western world, and consider all those bathtubs of water. It is a colossal figure.

Figure 1.3 Daily water consumption of a vegetarian diet: 2700 litres of water per day, namely 8 bathtubs filled with water.

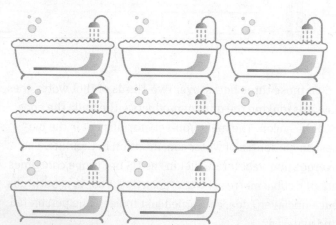

That's the industrialised nations, but what about the emerging BRICS economies? Let's look at what is for breakfast in India, a fast-growing economy and the 'I' in BRICS. For the vegetarian, breakfast will be grains, vegetables and vegetable oil. In Southern India, you might wake up to idlis, vadas, dosas, salty pongal, rounded off with some hot sambar and at least one variety of chutney. In all, this only costs about 300 litres of water. In China, breakfasts are slightly more indulgent and more likely to contain meat, as well as bread, noodles and porridge. They average 600 litres. Brazilians love their meat for breakfast, and so their breakfast costs as much as, if not more than, the average Western breakfast in water terms.

The other 160 or so countries in the world range from the very wealthy Arab oil nations to the extremely poor states of sub-Saharan Africa. In the Middle East, discounting the oil-rich countries, meat is rarely the cornerstone of the diet, as it is in the industrialised world. There, the average person requires a half to two-thirds of the amount of water each day consumed by the average person in the US and Europe. Throughout this book, we'll find that money and water (nearly) always flow in the same direction.

By now, you might be getting a sense of the amount of water you consume in the course of a year. If you are a meat-eater in the US or Europe reading this book, to get a rough sense of your water usage each year, imagine a house. A nice big three-storey house. With three spacious rooms on each floor. It's 10 metres deep and 10 metres wide. It's a large, generous-sized house, a family home. Fill it with water until every last room and corridor is bulging. Until the windows are rattling under the pressure and the whole thing looks as though it might suddenly explode. That is the amount of water you are using each year. Of course, you are *drinking* only a tiny fraction of that. A large wardrobe should slake the thirst of all but the most avid water-quaffer. Those other times when we

5

BRIC(S) AND WATER
Though well established in the discourses of economics, geopolitics and academia, the acronym BRICS may be unfamiliar to many. It stands for Brazil, Russia, India, China and sometimes South Africa. Occasionally, we see BRIICS, which is the same but with the addition of Indonesia. These economies are singled out as not fitting the model of either the industrialised nations of the Northern Hemisphere – plus Australia and New Zealand – or the less industrialised, developing nations of the South. We'll be returning to them throughout this book. Their importance both to virtual water and the world in general cannot be overplayed. It's no exaggeration, though an appalling piece of punning, to claim that BRICS are what will keep the global house standing in the future.

are clearly, consciously and directly using water – the baths, showers, cooking, washing up, cleaning clothes, toilet visits – account for a little more, perhaps a roomful. All the non-food commodities we buy account for another roomful. And the rest, amazingly, is food. It can't be reiterated enough: *most of the water you use comes through your food consumption*. Forget bricks in the toilet cistern: going vegetarian would save many lifetimes of toilet trips. Luckily, in the US and Europe, our jobs are pretty water-friendly. Service-sector salaries between $30,000 and $150,000 represent quite spectacular returns on only a couple of wardrobes of water. It is no coincidence that we in the developed world have managed to squeeze the greatest incomes from the smallest quantities of water. We might even put that forward as a definition of a wealthy industrialised nation: one that has maximised the financial returns per cubic litre.

6

Water is for life...not just for drinking

Water is one of the key components of life. Without it, we would be dead very very quickly indeed. All living things need water: it is the main building-block of the living cell. Water is also the basic ingredient of all bodily fluids: it flows in the vessels of our body and accounts for over 70 per cent of our bulk. Without it, we wouldn't be able to move nutrients around our body. Internally, we would pretty swiftly become a dried-up riverbed, with fish, boats and discarded boots sitting motionless in the mud. As should be becoming clear, water is also vital to food production. Food is essentially the result of nature's highly evolved integration of air, water and energy into vegetation. If we human beings are perched at the top of the food chain, then water is down at the bottom, making every last bite and gulp we take possible. If the bottom wobbles, the top falls.

Mother Nature is – like all good mothers – a bit extravagant and overindulgent to us children. When it comes to water, we have a superabundance. Seventy per cent of the world's surface is covered with the stuff. But most of it – 97.5 per cent – is salty and of very limited use to us. Of the remaining 2.5 per cent, only a small fraction is actually of sufficient quality to be used by the world's plants and animals. So much for mother's love, you might think.

Figure 1.4 Plenty of water but not as much as you might think.

Saltwater: 97.5%

Freshwater: 2.5%

Available for use: 0.1%

Each year, about 110,000 cubic kilometres of rainfall drops on the earth: that is a one-metre-thick blanket of water wrapped around the entire planet each and every year. Of this global freshwater, just over half evaporates or is transpired by vegetation and crops. Another 36 per cent ends up in our streams, rivers and lakes, and ultimately in the oceans. We humans now only make use of 6.5 per cent of rainwater.

As we clear away natural vegetation and redesignate land for crop growth, so too are we diverting water from nature and introducing it into our human economy. Yet somehow, while economists have been happily integrating land and raw materials into their theoretical factors of production, water has fallen outside their calculations. In this book, we are going to discover why that has to change. Water is already an invisible, potent force in the global economy, perhaps an over-riding force. Although, as we shall see, locally, even its near-complete absence can be mitigated. Just as our land-centric attitude enables us to name a planet predominantly covered in water Earth, so too we manage to remain wilfully blind to the pivotal role of water in our world economy. How do we manage this collective perceptual fraud? What is the explanation?

8

The answer perhaps lies in the history of our relationship with water.

A brief history of water use

Water scarcity has not been a problem. Until very recently in our history, our tendency to die early and reproduce poorly has kept global population below the one billion threshold. There were fewer of us and, in our pre-industrial state, we were using far far less water, about 1000 cubic kilometres a year worldwide, a fraction of 1 per cent of the freshwater available.

It has taken us most of our evolutionary journey to learn how to exploit water. First, we needed to come down out of the trees, which we did around seven million years ago. It was another five million years before we resembled current humans. But it was only in the Neolithic period, around 11,000BCE, that we developed arable farming. So was born virtual water. Until then, we only directly saw the water we used because we were either drinking tiny amounts of it or washing with very small amounts. By 10,000 years ago we were unwittingly diverting it via cultivation and embedding it in our food.

Like many fundamental behavioural seismic shifts, this one's significance with respect to water was not noticed at the time. Only with considerable historical distance can we see the importance of that change. It was another two millennia before we managed to domesticate animals. Until that time, we had to rely on two basic energy sources: fire and us. Now we had a slave race of animals: horses and cattle became our main energy force. They moved us and our goods around. They tilled our land. Those that didn't serve us fed us. And then, only two hundred years ago, a movement by turns economic, social, political and technological, definitively revolutionised our energy supply. Very recently, in the middle of the twentieth century – in the space of a few decades – most of North America and Europe was freed from a reliance on animals to farm and produce food, or to help produce goods and services or move them around.

Until this industrialising moment in our very recent history, for nearly seven million years we had not really learnt how to pollute. We were too few, too spread out, and aside from some low-level killing of flora and fauna we had yet to make our mark on the planet. From water's perspective, it was as if we didn't exist. The water system could absorb our levels of pollution and happily carry on, entirely unchanged. Amazingly, it has only been in the past couple of decades that people in the industrialised economies have listened to calls for stewardship of the water environment. There is a widening awareness that our industrial methods of exploiting our water environments come with serious costs that are not internalised in the prices we pay for water-intensive goods and services.

iPods, aeroplanes and water

We human beings are users. I don't mean that pejoratively. It is our great skill, which has enabled us to gain dominance (mostly) over this planet and all the other species.

9

WHAT'S IN A NAME?
What do Elton John, Bob Dylan, Marilyn Monroe and Virtual Water all have in common? They all needed a name-change to get noticed. I first began talking about 'embedded' water in 1988, but the concept seemed to have little or no impact. It was only a chance remark at an evening workshop in London in 1992 that led to the coining of the term 'virtual water'. A rose by any other name would certainly not smell as sweet from my experience. Perhaps it was the fashionable resonance of the word virtual in the digital-obsessed 1990s, but the concept took off very rapidly. Curious, not least us 'embedded' seems a more accurate and informative moniker than the ambiguous and nebulous 'virtual'. Yet the term stuck, and is now familiar to every water minister in the world. Goodbye Norma Jean…

We are capable of and comfortable using complex technology intuitively and without an understanding of how it works. It's the same with our own brains and the rest of our physiology. We do not understand them. But we use them. We are natural users and exploiters. I cheerfully listen to digitised music on my ergonomic iPhone, leaning back in the electronically reclining seat while travelling at biologically incoherent speeds and heights over the Atlantic; this troubles me little. I interact with the interface only. Mine, the shiny simple world of the iPhone touch screen and the duty-free magazine. Thinking about binary code, creating a flash hard drive, airbrakes and the angle of incidence would only confuse. And alarm.

So too with water.

We see the rain fall, the rivers flow, the waves surge. We find the arrival of water through our taps wholly unremarkable. We think little of what water gets up to between the cloud and the glass. Dredging our memories, we might recall classroom lessons on the water cycle – half-forgotten notes with large blue arrows charting water's progression through the soil. We might even remember the concept of evapo-transpiration, though we probably only hold a very woolly definition in our heads: plants return water to the atmosphere somehow. We don't view this knowledge as essential. Its best purpose seems to be to gloss impressively a TV documentary for our friends and family, or to nail the tricky geography question in a game of Trivial Pursuit. We don't consider this knowledge as an important context for our daily, indeed hourly, water use. We are very wrong indeed.

At the start of the industrialised age we knew only four big things about water: rain falls; streams and rivers flow; seasonally moist soil can raise crops; oceans are salty and not good for drinking. As our intellectual curiosity grew, driven by the resource-hunger of industry, we learnt more about water. We discovered that shallow-depth wells were

10

EVAPORATION OR EVAPO-TRANSPIRATION?
Both are routes by which water is returned into the atmosphere. Evaporation is from water surfaces, evapo-transpiration from vegetation and crops.

A SEAT AT THE WATER TABLE
The water table is the subterranean level of soil or rock that is saturated with water. Beneath the water table, every gap or space is full of water. Almost every gap. There is a little bit of air down there too.

just a taster of the vast subterranean water waiting to be exploited by our newly invented drills and pumps.

What comes down must go up

Pulling itself up by its bootstraps...
Water systems operate vertically, globally and regionally, over both land and water. Water vapour condenses in the atmosphere until gravity can get its ever-greedy paws on it. Then it falls. But gravity doesn't stop there. On land, it pulls the water through the soil and – if there is enough water – down into the subsoil, adding to the reserves of fresh groundwater deep underground.

11

But water also goes up. If it didn't, we would have a very big problem indeed. And here is where we get to the important, complex and occasionally mysterious processes of water that take place behind the scenes.

In the first instance, water likes going up. It wants to rise. Pour yourself a glass of water and look at it through a magnifying glass. Where the water touches the sides, you should be able to see it rising up slightly, as though trying to climb out of the glass. That is in fact what it is doing. In tightly packed soil, this tendency to rise – called capillary rise – is far more significant. Water can move vertically upwards through some soil by more than a metre. But that's pretty small potatoes compared to the strongest pump in the world.

The strongest pump in the world...
What is the world's mightiest pump? You might think of the great engineering achievements of imperial Britain and Brunel. Or perhaps major American civil works, moving water from one river basin to another. Or possibly some incredibly clever Japanese technology, compact and potent. You would be looking in the wrong place. Very likely, you are within walking distance of several of these

powerful pumps. Nature left them lying around all over the place. They are called trees.

Some trees have the capacity to exert forces equivalent to pumping water upwards over 200 metres. As a point of comparison, no human-designed technology can pump at even a significant fraction of the strength exerted by a forest. It is a phenomenal and vital natural technology system. And, naturally, we take it entirely for granted. Natural vegetation systems are able to divert and move water in volumes and over distances that engineers can only marvel at. As we will find as we explore the idea of virtual water, economic systems can do this as well. Importantly, both the natural and economic hydraulic capacities are invisible. They are not of our control or our design, but they are known. Now we need to understand them.

Backseat drivers

Science has made it abundantly clear. We are not drivers on this planet. We are passengers. And it would be a good idea if we stopped carping at the driver, kicking the back of their seat and nudging their arm while they turn the wheel. When it comes to water, it is gravity – a physical system – that brings it down, and plants – a biological system – that puts it back up. Similarly, when water moves horizontally, it is mostly due to natural systems of pressure gradients and winds. Again, we see the movement of vast quantities of water through the air across thousands of miles as though this were an easy, simple and eternal process. It is not. If the system were to break down overnight, there is no way in which human technology could replace or replicate it.

Dumb with water

In the context of the rise and fall of societies, you lose water and you are out of the game. Water security has been the *sine qua non* of human civilisation. It is no coincidence that writing developed in the four great river valleys of antiquity: the Nile, the Indus, the Yellow River and the Fertile Crescent of Mesopotamia. If you had a guaranteed water supply, you had food and you had a trade advantage. In turn, this brought wealth, power, richer diets and the time and money necessary for cultural development.

Droughts and floods kill harder and faster than wars. They can shatter countries. To be crude, societies will either sink or swim based on their interaction with water.

13

But, to reassert, we humans are not too dumb, provided we are not trying to be too clever. Instinctively, we have gravitated towards reliable water resources. Human history can be analysed in terms of a movement to water security. From the great prehistoric migrations to the current power politics of the Middle East, humans have been testing their water environments and supplies, trying to understand water's limits and productivity.

Often, these tests have seemed sufficient. But we are learning that our findings were erroneous. It didn't matter that we misunderstood hydrological and plant systems. They rattled along happily, uninterrupted by us. Similarly, we merrily marched on in a reassuring ignorance. What did it matter that we didn't truly understand how rain fell or where the water in wells came from? All that mattered was that water did its part and, for our ego's sake, we fooled ourselves into thinking that we were wisely exploiting nature. We were not. It was only that our impact was so small that it mattered not how wrong-headed it was. Now our impact is far greater, but no wiser. When we didn't understand the system but our demands remained sustainable, our ignorance was benign. It is now highly dangerous.

14

The salutary lesson of the Mesopotamians, or 'How water caused a dark age'

The great empires and city states of Mesopotamia were often determined by their thirst and their water security. Arguably the cradle of civilisation – at least in our Eurasian tradition – Mesopotamia had an ambivalent relationship with its water supply: it was both its making and, ultimately, its destruction.

Water was fundamental. The name of the region itself comes from the Greek meaning 'between two rivers', the rivers in question being the Euphrates and the Tigris. The Mesopotamians knew the importance of water and they – relative to rival human civilisations – knew how to use it well. They were geniuses of irrigation, water storage and transportation, and used technology that would not reach Western Europe for several millennia.

But their understanding of irrigation was not as complete as they believed. They had focused their intellect on drawing water from the raised rivers to the low-lying fields. Being humans, they marvelled at their intelligence and achievement, little accepting that they had not done much more than exploit the simple relationship between gravity and water. What the Mesopotamians hadn't bothered to think about was where the water was going. They knew that the crops were drawing water out of the soil. That had been their goal and so, in their thinking, water became irrelevant once the crops were nourished. Happily, their fields didn't seem to be too waterlogged, despite the impossibility of the irrigated water re-entering the rivers themselves. In their simple equation, irrigation brought the water and the crops took it away.

But evaporation from the soil surface had invisible and gradual effects that ultimately poisoned the soil, devastated the economy and destroyed the once-mighty empire. Here is the knowledge that was invisible to the Mesopotamians: when water evaporates it leaves deposits of mineral salts in the soil. It also draws mineral salts in the soil from the lower to the upper levels. Slowly, over generations, the mineral salt content of the topsoil grew, unnoticed. Just as a frog dropped into a pan of boiling water will leap out to safety, but a frog placed in cold water that is gradually heated will allow itself to be boiled alive, so did the Mesopotamians steadily, diligently and unknowingly poison their fertile soil until it became toxic and unusable. The water and food security that had been the bedrock of this powerful civilisation was eroded and undermined. Peace and prosperity gave way to starvation and poverty. Trade collapsed into war. If you could not import your food and water through trade, you would have to take it with the sword. Mesopotamia imploded towards the end of the second millennium BCE; it would be centuries before it was rebuilt. Water had claimed its first imperial victim. It was not to be the last.

15

It's water for lunch...water again

We need to understand one very big and seemingly simple idea: we 'eat' a lot of virtual water. Humanity has deluded itself since the beginning of time about the biological and physical processes that deliver renewable water. We have equally deluded ourselves about the important connection between food and water.

Prehistoric self-service restaurants

In the early days of humanity, we were dependent on vegetation for food. This was mainly because it neither ran away nor bit us. Other mammals in the African grasslands were significantly faster than us (they still are). This had a double effect: they were good at getting away from us, and also better than us at escaping mutual predators. When it came to prehistoric meat-eating, man was most often on the menu, not seated at the table.

It was not until two million years ago that we became broadly human. By then our brain capacity had grown considerably. So too had our capacities for self-awareness, social organisation and communication. As slow, clawless creatures in a hostile world, we applied our intellect to the important task of survival. Though biologically ill-suited to hunting, our brains made us successful scavengers. The history of the human diet can be understood as the history of human technology, predominantly weapons technology. The ability to throw stones most probably gave early humans their first sustained access to meat, as these were used to chase away rival scavengers. The development of clubs and spears gave us a powerful advantage over most other mammals. We could now kill our own quarry and transport it to a safe place. With fire, we could soften the meat and so eat more. Technology and meat went hand in hand. The technology improved access to meat. The meat increased our brain size. And our intellect improved our technology. A virtuous circle had developed.

But where does water enter the equation?

Diversifying diets and economies

Neolithic farming methods prompted the first instances of urbanisation and economic diversification. Not everyone needed to be a spear-chucker, but the urban centres needed the food produced by farming and hunting. Trade was born. At the very outset, food traded into towns meant virtual-water 'trade'. As farmers brought their grain, vegetables and livestock into the urban areas, they also brought embedded water. Today, each tonne of grain has a virtual-water content of about 1000 cubic metres; this figure gives us a decent notion of the volume needed in the past. From the word go, those living in urban settlements have been blind to the true extent of their water consumption. The delusion about urban thirst is as old as urbanisation itself.

As societies and economies developed, so did international trade. The early Mediterranean, North African and Asian civilisations traded staple foods and vegetable oils. They did so, unknowingly, to compensate for the water shortages that existed at that point in history because they did not have the knowledge to develop their green and blue water resources to achieve food self-sufficiency. Virtual-water 'trade' is not new; it is as ancient as the diversification of jobs.

Thirsty browsers

Thirst informs our behaviour in ways we rarely see or understand. Recent years have seen growth in shopping science, with research and evidence-backed studies on product location, consumer behaviour and in-store architecture. Anecdotally, we hear about supermarkets pumping bready smells into the bakery section or moving key products around to draw us into unfamiliar and unvisited parts of the shop. Much is made of the human browsing tendency, again with little understanding of what underpins it. All the supermarkets need to know is that we are drawn to sweet treats in bright packaging hanging at unexpected intervals in our journey around the shop. They don't need to know why.

But the answer is water. Very early in human development, much of our water need was satisfied not by directly drinking but by indulging in brightly coloured red, orange and blue berries hanging on shrubs we passed. This fruit brought water to our ancient ancestors in a way that was convenient, cool, refreshing and, most importantly, utterly invisible. Their modern in-store equivalents, while economically and nutritionally punishing, still mimic their natural forerunners' colour schemes. Consider those bright reds, oranges and blues on the cans of the leading soft drinks.

As we will continually see, it is a mistake to allow ourselves to be fooled by the invisibility of water in our food. We have been making this mistake for millions of years. Thinking in

17

> *terms of virtual water enables us to understand our reliance on trade and economic forces to meet our water requirements. Those of us in the urban areas of the industrialised world depend on a complex network of virtual-water 'flows' to quench our thirst. There truly is water everywhere.*

So, why this book and why now?

18

The invisibility of water in food has its roots in human prehistory. The superabundance of water and the relative insignificance of human population size has meant that this invisibility was harmless. Not so for us as we face the water-demand predicament of the twenty-first century.

Virtual water has been, and will remain, the remedy to regional water scarcity. Getting people to grasp the significance of their collective impact on the world's water resources can only be achieved if they first grasp the concept of virtual water. Information is power, and I want people to be more informed about water. Note, it is information and not simple facts that empowers. Virtual water is a concept that people should be able to grasp easily. And once grasped, deploy.

New concepts are always resisted. And virtual water has been no exception. But after nearly twenty years of increasing currency, it has become a term that can help individual consumers understand their collective impact on their national and even on the very-hard-to-conceptualise idea of global water security. If we get behind the concept and try and understand it, it should help us to consume more sensibly. Sensible food consumption is one of the commandments for twenty-first-century society. Walk more. Reuse goods wherever possible. Never buy automatically anything you've seen advertised. Any offer of easy money is a con, of which you will be either the perpetrator or the victim. Understand that the greatest differences between people and cultures are little more than superficial. And eat sensibly.

Awareness of the concept of virtual water will not provide a magic answer to the world's water problems (although it will point society in some useful directions). But the concept will allow us to see characteristics of water, its nature and our (mis)use of it, to which we have been blind since our time as pre-Stone Age scavengers. Once we see and accept these qualities and vulnerabilities, we stand some chance of being able to make decisions individually and collectively that are consistent with the underlying hydrological and economic fundamentals of water resources. Simply put, once we understand water truly, we will be able to use it wisely.

19

That is the *why* behind my concept and this book. And the reason for why now? There is no one single reason for the urgency of this measure. There are 6.8 billion reasons, 6.8 billion thirsty human beings unwittingly consuming between 2 and 5 cubic metres of water each day.

'Water flows uphill to money and power'

This powerful and astute observation was made by Marc Reisner, an American environmentalist and journalist tragically lost to cancer at the start of the century. Without doubt, he was a brilliant analyst of the water predicament of the US. My assessment of California in Chapter 3 owes much to his work and insight. Don't feel obliged to take my word for it: investigate his writings for yourself. You will not put his book *Cadillac Desert* down until you reach for your laptop and email everyone you know and tell them to read it too.

Historically, water has flowed from the poor to the wealthy. The wealthy urban areas of the industrialised world have an immense hunger for water, which is satisfied by a global trade network that allows for virtual water to 'flow', inside imports of food and other products, disproportionately to the rich. Uphill indeed.

Here is the central problem of the misallocation of this vital resource: it happens invisibly. However, here too is the solution. Once we understand these virtual-water 'flows', we can with enough political will use trade to manage more effectively this resource, thereby ensuring mutual water security. The market alone will not be able to.

Over the coming chapters, we will see how 'trade' in virtual water underpins the water and food security of the water-scarce populations of the world and how this miraculous, invisible economic process has even pulled us away from the brink of often-predicted water wars.

20

As the problem of ignorance offers a solution to itself once seen and understood, so does virtual water offer the conceptual key to seeing and thereby addressing our water dilemma. We humans have a poor track record of predicting the future: we too often use the model of the past, which is by definition inadequate to meet unknown demands. We are at our most ingenious and potent when we discover and transgress the ever-advancing boundary of our ignorance. We can observe, understand and adapt only in that order. This book, and the concept of virtual water, will allow us, as readers, citizens and civilisations, to see our misuse of water more clearly than ever before. From there, the onus is on us all to understand and to adapt.

And fast.

CHAPTER 2

Beneath the surface:
a guide to getting water wise

When the well's dry, we know the worth of water.
BENJAMIN FRANKLIN

Dear reader...

Most likely, you are one of the highly privileged persons of the world fortunate enough to be living in a country with safe running water and treated sewage. Only one in five of the global population is in your lucky position. But if you are living in one of the rich, industrialised nations of the world, then you and your ancestors will have been enjoying such amenities for five generations. This is the exception, not the rule.

The nations with long-established water and sanitation systems are not those with the greatest and most reliable water resources. Nor are those nations with the most water the ones with the best track record of getting high-quality drinking water to its population. What does this tell us? That access to readily available water resources is not the key determinant when it comes to modern, reliable water services. Rather, the quality of a society's water supply depends on its technological nous, its management skills and – most importantly – its money. Again, water follows the money.

How the industrial revolution delivered (and muddied) the waters

The great failure of private enterprise
The success story of drinking and domestic water provision in the industrialised nations of Europe and Northern America in the nineteenth century is built upon a significant but often-ignored failure. By the latter half of the nineteenth century it had become patently clear that the private sector could not deliver adequate water services. The organisational and engineering requirements were simply too burdensome for any private endeavour to bear.

It may be anathema to modern ears, but where the dynamic private sector proved impotent, the public-sector bureaucracy was triumphant. Across the industrialising world, local urban authorities simultaneously started developing water services. Where private capital and the profit motive had stalled, civic pride and tax monies thrived. In a short space of time, residents, workplaces and factories in cities across North America and Europe were provided with high-quality water and even more costly sewage facilities.

But a mistake was made. A mistake that has become so accepted a convention that we might find it hard to imagine it could have been otherwise. It was decided, across different cities and nation states, that all domestic water supplied would be at drinking-water standards.

Pause for thought. You might only fill your glass from the kitchen sink, but there is no reason (or no *health* reason at least!) why you couldn't take it from the bath, the feed pipe to the washing machine or even the toilet cistern. All mains water is of the same quality. With the wisdom that history brings, we might now criticise the understandable folly of these nineteenth-century architects of our water services. Their choice means that we now wash our armpits and bedsheets and – worse still – flush away our

22

POTABLE WATER
Water that is safe to drink, coming either from pure springs or (most likely) having been treated and purified. In both cases, the water is subject to tests to ensure that it is not contaminated. Delivering potable water costs money – not so much for the water itself but for the treatment, and especially for the installation and maintenance of the network, with its pipes, pumps and meters, as well as the army of engineers and IT and other staff who make sure the high-quality and safe water keeps flowing. Remember potable water is the small water in our lives. It plays a much bigger part than is needed because we use potable water to wash the car and flush the toilet. But it is still only between 100 and 200 litres per day per person in an industrialised economy – only 10 per cent of the water we need for food.

own waste in water that has been expensively treated to be drinkable. All this while, by the World Health Organisation's reckoning, over a billion people worldwide lack access to safe drinking water. It's a frighteningly large figure, and it's no surprise that it's the poorer, developing nations that lack reliable supplies of drinking water.

Yet, in the industrialised and post-industrial nations we unthinkingly spray our gardens with costly, treated potable water.

Dangerously, as discussed in the last chapter, we give little or no thought to how much water we are using. We are blind to waste. This waste is made all the more poignant by the fact that the water has been expensively purified to drinking standards. Stop and consider for a moment: every time you shower, bathe, flush, clean up or wash the car, you are using a precious resource that others are literally dying to get their hands on. The extravagance of watering the garden suddenly borders on the repulsive. Don't believe me? Fit a water meter and discover for yourself whether domestic irrigation is a financially prudent use of water.

23

We do not know the amount of water we use. Nor do we know its value. And that is because, in the developed world, water is cheap. Rarely does water account for more than 2 per cent of the household income in advanced economies. Any economist can see the problem immediately: the financial incentive to learn about water and economise is weak. It is bad that we do not understand or take sufficient care with the 5 per cent of water used in the home. We flush, we sprinkle, we hose with wild abandon. We leave the tap on while we clean our teeth, or refuse to use a plug when doing the washing up. All with water that is of the highest possible quality. However, if that is bad, it is worse that we are completely ignorant of the unfathomable volumes of water used to make our food. An astounding 90 per cent of our water usage is hidden in our food. We are blind to its presence and blind to its cost.

But many people in the world are not blind to the cost and the value of water. The truly impoverished understand: for them, the well is dry, the water scarce, the price terrible.

They don't read books such as this or have the chance to write one that would tell us the basics of the value of water carried home each day, or of the water they use to irrigate their crops. If such a first-hand account were available, I would recommend it over this book currently comfortably in your hands.

And the poor subsidise the rich

24

Few families in advanced economies live in water poverty. That is not to say there is no water poverty in rich countries. The poor are threatened with water poverty everywhere. In the UK, the Consumer Council for Water defines any household spending more than 3 per cent of their income on water as being in water poverty. By contrast, in developing nations some families pay 25 per cent of their income for insufficient quantities of poor-quality water. Remember, it is not a lack of technology or resource, but a lack of public investment and purchasing power that prevents access to water. The wealthy of every nation enjoy almost identical water services, on the model developed by the industrialising nations of the nineteenth century. But in developing economies, the wealthy get more and better water, with greater ease and, often, at lower cost.

Advanced piped water systems are simply unafford-able for the large numbers of people in Africa and Asia surviving on a dollar a day. Location is also an issue. The poorer areas of cities are less likely to have proper water infrastructure. Isolated rural areas are left to fend for themselves. Wealth draws the water infrastructure like a wasp to sugar; water infrastructure ensures that water is potable, plentiful and affordable. But it only reaches established households. Our world is ordered according to the ownership of property. No private company or local authority will send pipes to an illegal homestead. Therefore, for water supply, the inhabitants of urban shanty towns and rural communes often have to rely on private water vendors. These vendors charge more, and their water quality is not guaranteed. But thirst is the ultimate imperative of life – we'll drink water that will kill us tomorrow in order to survive today.

Not only do the poor of the developing world appreciate the importance and value of water, they also understand the volume of their consumption. And the weight. That is the one clear advantage of having to carry your domestic water: you get a very good idea of how much you are using. It is interesting to consider how such a stricture might serve to lessen water wastage if it were to become suddenly necessary in the developed world. Fewer showers, fewer half-full dishwashers, fewer over-liberal garden sprinkler systems. For all our assumed knowledge, it should be humbling to note that the severely impoverished women of the developing world have a far more acute and complete understanding of their water consumption than we do of ours. Note, most often, it is the women of the household who fetch the domestic water. Here we have vital, intuitive knowledge in the hands of the most unempowered demographic on earth: the poor women of the developing world. Collecting water is the task of the powerless. The political agenda responds to the needs of those who are blissfully unaware of their water needs. How foolish that the ignorant are heeded to the detriment of the wise. How foolish, and how dangerous.

Even the rich might notice the weight of their water use when buying containers of expensive bottled water from the supermarket. They would not try it without a car.

A Royale with cheese

Readers like stories. They don't like numbers. More, they don't want to handle complex situations. Worse still, the angry switch off when asked to juggle two systems.

Politics is all-pervasive. The world of measurements and metrics is not immune. That we endure so much difficulty wading through different systems of units, whose spread provides a mini-history of the twists and eddies of European imperialism, would be amusing if it were not so counter-productive.

We are deaf to the measurements of others. This is a problem because, when it comes to metrics, we are still on day one after the fall of the Tower of Babel. The dominance of the British empire and its American successor has left an unbridgeable rift in the international language of metrics. It is not within my remit to attempt to heal this. That the foot remains the essential unit in aviation reminds us that the rules by which society is ordered are dictated not by common sense, logic or suitability but by social convention, influence and good old-fashioned power. And an intuitive view on safety. Resistance to the metric system in the UK for many years seemed to form the central plank of any argument against greater European integration.

'Please all, and you will please none,' warned Aesop. Regardless, we shall attempt to please all and show here how metric measurements relate to those common in the US and UK, quaintly called the imperial system.

Rounding numbers saves some pain. A pint is half a litre. A US gallon is 4 litres. There are 250 US gallons in a cubic metre. An interesting and distinctive measurement popular particularly in Australia is the gigalitre. Giga is the metric equivalent of the US billion. Hence, a gigalitre is a billion litres, or one-tenth of a cubic kilometre.

For small water, the problem is not so acute. The imperial pint and the metric litre both serve us well. A pint or litre of milk is an everyday experience. We can visualise the quantities and move between the two with relative ease. Thanks to the ubiquitous automobile, we are also used to measuring out in US gallons or metric litres when performing our weekly fill of gas or petrol. For reasons of historical context, imperial measures are not so good when attempting to capture large volumes. This forced energy producers and traders to invent a new unit – the barrel – which is almost the same as the metric tonne.

METRIC MEASUREMENT	US IMPERIAL MEASUREMENT
1 LITRE (l) →	2 PINTS
1 CUBIC METRE (m³) →	250 US GALLONS
1 CUBIC KILOMETRE (km³) →	800,000 ACRE-FEET

US IMPERIAL MEASUREMENT	METRIC MEASUREMENT
1 PINT (pt) →	0.5 LITRES
1 US GALLON (gal.) →	4 LITRES
1 ACRE-FOOT (ac/ft) →	1200 CUBIC METRES

Table 2.1 Rough equivalents, metric and US imperial units. Exact equivalents are given at the end of the book.

Big water cannot be measured in pints, gallons or litres. We are dealing with quantities beyond that of which we might have direct experience. At the risk of seeming partisan, it is here that the happy logic of the metric system comes into its own. Talking of daily individual water consumption as being in the range of 2500–5000 litres is clumsy: the numbers seem inflated and the digits look isolated and incoherent on the page. So, the metric system yields up 2.5–5 cubic metres instead. Far easier to get the mouth, the eye and the brain around. Better, the metric system is a system of convenient joys. For example, a cubic metre of water weighs a metric tonne.

The imperial system offers no such conveniences. The foot, the yard, the chain, the furlong, the mile and the acre all exhibit a certain character, but they lack arithmetic grace. In place of the cubic metre, the imperial system offers the acre-foot. Equivalent to about 1200 cubic metres, the acre-foot is an invention of farming and engineering, in which professions it is intuitive and useful. Not so in capturing quantities of water. It is no surprise then that water professionals – myself included – have gravitated to the metric system's cubic kilometre when addressing big water in huge river basins, national economies or virtual-water 'trade'.

The importance of water security

The infinite breast-milk dilemma

It's fair to say that babies don't understand breast milk too well. A slightly unhealthy relationship develops between the baby and the milk. Every time the baby cries, and even sometimes when it doesn't, the milk is supplied and continues until the baby wants no more. For a period, the baby is sated. Then the hunger rises again, and the cycle is repeated. The baby's intellect is too underdeveloped, its knowledge too incomplete. Hence, it is incapable of separating cause from effect. The milk exists to satisfy the hunger. As it has done on every occasion, so it will continue. Seemingly, only the need is necessary, and the supply inevitably follows. The unbroken presence and

unfailing availability creates an illusion: that the milk is
infinite, conjured by hunger.

So too with early man and the natural world.

There was always more space. Always more animals.
More vegetation. Water.

We've shaken off most of these illusions. Scarcity,
and the formalisation of scarcity into economics, has
given us both the theoretical and practical framework
for valuing land, animals and vegetation. Land is owned.
Even public land, such as parks and coastlines, is held by
benign authorities who grant us access. So also the useful
animals, those desirable as pets or dinner. Each with an
owner. Similarly plant life. But who owns the rain?

Like wind and sunshine, the rain cannot be control-
led. However, our economic systems, our societies and our
very lives rely on the benefits all three bring. When incor-
porating them into our economic system, we must codify
these elements in a way that might seem strange to any
born before the industrial revolution. Wind and sunshine
are public goods, non-excludable and non-rivalrous, and
gifted to us by the universe. Using them doesn't deplete
them; it is fair to consider them infinite. Not so with water.
To mistake water for a public good is to employ the reason-
ing of the baby at the breast. People have sensibly and
intuitively gravitated towards water supplies; those that
have not most often perished. They are not available to
give testimony to the truth that water security is the key
criterion for survival in primitive economies.

Very soon, we will need to find a way of costing water.
If we do not, even the industrialised economies will not be
able to get enough food and water. The illusion of national
water and food security will evaporate. Efforts are already
being made, and we'll return to this idea in the last chapter. Without success in this area, we will never be able to
express economically the value of water. Without an economically expressed imperative, little will be done.

29

But why?

Because we aren't worried about water. We don't understand that it isn't free. We have a vague sense that we are
paying for it at some point, but the connection between
our water use and our financial contribution to the costs is
very weak. Not only do we think water is free, but we aren't
able to remember that there are additional costs associated with delivering the stuff. Water doesn't grow on trees;
nor does it naturally dwell in taps. Until we start thinking
about water (including embedded water) as an actual, hard
cost, we stand no chance of understanding the economic
and environmental price tags attached to water. Currently,
these tags are absolutely invisible to us. But every time
we use water, someone somewhere is paying both these
bills. Globally, we are drawing on an account we don't even
know about. With each drop, the debt deepens. No image I
know summarises the situation better than this.

30

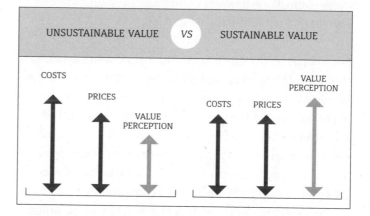

Figure 2.1 Valuing Water:
unsustainable versus sus-
tainable value positions.
Source: Jack Moss, Gary
Wolff, Graham Gladden
and Eric Guttieriez (2004),
*Valuing Water for Better
Governance: How to pro-
mote dialogue to balance
social, environmental and
economic values?,* Geneva:
World Business Council for
Sustainable Development.

In our current, unsustainable situation, costs outstrip
the price of water, mainly because the environmental cost
of water is not being included in the economic formula,
and is therefore unrepresented in the price. However,
value-perception lags well behind both cost and price. We
think water is worth even less than that which we pay for
it. Our perception then is the exact opposite of the reality.

This is the epitome of human error. Always, we favour the faulty perception over the uncomfortable reality.

To move to a sustainable use and valuation of water resources, costs and prices must be aligned. Otherwise, the economic forces of supply and demand will drive us (further) into environmentally and economically reckless water use. Most importantly, we have to value water more. In fact, our value-perception should not merely align with the costs and prices (though this would be no small improvement on the current situation). Rather, value-perception must exceed costs and prices. Water is worth it. It's vital. And not just for drinking. Water is also food.

31

Water isn't just about water

It's an important point and one to which we will be returning throughout this book: water is essential for food. Getting decent potable water is not too hard, though it unnecessarily eludes many. It is not too hard because the quantity we require on a daily basis is very modest. We require only about 3 litres each day. Rarely is it a challenge for any but those in the most deprived areas of the poorest countries to secure 3 litres of potable water each day. Drinking is not the problem. Eating is. Ancient settlements were close to water not just so that they could drink, but so that they could raise crops, eat and – later – trade. For this they required about 2 or 3 cubic metres per person per day: roughly a thousand times the 3 litres needed for daily drinking. So food is the big issue. Reliable rainfall and natural flood irrigation were the prerequisites for food production in the early millennia of human existence. The Nile and Asian river basins supported the first sophisticated communities precisely because some of their major rivers tended to flood annually. We have wandered around for thousands upon thousands of years, scooping up water (directly or embedded in food) with the same casual ease with which we inhale air. As we mammals evolved noses and lungs to catch air and absorb oxygen, so did we evolve mouths and digestive systems. We've used these systems in the same way; biologically, we have been fooled into equating water's ease of consumption with air's ease of availability.

Today, living in London, I pull oxygen from the air with almost identical ease as I might have in this same spot two thousand years ago, when it was, as Joseph Conrad rightly observed, 'one of the dark places of the earth'. Though air pollution might prompt fears of respiratory disorders, only the most obsessive hypochondriac would wish to treat or purify the air in some way. Essentially, the air is there, free and accessible. It is unmediated, inexhaustible and to hand. No one need do anything other than inhale. But much is done to the water. It has travelled a long and complicated route to reach my stomach. For potable water, flocculation, sedimentation and filtration are but the three best-known stops on a complex journey. For virtual water embedded in food, that complexity is almost incalculable. I – like many of you perhaps – consume a diet dependent on commodities produced in scores of countries spanning the globe, brought together and then onwards to me through the interconnecting international trading systems. The transactional history of this water is unfathomable, its transactional costs incalculable.

After self-sufficiency

Time was, prior to the early industrialisation and trade of the nineteenth century, that every proto-nation state was broadly food- and water-sufficient. A global population of nearly a billion, and each soul enjoying local water and food security. How this has changed. By the close of the last century, only ten countries could consider themselves to be enjoying surplus water resources. Population growth has pushed most political economies into water deficit. Fortunately, the rich nations have been able to trade; trade in food has enabled the water-scarce to remain food-secure. In doing so, it has sadly obscured the relationship between society and its water resources. Only those families who depend on irrigation have practical experience of the sheer volumes of water required to raise crops. Given that most crops are raised with water in rain-fed soil, we can easily see how even those farming the food are blind to the volumes and costs of water. What chance for those of us consuming the food thousands of miles away in our city restaurants?

Why a pessimistic Anglican reverend from the end of the eighteenth century can point us in the right direction on water use...

The Reverend Professor Thomas Malthus has not been treated kindly by history. Most probably this is because he provoked the ire and criticism of bigger names, famously Karl Marx and Percy Shelley, who castigated him as an 'enemy of the people' and a 'eunuch' respectively. Why the hostility?

Malthus's reputation, for better or worse, hinges on his expression of a simple axiomatic truth: while population growth is geometric, subsistence growth is arithmetic. What does this mean? Population growth will always outstrip increases in food production. Bluntly, human beings will, if unchecked, reproduce so frantically that they will starve. As Malthus more eloquently phrased it in An Essay on the Principle of Population, *'The power of population is indefinitely greater than the power in the earth to produce subsistence for man.'*

Combined with Malthus's uncompromising religious views, that the pain of famine and the spectre of starvation looming over the great masses of the world were divine instruments to guide humans onto the path of virtue and hard work, it's easy to understand why these findings caused offence. But repugnance at Malthus's moralising shouldn't discredit the essential truth of his main idea. He lived in an age of idealistic utopianism. Advancing social, philosophical and

34

political understanding were running concurrent with great (and seemingly unending) leaps forward in technology and industry. No one wanted to dampen the mood and take notice of this unbending, grumpy, pulpit doom-monger. A brave new world was lurking around the corner: industry, economics and Enlightenment thinking were to eradicate unnecessary poverty, improve living standards for all and herald a true golden age for humanity. Each of these achievements was underpinned by vastly improved farming, both at home and in the new lands over the seas.

Not wishing to ride on the coat tails of another's greatness, there have been moments – on finding the ears, eyes and minds of politicians, civil servants and captains of industry firmly closed to the perils of water mismanagement – when I have felt a real affinity with the Reverend Malthus. Cassandra's curse was not to be always right, but to be always ignored.

Thinking about ignorance and sustainability

Two types

We are facing two types of ignorance about environmental sustainability. The first is excusable, the second unforgivable.

First, we are naturally ignorant of what advances the future will bring. Little is certain. Humanity has a flair for invention. It began with Neolithic tools and weaponry – as discussed in the previous chapter – and continues in our world of keyhole surgery, electric cars and ever-tinier and more multi-functional mobile phones. Technology could very easily provide, if not a cure, then some mitigating intervention for our sustainability malaise. I might hazard a guess at the potential positive impact of solar energy and desalination technologies but, excitingly, there no doubt remain technologies which will be vital to our future existence that are currently unproven or not yet even conceived. We cannot be criticised for our ignorance, though we can regret we shall never get to see these great future advancements, always beyond the final corner of our lifespans. Not wishing to echo too closely the words of former US Secretary of Defence Donald Rumsfeld, future technology is an enigmatic rattlebag of known and unknown unknowns. Given that the second half of the twentieth century was an exceptional, unprecedented and entirely unpredictable period in terms of population growth, increase in the lifespan of the rich, change in diets and food trade, and developments in technology, the only bet I would care to make about the future is this: it will be surprising. A joy, albeit an intimidating one. I intend to catch as much of it as I can, and advise you all to do the same.

35

Our second area of ignorance, which is less wondrous or forgivable, is *WAVSE non-awareness*. Acronyms cause a common knee-jerk reaction in the human brain: apathetic acceptance. Acronyms are rather like workmen in high-visibility jackets. As soon as we see one, we switch the questioning part of our mind off and assume that they are performing some useful function, about which we need not worry. Best to let them get on with it and do the work. We know that further down the line we will be (ignorantly) reaping the benefits. Let's stop this lazy thinking now, at least when it comes to water sustainability.

What does WAVSE stand for? Water, air, vegetation and solar energy. Basically, it's the environment. The impor-tant idea behind the acronym, though, is that all the disparate elements actually work together as one inte-grated, highly complex whole. Whereas future technology is unknowable for the most part, the WAVSE environmental system is most definitely knowable. That is not to say that we have charted all this territory. Science has much work to do before we have assembled an exhaustive, comprehensive view of the WAVSE system. At the moment, we simply do not have the ability to calculate, with any scientifically acceptable precision, the volumes of air, water vapour, water and carbon in our planet's natural systems. If anyone has a proven method, there are plenty of scientists who would be excited to hear it. We shall see in later chapters that it is actually almost as hard to calculate the volumes of embedded virtual water in commodities. Again, suggestions on a postcard please.

However, the fact that our knowledge is imperfect – both in terms of being incomplete and being based, in places, on unproven assumptions – is in no way an excuse for the general levels of public ignorance. It is time to get interested and to get understanding. Importantly, preconceptions must be checked at the door. It is hard to identify the evolutionary gain in WAVSE being invisible to us. It is the case that WAVSE non-awareness is hard-wired into our genetic make-up. It is as deeply ingrained as flight from a roaring lion, dancing to music or the capacity to flirt (and engage in flirting's aftermath).

Concepts like WAVSE awareness or the food–water link are Big Ideas. Humanity has a very bad track record of absorbing Big Ideas into public discourse. Consider Darwin's theory of natural selection. It was first ignored, then ridiculed, and finally fought in the law courts, schools and pulpits, before becoming widely accepted. Note that even today in the US and UK, there are some struggling to force the introduction of Creationism or Intelligent Design theory onto the science syllabus. Societies construct knowledge. Once this is done, they resist through inertia and prejudice anything that threatens long-constructed knowledge.

Toddlers and water consumption

We are not good with the concept of need. I'm always amused to hear small children explain how they need a lollipop or need to play on the swings or need a new toy. This inability to distinguish between a want and a need

is somewhat less endearing in adults. In national governments, it is a terminal, environmental menace.

So how much water do we need? Basic needs have hardly
changed over the past two million years. And why should
they? Physiologically, we are not much changed. We've
made no serious evolutionary progress in that time, except
for some very impressive (but nutritionally irrelevant)
improvements in brain size and capacity. A rose bush needs
no more water now than then. Nor we. This is reflected in
the figures for consumption. Taking a global average, each
human needs about 1200 cubic metres per year. (And by
'need', I am only saying 'consumes'. As intimated, 'need' is a
moot point, and one to which we shall return.)

37

Until the industrial revolution of the nineteenth century, this figure was around 1000 cubic metres per person
per year, and seemingly had been back down into our
prehistory. Our current global average is slightly disingen-
uous. The average US citizen consumes around 2400 cubic
metres annually (though this is declining), whereas the
average Chinese requires a mere 700 (though this is rising).
There is much that is interesting in these simple statistics.
That water use is declining from its recent (unsustainable and morally indefensible) high in the industrialised
nations is a reassuring, if overdue, change. That Chinese
usage is rising is a less-encouraging vindication of our
hypothesis: water flows to the wealthy. GDP and water consumption tend to grow in parallel. We shall return to both
these statistics later on. We will also see that this example
of China effectively subsidising the water consumption of
the industrialised nations is no isolated incident.

The idea we need to get clear is that the readers of this
book do use more water than their prehistoric forebears,
but it is mainly because of what they eat – through the
extra water associated with the consumption of beef and
livestock products. Such changes in diet can account for
increases in water consumption of between 20 and 30 per

cent. The extra water used at home to protect health and improve lifestyles as societies develop, accounts only for a tiny increase in water consumption: from less than 0.5 per cent in prehistoric societies to about 3 per cent. It is the water footprint of our food that dominates individual and national water budgets. Saving water at home is economically important but it will never underpin the water security of a society or do much to address the stewardship of the water environment. In addition, about 70 per cent of domestic and industrial water can be cleaned up and reused.

Of the average individual annual water consumption of 1200 cubic metres, all the water consumed in the home or in non-agricultural industry has to be freshwater. These *small* freshwater demands – a miniscule proportion of our total water needs – have risen exponentially since industrialisation, from between 10 and 20 litres per day in the early nineteenth century to our present-day demands of around 200 litres daily. Yet amazingly, this is not the problem. Almost every nation in the world is still small-water self-sufficient. Meaning that nearly every nation has enough water for everything except agriculture. The problem is the *big* water. The water used for food. In 1960, world population stood at three billion. Today, it is more than double that figure. Diets have become more water-intensive. Given that there is a fixed amount of water in circulation, and that figure will not change, we have a clear numerical problem ahead. Our big-water demands, as currently expressed, cannot be sustained in their present form.

A sudden and dramatic drop in population is hardly humanely desirable. An increase in water is a geographic impossibility. The only variable left in the equation is diet. There are already sensible social forces acting on us to eat more wisely, for reasons of personal health. But there are more potent forces, often what we call market forces, pushing us in the other direction: to consume more and to consume badly. And this is bad for the health of our water environment.

2 | Beneath the surface

A big glass of water vs a glass of big water

From this point onwards, I am going to start talking about big water and small water. And it is very unlikely that you will understand instinctively what that means. So I shall gloss. Small water is easier to define. Every time you directly interact with water in its purely natural form, that is small water. If you drink it, flush it, wash in it or sprinkle it on your car or hollyhocks, it's small water. And big water? Big water is food. All the water required to raise food and underpin the livelihoods and mechanisms that bring it to your mouth. Obviously, if we think about if for a few seconds, we know that the tomatoes on our table required some water to grow. 39 *Perhaps we even have a small tomato vine in the garden. We water that, don't we? We understand how this works; at least, we understand enough. Less likely is it that we can instinctively comprehend the massive water cost of our clothes, our car, our T-bone steak. Here's the terrible paradox at the heart of big water: it accounts for about 90 per cent of our water use and it is completely invisible. Discussing water scarcity and usage but only in the context of small water – as most politicians and people are sadly inclined to do – is rather like developing an energy policy but restricting ourselves to a consideration of AA batteries.*

So, when you drink a pint glass of water, it's small water. But a little mug of hot milk before bed, that's big water. Why is one big and the other small? It's very simple. With small water, what you see is what you get, in terms of water consumption (give or take a few leakages and losses in the treatment and delivery). But big water? Even that splash of milk in your tea represents far more water consumption than your daily small-water needs. We call it big water because, to be blunt, it's really a lot bigger.

The opposite of freshwater

You may in your head have an old school-lesson dichotomy: freshwater and saltwater. Discard it. We are indeed like Coleridge's ancient mariner, with 'Water, water, everywhere/ Nor any drop to drink'. The almost incomprehensible quantities of water in the world's oceans and seas are all but useless to us. I add the qualifier 'all but' as the oceans are a key stage in the water cycle. It's a humbling thought, but taking a universal (rather than a species-centric) view of the earth, its story is that of the movement of water. Each drop of water will, in time, have occupied every place in every ocean. However, for a discussion on human water consumption, these vast pools of saltwater are barely relevant.

The dichotomy you need to hold in mind is: freshwater and soil water. This dichotomy, for the purposes of this book at least, maps directly onto another: blue water and green water. Freshwater/blue water is in the rivers, streams, lakes and underground pools. Soil water/green water is the water held in the soil after rainfall. The rainwater infiltrates the soil and gets sucked up by (and stored in but mainly transpired by) thirsty flora. We've managed to cost freshwater. As with most natural resources, as soon as you start to move it around, it acquires a clear and easily calculable – if unwelcome – economic value. We treat freshwater and supply it to homes or bottle it and send it to shops. We use it to irrigate crops. Whenever this happens, someone tends to charge someone else for the transporting. (Though it would be wrong to assume that these prices reflect accurately the costs of delivery or the value of the water.)

But our tendency to believe that all water is like rainfall – and free – equips us badly to engage in water markets. Only bottled water is accepted as a natural candidate for selling, buying and profit-taking. Other small water delivered in pipes to our homes – despite being as safe and at least a thousand times cheaper – has to contend with elemental resistance to economic pricing. Odd that we'll resent incredibly cheap water piped directly into the house, yet will trek back and forth to the supermarket to load up on implausibly overpriced water in environmentally unkind plastic bottles. But if resistance to the economic pricing of piped small water is elemental, then we need an even stronger word to capture the universal opposition to charging an economic price for big water in irrigated farming. Perhaps 'existential' is the word. Sometimes, the news will tell of a local urban riot in a poor country, where people feel they cannot afford the piped small water on offer. Compared to these tiny skirmishes, the conflict over charging for big water is an ongoing cold war without evident end.

41

But no one has managed to cost soil water. Hydrological and biological processes move it around. No one has to do anything – indeed, no one can do anything. Ask a raindancer in the middle of a drought. It is outside our control. This is not a situation whose truth is compatible with the prejudices of the individual or the collective human ego. Currently, soil water has not been codified into our economic models. It's under the radar and taken for granted, as we might take for granted the air which fills the lungs of our factory workers. This is a very foolish stance. By volume, soil water is the most important single component in food production. Let me reiterate, with some more detail: soil water is the most necessary resource on the planet. It stops us from starving. It is vital. And yet it is politically and economically invisible. It is ignored. Like sleeping children in the back seat of a car, we are ignorant of what is carrying us forward.

Colour-coded water

Blue or green?
Blue water can be drunk and pumped. It's there, available as water. Green water is hidden inside trees, shrubs and other plants and biota. There is significantly more

Figure 2.2 Lots of water, but not always where it is needed.
GREEN WATER: infiltrates into soil and is taken up by natural vegetation and crops. Much is transpired by natural vegetation back into the air.
BLUE WATER: flows through the landscape into rivers, lakes, aquifers. Can be dammed, stored, pumped and metered and used to irrigate.

green water than blue: the ratio is 61.2 to 38.8 per cent. Both types of water fall on the earth as rain. At this point, blue water goes in one of two directions. Some stays on

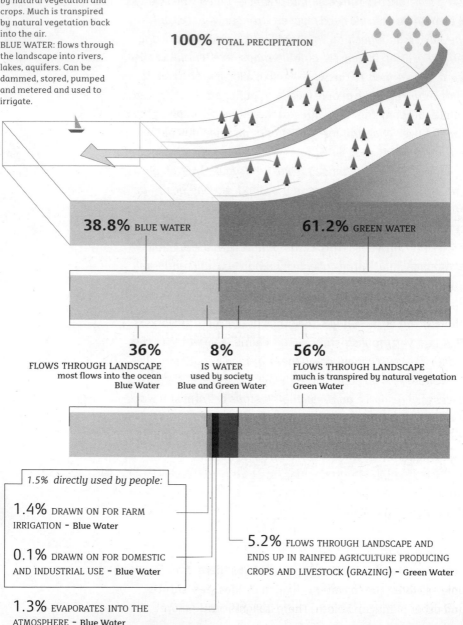

100% TOTAL PRECIPITATION

38.8% BLUE WATER

61.2% GREEN WATER

36%
FLOWS THROUGH LANDSCAPE
most flows into the ocean
Blue Water

8%
IS WATER
used by society
Blue and Green Water

56%
FLOWS THROUGH LANDSCAPE
much is transpired by natural vegetation
Green Water

1.5% directly used by people:

1.4% DRAWN ON FOR FARM IRRIGATION – Blue Water

0.1% DRAWN ON FOR DOMESTIC AND INDUSTRIAL USE – Blue Water

1.3% EVAPORATES INTO THE ATMOSPHERE – Blue Water

5.2% FLOWS THROUGH LANDSCAPE AND ENDS UP IN RAINFED AGRICULTURE PRODUCING CROPS AND LIVESTOCK (GRAZING) – Green Water

After Peter Rogers 'Running Out of Water', Scientific American, August 2008.

the surface in rivers, lakes and streams. This is the only truly visible terrestrial (as opposed to oceanic) water. The remainder (and the vast majority) of blue water percolates down through the soil to form pools of groundwater. Like green water, this too is invisible.

Figure 2.2 is a simple but instructive illustration answering that childhood question: where does all the rain go? Amazingly, only 1.5 per cent of all rainfall is actively used by us humans. Most is absorbed and transpired by plants. Much of what isn't ends up in the oceans.

Green water is found everywhere except the most arid regions, by which I basically mean the desert. Anywhere you see a flash of green – be it ever so humble as a blade of grass – that means there is green water present. Blue water is hard to remember when it is stored in underground pools. It is available everywhere that has rain. A big difference between the two is their availability for withdrawal and use. We can't really do much with green water, except sit back and admire nature at work. Green water gets absorbed by plants from the soil, and is eventually released back into the atmosphere. Blue water, however, can be stored. It can be used to irrigate. It can be dammed. It can be pumped and metered.

43

This reveals a rather shocking fact. Humanity is almost entirely reliant upon a gift of nature that is totally outside our control or command. If green water were suddenly to vanish, we would swiftly follow it into the void. The forests and grasslands of the world are fed by water that is free at the point of use. Mother Nature picks up the tab. The same is true for nearly all the crops raised by farmers and the cultivated pastures for our livestock. If our benefactor pulls the plug, we're finished as a going concern.

Green water has been of great, consequential and essential importance to humanity throughout its history. But only now are we beginning to conceptualise and discuss it. Despite the fact that it is the key determinant in whether we live or starve. And despite the evidence that human societies, for much our development, have risen where green water was sufficient and accessible to produce food.

Figure 2.3 Green-water and blue-water flow.
Source: After Rockström and Falkenmark and developed by Phillips. Consumptive water is not available for reuse. The big consumptive water use is in food production. The water goes into the atmosphere and is unavailable for reuse locally. A high proportion of small water can be reused. One cubic metre of water used for domestic purposes is worth 1.7 cubic metres, as 0.7 cubic metres can be reused.

GREEN WATER
The eminent Swedish hydrologist, Malin Falkenmark, conceptualised blue and green water. By highlighting the volumes and significance of green water in crop production, she transformed the way we think about water and water security.

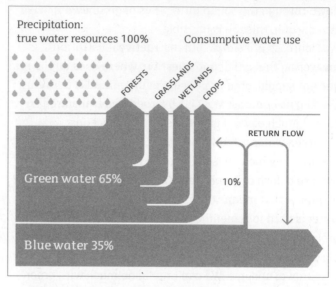

Naturally, instinctively and – until now – unproblematically, we have drawn our drinking water from the blue water and used green water to raise our crops. In the past two hundred years, we have begun to use significant amounts of blue water in growing crops, mainly through advanced irrigation techniques. By the close of the last century, farmers were using considerable quantities of blue water. Wherever we have irrigated using blue water, we have run out of water. The crops upon which we feed are unimaginably thirsty.

The time we left the tap on...

In the second half of the last century, humanity turned a tap on. And left it on. We slipped out of accord with the blue-water resources of the world and have done nothing to get back in step. What we don't seem to understand is that when we slip out of step with nature, we, not nature, suffer.

Sixty years ago, we seemed to be in a position to actualise the biblical belief that we as a species were to be master of this planet, and nature our subordinate. This hubris was not restricted to water. The environmental disasters looming in our future stem from the misplaced righteousness of our plundering. The earth was to yield up its bounty and its secrets. From the deepest oil reserves to the hidden power of the atom, everything was to be ours to command. On the back of such enhanced exploitation of the planet, we demanded that the world support a population vastly greater than anything it had ever previously been forced to bear. The narrative was one of eternal progress: the earth would be made to give forth the means of support. If we had the will to become so populous, then we would concurrently develop the ability to mine the earth for materials to feed that growth. In a sentence, we truly forgot the teachings of Malthus.

45

That is not to say that we haven't become expert exploiters. The productivity levels for land and water use have increased steeply. Often, in localised geographies, population has not outstripped crop yield. Rather the reverse. In the UK, the population has increased by a factor of five since 1800; the productivity of rain-fed wheat has increased by a factor of ten. It's hard to get a complete picture of how improved productivity relates to increased demands. Pardon the pun, but water is slippery. Getting the measure of it in sufficient detail is a big and complex undertaking. It is financially and scientifically daunting. Also, there are political and social imperatives to let the issue lie.

Here is the central problem: with their water-using preferences and their under-informed politicians, populations continue to bumble along, relying on uncritical beliefs and assumptions. It is easy and natural for them to do so. It was ever thus. The uncritical approach is politically expedient in the short run but exacerbates the potential problems in the long term. Politically and socially constructed knowledge is based on a straightforward and perfectly flawed assumption: past experience validates future policy. It seems remarkable that we should be happy to move forward, with our rapidly growing population, with such a willfully cavalier attitude. We are driving off a cliff edge in the blackness of the night with the lights off, so afraid are we of what we might see. So illusionary is our water security. So foolish is our stubborn refusal to acknowledge our situation that it constitutes the greater and more pressing danger. No matter how terrifying it might be, I strongly advocate that we at least switch on the headlamps. It will shock us, but there is no other way to discover in which direction we should turn.

46

How to switch them on? Though many are working hard to rectify the position, there remains an irresponsible dearth of research. We need a political policy that is informed by – rather than works against – the observation and monitoring of actual resources, of actual trends in use, of actual levels of resource-use efficiency and of trends in such efficiencies. All in the context of the actual degradation of water environments through pollution. I am a scientist not a politician, so it is perhaps natural I should argue thus: we need an approach based on the actual and not the ideal. The ideal is an illusion, but is one that is deeply embedded. It has been constructed by politicians and society because it is comforting. The truth is far from comfortable. We need to blink the illusion from our eyes and square up to the uncomfortable reality.

My science footprint is currently very different from what it was two decades ago when I was struggling to understand the water-resource security of the Middle East. During the 1990s it became clear to me that the currency of politics and society was constructed knowledge. Not science. Constructed knowledge – based on misleading experience, history and culture – was unsafe but always prevailed over observed science. This book attempts to help readers both from society and the political classes to question their dangerous faith in their constructed knowledge on water resources, and particularly on water security.

What ever happened to the water wars?

Happily, the oft-predicted water wars have failed to materialise. Unhappily, this good fortune serves as further encouragement to our dangerous *laissez-faire* approach. What has (for the moment at least) staved off social unrest, international conflict and greater levels of starvation?

Broadly, luck.

Specifically, that luck has been in the form of virtual-water 'trade', a solution that came together invisibly, spontaneously and quasi-economically. Rather than a top-down, policy-led hydrological solution, we had that capricious, unknowable and flighty force without a moral compass, the market, somehow deliver an answer while we were still stumbling over the question.

Already, the water demands of current and future populations have outstripped the available water resources in many countries and regions around the world. In the Middle East and North Africa – which the military have acronymised into MENA – all twenty or so economies suffer from some degree of water scarcity. So do the semi-arid and semi-humid countries of Africa, Asia, Australia and North America. The water resources of Ethiopia, Kenya and the Sahelian states are especially under serious pressure. The strategically important rivers of the Nile, the Yellow River, the Indus in Pakistan and the sacred Cauvery River of southern India are all drying up; comparatively minor rivers such as the Jordan and Orontes are faring even worse. As we are coming to understand as we move through this book, a lack of water doesn't mean hosepipe bans. It means starvation.

47

THE SAHEL BELT
An ecologically distinct region running from the Atlantic to the Red Sea and sitting between the Sahara (to the north) and Sudan's savanna (to the south). Senegal, Mauritius, Mali, Burkino Faso, Niger, Nigeria, Chad, Sudan and Eritrea are all within (or partially within) the Sahel.

SEMI-ARID
This compound adjective is going to be used a lot. Sometimes called a steppe climate (because it is the climate of steppes!), semi-arid climates see low rainfall, around 250–500 millimetres per year. Think the Australian outback or any Western movie you've ever seen.

The concept of virtual water is a child of the contentious debate over the imminence of water wars. Those who predicted them believed the MENA region would be the main theatre of conflict. The reasons are obvious and understandable. Here is an area with terrible wealth inequalities and a strong recent narrative of civil unrest and poor relations between nations. Worse, many of the economies are dependent on a few strategically important rivers, such as the Nile or the Tigris-Euphrates flowing into the region from more humid regions. Some of the economies are very unhappy partners contending for the scarce waters of the Jordan and its tributary the Yarmuk. From the 1970s onwards, senior MENA leaders and officials have been issuing grave warnings that water wars were coming. These people were not fools or cranks or hysterics. King Hussein of Jordan was one. Boutros Boutros-Gali, the respected Secretary-General of the United Nations, was another. Indeed, to this day, Mr Boutros-Gali will prophesy water war.

He's wrong. The last water wars were minor skirmishes between 1962 and 1964 between Syria and Israel. No one has waged violent conflict over water since. Relations over scarce shared water are always conflictual but there is no armed conflict. There have been no further wars, despite a worsening global water-resource crisis. Economically invisible and politically silent virtual-water 'trade' has circumnavigated the need for actual conflict. There are still constant rumblings around the world, but never open war. The apocalypse has been postponed. A version of food security has been achieved in all these water-scarce hotspots. And it has been achieved without the political leaderships either doing anything deliberate or under-standing fully what has taken place. Local water scarcity has been ameliorated by invisible and politically silent trade in water-intensive commodities. While we weren't looking, virtual water has snuck into our global house. It's done an awful lot of tidying up and (temporarily) resolved conflict. As in the fairytale of the elves and the shoemaker, virtual water has been beavering away while we slept, averting disaster, keeping the wheels of the world turning, feeding those who would otherwise starve.

Importing water?

By the 1950s, several MENA economies were out of water. Population growth meant that they were simply no longer water- and food-secure. By the 1970s, the whole region was suffering a severe water deficit.

But if I presented these facts to anyone living in the region at the time, they would accuse me of being several glasses short of a gallon. I can imagine the indignant questioning cries. Where were the food shortages? When did the taps run dry? Where is the impact of water scarcity on economic development? In truth, I don't need to imagine these cries. I have heard them often enough in reality.

And how have I always answered them? Thus: 'My dear brothers, you've been importing water all this time.'

The responses come even harder: importing water, what nonsense! Show us, where. Show us, how.

Let us take Egypt, the most populous MENA economy. The country has been in extreme water deficit since the early 1970s, but no one would know it. Egypt is a huge country which can produce food and other crops on about 4 per cent of its area. The tracts irrigated until the 1970s were the rich soils of the Nile and its delta. The sandy tracts beyond the Nile lowlands can be made productive with water and other inputs. In the early 1970s, Egypt attempted to expand the irrigated area by 20 per cent and simultaneously began to import food staples such as wheat and later maize and soya. The former project failed, but trade proved to be a silent and very effective remedy to running out of water. We can easily see these food imports. They arrive in large very visible ships. They

49

are highly visible and apparent. But that visibility, served to conceal. They thought they were simply importing food, and were blind to the virtual-water content.

So Egypt has been importing water.

This was not deliberate or planned. Amazingly, it was not water policy-makers in Middle East who provided the remedy; rather, it was food subsidies in the industrialised economies of North America and Europe. The European Common Agricultural Policy (CAP) is well known. One might even call it notorious. It is perhaps the greatest single example of market distortion in history. Most

50 casual observers note that global free trade, as it stands, is very far from free and light years from fair. The EU and US provide considerable trade and production subsidies, enabling their agribusinesses to dump vast quantities of cheap produce on the markets of other economies. This is a theme to which I shall return later. For all the negative outcomes of this policy – and there are many – it did serve to incentivise food importing by water-scarce economies. These staple foods are incredibly water-intensive. So, in Egypt, neither the politicians nor the general public were aware that they were engaging in water-securing processes. They thought they were just importing cheap food. The water was invisible.

Just as problems can be persuaded to bear the fruit of their own solutions, so do solutions often contain the seeds of further problems. International trade brings food and water security, but not self-sufficiency. Also, it brings the remedy so swiftly and so effortlessly that it becomes easy to ignore the downside. Easy, and dangerous. The indignant, defensive responses I get from those living in countries with severe water deficits are made possible by the invisibility of their water imports. When I call them water importers, they call me delusional (sometimes worse). But it is they who are delusional. And when it comes to politicians it is survival. Imagine the political fallout from announcing to your electorate that you are in water deficit, that your apparent water and food security depends on the caprices of other economies, that any self-sufficiency is illusionary. Imagine that announcement. And then imagine the uproar.

I don't blame the politicians. They and I see things differently, each according to her or his own job description. What is the role of the politician? The politician is the dance-partner of Uncertainty, that ugly but inevitable uninvited guest with whom no one else would ever dream of dancing. To meet Uncertainty's demands, politicians are sometimes forced to reorganise the allocation of resources, or even the regulation of behaviour. Our uninvited guest might demand the floor to herself. She might require exclusive use of the waiting staff. She might drink the bar dry and fall asleep under the buffet. And the politician has to ensure that this fickle partner is made comfortable and welcome. To fail to do so would provoke Uncertainty's ire, and the smashing of the whole party in a fit of pique. Yet, in managing Uncertainty, the politician is always facing the hazard of unpayable political costs. We do not like the politician suddenly restricting our share of the vol-au-vents or turning off the champagne tap. Even less do we like the politician telling us that we must change our ways to accommodate this new, unwelcome guest. Politicians stay in power by avoiding political costs.

51

But the plodding scientist, working in the relatively certain domain of probability, is most usually blind to the uncertain and hostile political landscape that can scorch the feet of the politician. The scientist has never paid much attention to the gilded invite to the glamorous ball, attached as he or she is to the microscope, the test tube, or the word processor.

In their behaviour, MENA politicians have been nothing but rational and expert. They have observed that water-resource-management problems are no more stressful than a decade ago. Politics has to be in the here and now. Only a fool starts managing tomorrow while still smack bang in the middle of today. For the politician, a problem removed is a blessing counted. That is more political capital to be offset against the inevitable costs incurred by capricious Uncertainty. Where is the politician's incentive to converge on the message of precautionary, probabilistic and politics-blind science? Nowhere. The politician and the scientist ride parallel lines which only meet when societies are secure through building a diverse and strong economy able to 'import' virtual water. Economic diversification is another mighty invisible.

52

But I am not by now just a scientist. I like sticking my fingers into the nitty-gritty of reality. And out there are politicians who are just politicians. Some politicians enjoy being visionary. They enjoy saving the world rather than fighting the little fires. And that's how change becomes possible.

'Maybe it's the third world; maybe it's his first time around' When singing that line in 'Call Me Al' from the Graceland album, Paul Simon was expressing a spiritual wonderment and emotional connection belonging to the naive but benign central character of the song. A lost figure in a strange and bewildering physical landscape that somehow mirrors his alienated internal emotional landscape.

More banal, though, he may have been expressing a legitimate critique of the (then) categorisation or league-tabling of nations into the first, second and third world. The disappearance of (much of) communism at the end of the 1980s put paid to this slightly arrogant formulation. The poorer nations of the world have successively been labelled the 'undeveloped', 'underdeveloped' or 'less-developed' economies, in attempts to express tactfully the relative weakness of their economies. The more hopeful and acceptable moniker 'the developing world' has also gained much currency in recent decades.

However, this study also uses a three-fold categorisation.

What is often wildly inaccurately (given the inclusion of nations such as South Korea and Australia) referred to as advanced Northern economies requires a label. I bundle them into a catch-all term: industrialised or OECD economies. These are nations with advanced, diversified economies. They are wealthy, well-fed and most of their jobs bring very high returns to water. The BRICS nations are the easiest to categorise, the name being simply an acronym: Brazil, Russia, India, China and South Africa.

Implicitly, a three-tier hierarchy exists even in this more even-handed formulation. In Figures 2.4 and 2.5, they are ordered top to bottom thus: industrialised, BRICS and less developed. It's hard to shake off historic and ingrained prejudices and modes of thought. In my defence, let me observe that in 2.4 at least, the figures plotted arguably justify the order.

53

Follow the money

The luck of the wealthy extends to all areas of life. Water is no exception. The water story of Singapore is breathtaking and one to which we shall return. The headline fact is astounding, though: Singapore has only 5 per cent of the water it needs. Yet there is no hint of water shortages, nor of the constrained economic development that many feel ought to be inevitable for a seriously water-short island economy. Ninety per cent of the total water needed is brought in through trade in food commodities. The other non-native 5 per cent has until recently been imported across the straits from Malaysia. This dependence is now being reduced by investment in desalination, an increasingly affordable technology. All these options are easy (well, relatively easy) for Singapore. It is a rich nation with a diversified and developed economy.

Figure 2.4 Virtual-water 'exports' and 'imports', volume per annum, 1997–2001

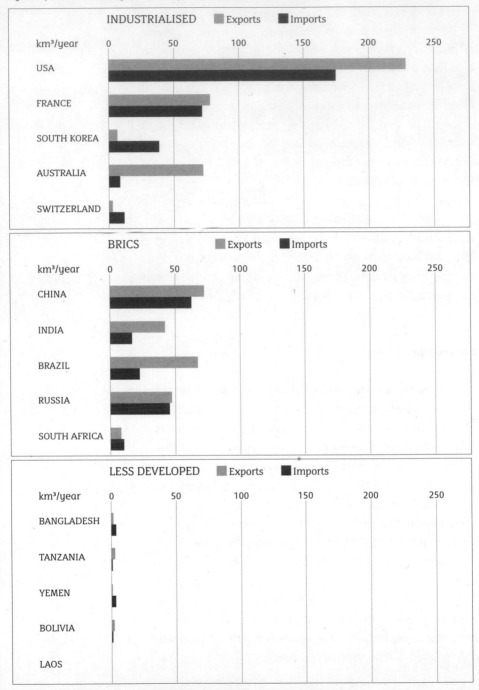

Source: A.K. Chapagain and A.Y. Hoekstra (2003), *Water Footprints of Nations*, Delft: IHE.

Figure 2.5 Virtual-water 'exports' and 'imports', volume per head, 1997–2001

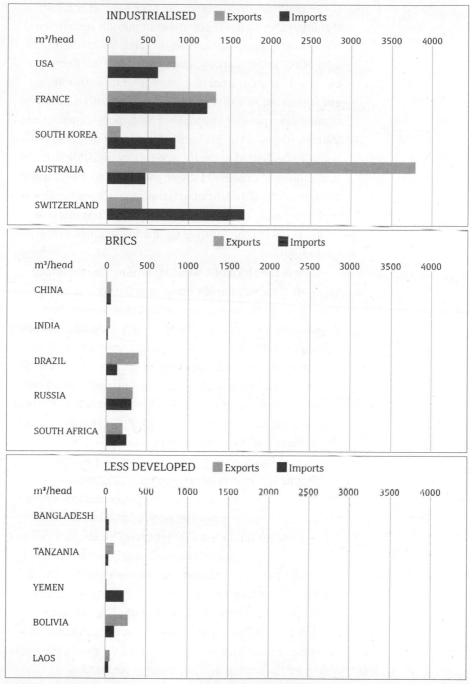

Source: A.K. Chapagain and A.Y. Hoekstra (2003), *Water Footprints of Nations*, Delft: IHE.

Singapore managed to head off its water scarcity through exceptional investment in human resources. It is not intuitive to solve a water crisis by investing in education. But it worked. The investment in education, along with a great deal of imaginative investment and enterprise led to a diversified economy, with a powerful trading arsenal. The example of Singapore demonstrates that solutions to the problem of water security can lie outside the field of hydrology. A mix of invisible social and economic processes prove silently effective. Consider the hydrological horror of attempting – for example – to mobilise water locally to meet Singapore's needs and contrast it with the relative ease and elegance of the trade solution.

56

Such is the story of a wealthy nation. The poor fare less well. Poor economies often only manage to import enough water to meet 10 per cent of their needs. And these imports are most often infrequent and irregular, and often damaging to the local rural economy. Sometimes, it takes a natural disaster to bring in the necessary water. Ethnic violence, civil war and other forms of armed conflict are frequently accompanied by death and starvation. Conflict disrupts trade. A disruption in trade leads to a disruption of the illusion of food and water security.

So, who has the water and who uses the water?

Graphs and charts are the scientist's constant companion. But they are the enemy of the general reader and, so my editor informs me, the bane of publishers. Nothing haemorrhages readers quicker than an injudicious reliance on graphs. I hope you will praise my restraint. For here we are, well into Chapter 2, and only now do I deploy this too carelessly and frequently used device of academe. Don't be daunted. Let me guide you through. The first graph – Figure 2.4 – shows water trade by country, in cubic kilometres per year. The second – Figure 2.5 – shows the same thing, but measured in cubic metres per head.

On the industrialised economies selected, a brief word. The 30 OECD economies are home to about 17 per cent of the world's population. Contrast that with the whopping 38 per cent who live in the five BRICS economies. The remaining 45 per cent live in the oil-rich Gulf or the poor economies of the world, which we group together as the developing economies.

France, the US and Australia are three of the major food exporters in the world. This is borne out clearly by the graphs. The wild spiking of the figures for Australia in Figure 2.5 are the simple result of being an awfully large, awfully empty country with few people. Figure 2.4 highlights another important issue: the less-developed world is not in on the virtual-water game. Probe a little deeper and we can see another headline trend: the big, rainy farming countries (Brazil, India and Australia) are exporting 'water' (concealed in food) to the populous smaller nations such as Switzerland and South Korea that have neither the land nor the water to meet the food needs of their populations.

The graphs throw up other useful snippets of information and insight. Russia and South Africa have higher per-capita levels of imports than the other BRICS nations, but for wholly different reasons not expressed in the figures. Russia has a relatively underdeveloped agricultural economy; South Africa is water-scarce.

57

ACRONYM-DROPPING: THE OECD
The Organisation for Economic Co-operation and Development comprises 30 member nations. These are essentially Europe – bar the Baltics, the Balkans and the former USSR states the Pacific Rim economies of Japan, South Korea, Australia and New Zealand, and the US, Canada and Mexico.

China quietly saves the world

There is a lot that can be said about China, this frequently silent monolith. Anything I say in praise should not detract from legitimate criticisms on issues such as freedom of speech and human rights. In this, China certainly lags behind the industrialised nations, whose recently acquired standards make their leaders and inhabitants forgetful about the spasms of industrialised killing that characterised the first half of the twentieth century.

However, China has saved the world. In water terms, at least.

While the rest of the world has been ignoring its water crisis, China has quietly addressed its own insecurity, and incidentally the world's, by managing its own demand for water.

And it has done this on three ostensibly unconnected levels. First, in straightforward hydrological policy, China is a world leader. It has driven water productivity across the domestic, industrial and agricultural sectors with the kind of focus and determination that only comes after sixty years of strict Communist top-down governance. Second, China is 'importing' virtual water through low-value, water-intensive food imports.

Yet this is not how it has saved the world. It saved the world in 1979 through the adoption of a policy which was at the time – and has been frequently since – criticised for being inhumane, totalitarian and unnatural. That policy was officially termed the Family Planning Policy, but unofficially and internationally is known as the one-child policy. For those unfamiliar with it, it does what it says on the tin. Families are limited to one child only. This policy is enforced by law, backed by punishments, including fines and imprisonment. A tough means of regulating population growth, and one totally unachievable in a democracy where the legislators are accountable to the public at the ballot box.

What effect has the one-child policy had? It has reduced births, and the subsequent reproduction by those unborn persons. Estimates suggest that a population increase in the region of three hundred million has been avoided. That's enough people to repopulate the US (with Canada thrown in for the high end of the estimate range). And what's that in water? It's a roughly 20 per cent decrease in water usage compared to what it might have been. In other words, there's 300 cubic kilometres of water going spare each year, a volume of water sufficient to meet the needs of all the MENA economies combined, of Old Europe and half of Africa. These are globally significant numbers. Be clear: no other society has made such a contribution to global water security. Only economic diversification has had a positive effect on water security comparable to that of China's collective social experiment. And in China, population control has run concurrent with a highly ambitious enhancement of human resources, and the consequent surge in industrialisation.

The bottom line: there's a very strong argument for the assertion that no one other decision has had so great a positive effect on global water management than China's one-child policy.

A very quick peek at the future

59

Feeding the five thousand

The human race is getting too good at reproducing and too bad at dying. Since 1950, population growth has tended to be exponential. Globally, the population has grown by four billion in six decades. This is bad news, and little mitigated by the tendency that the populations in industrialised economies have of levelling off or even declining. The 100 poorest economies in the world are growing rapidly, and will bring another two billion to the population within the coming decades. This isn't nearly as much of a problem as the extra four billion added to the world population since 1950.

But while population technically knows no limits, water most certainly does. There is a finite amount in circulation on this planet. And there won't be any more. The more of us, the less for each. We need to learn a simple lesson. Those of us over-consuming (especially meat) are using up too much water. It's bad for our personal health and bad for the health of the environment. Pre-emptively, our diets need to change, so that we are consuming at the levels available for the future, rather than riding on the ignorant excesses of the past. All nations will have to reduce their water consumption as groundwaters are exhausted and river flows have to be restored. And a reduction in water consumption means a reduction in food production. We are all going on a diet, whether we like it or not.

Conversely, there will be strong economic drivers for increased water consumption. In the industrialised nations, we are using as much water as we possibly can. We do this without a moment's thought. We have our meat-rich diets, our comprehensive water and sewage amenities, our various water-intensive commodities. But the BRICS and less developed economies have yet to reach this level of water profligacy. They will. Or they will certainly try, at least. Already, as living standards improve, so water consumption rises in tandem. Such is the human condition, as cultivated by the market. Consumption is the ultimate good.

60

It's not all gloom though. Improvements in the water efficiency of agriculture are very hopeful. Russia and several African economies have considerable food-production potential currently untapped. Even a pessimistic appraisal allows for an increase of 30 per cent in global food production. That's no bad thing, given that the global population is also predicted to rise by 30 per cent by the middle of the twenty-first century. The problem comes at the point when there will be few further efficiencies to be had on a planet sagging under the weight of nine billion people – some hungry and some over-fed.

A diet for the world

It sounds glib, but we can eat ourselves out of this problem. Or rather, we can stop eating ourselves into a corner. There is much number-crunching to be done, but research suggests that diet changes could reduce per-capita water consumption in the industrialised countries by up to 40 per cent. Basically, dear reader, this means you. It's your diet that we are talking about. It's the meat you eat. It's the food you throw in the bin. It's the water you are squandering. I don't mean to be abrasive. Perhaps it would be fairer to say that it is *our* diet. I am trying to wean myself off water-intensive meat and onto less wasteful foods. It isn't easy. It involves swimming against the tide both of one's own life habits and against the broader culture. But together, we can change that culture. The past decade has seen astounding quantum leaps in popular attitudes towards recycling and energy use. Why not water? It is every bit as urgent, and arguably far easier for individuals to do something about. Less meat; more water. Perhaps I ought to get that on a bumper sticker.

Things are trickier for the BRICS nations. Predominantly vegetarian India can do little to reduce the water impact of the national diet. While the emergence of an affluent middle class is driving meat consumption in China, the Chinese government has the strength and inclination to curtail personal freedoms for the sake of the collective good. China will also meet any water shortfall by importing food commodities. Brazil has a lot of water. More than any country on earth. Brazilians really can indulge their meaty appetites with impunity.

61

Naturally, it is the poor and water-scarce nations of the Middle East and Africa which have the most uncertain futures. Their rivers are often dry; their economies are frequently far from robust. Here – as so many times before – is where human suffering will be most acute. Those nations that are neither oil-rich nor sufficiently swift to diversify their economies will bear the brunt.

But I love my hamburgers...
Cutting back on meat is not the only answer. Other solutions come to mind. But they are too remote at the moment. They lack the impact and ease of diet change.

Cheap renewable electricity is the holy grail economically, ecologically and politically. Low-cost solar energy could produce affordable water. And it would do it without polluting the atmosphere. Desalination plants fuelled by oil and gas pollute the atmosphere. Affordable water produced with clean solar energy which does not pollute the atmosphere would be ecologically sound and would help ensure that the price of food would not skyrocket. But clean solar-energy-driven desalination is decades away from realisation and application. High-quality water is being produced in desalination plants across the world for domestic and industrial users. But at between $0.5 and $1 per cubic metre the water is too expensive for irrigated crop production. In the coming decades, however, solar energy in the different energy economies of the future will enable water to be desalinated without negative impacts on the atmosphere.

62

Let's do lunch

In Chapter 1, we talked about breakfast. Now let's do lunch. Because lunch is going to be our way of changing, and saving, the world.

Bathtubs and buckets: some observations on how change happens (or doesn't)

I have had quite a few decades' experience watching how change does – or does not – occur in the scientific, political and commercial spheres. When I feel despondent, I consider myself cynical as a result of this experience; when I feel positive, I consider myself wiser. Here is what I have learnt. Effecting change is not a linear process, with regular, incremental steps, evenly accumulating towards happy completion. It is not, in short, like building a wall. When building a wall – or at least, when building one *properly* – you position a brick and hold it in place with cement. Every step, once achieved, is fixed, and forms an unambiguous foundation for the next step. This is not how political and social change occurs. Effecting change in our world is like filling a very leaky bucket. Much effort will be lost. If you drop your pace, you lose important ground. The input-to-outcome ratio is not one, as with building the wall. A great deal of what is put in will leak away.

The process of change can be summarised into three key stages, as so many things can. The first leg of the tripod of change is knowledge. People need to know about a problem or an opportunity or a new way of thinking. The next leg is wanting. It's not enough that people know about the need to change; you always need their buy-in to the process. (Except, as mentioned earlier, in China, where all you need is totalitarian rule.) Finally, the political system has to allocate resources to incentivise change.

63

The social change in attitudes and behaviour towards smoking are a helpful example. It is over fifty years since science first established a causal link between smoking tobacco and lung cancer. Consider the mass of research, campaigning and resource allocation required over the last half century. Scientific studies, pressure groups, anti-smoking adverts. The process has been driven from many different places and in many different, often conflicting, ways. We have not been building a wall; we have been filling a leaky bucket. Still, things slosh. People argue for illegalising tobacco, for raising the tax, for lowering the tax. But one can't help but feel in the face of ever-dwindling numbers of smokers that the tide has turned. Tobacco companies might try and junk the science behind passive smoking, but the days of doctor-endorsed cigarette brands are long gone and will never return. 'Nine out of ten doctors recommend Camel cigarettes for a smoother smoke!' Not likely in 2011. Change happened. Haphazardly. Sloppily. Too slowly for the impatient. Too swiftly for the conservative. But it happened. And is still happening now.

As Sam Cooke so rightly observed, it is in the nature of change for it to have 'been a long, long time coming'.

So, why lunch?

Because what I am trying to start here is a discourse. Or, more simply, a conversation. We're at that first step of effecting change: disseminating knowledge. I'm doing my equivalent of shouting from the rooftops.

Water by numbers

And the winner is...

Oscar speeches are often tedious for their gushing sentimentality, but I am always intrigued to hear about the invisible cast of extras 'without whom this would never have been possible'. There is something wonderfully mysterious about these unseen backroom figures, like the surprisingly lengthy catalogue of names in the acknowledgements of a book or the administrative team beavering away behind the backdrop behind an American President. You realise on inspection that what seemed the work of one person proves a collaboration. A community of talents. It is so with virtual water.

I'd like to take this chance to introduce you to a very important contributor to establishing the concept of virtual water: Arjen Hoekstra. Arjen is a prominent water scientist who manages a team of modellers. His modelling has made a very important contribution. It has also been very significant in getting the attention of water scientists in particular. For many scientists, modelling is the language of science. But what is a modeller? They produce results that make other scientists sit up and take notice: 'That Professor Allan might just be onto something here.' There are very few days when I do not thank my good fortune that Arjen and his international team in the Netherlands chose to turn their attention to virtual water, and soon after to individual and national water footprints. He could easily have devoted his skills to some other equally deserving field of enquiry.

A quick-warning

The rest of this section will be dedicated to an analysis of Arjen's modelling and the implications of his work. Many will find this fascinating. Those in the science community will find it absolutely vital. However, some readers may not require hard evidence. They might be willing to take my assertions about the virtual-water 'trade' on trust. For them, the big ideas. No need to check the numbers: they only want the ride. I understand such number-aversion, and I happily tell such readers that they can skip straight to the next section, missing nothing other than that they would wish to avoid.

65

What the modellers did...

Arjen and his team looked at the levels of water consumption and trade in 140 of the 200 world economies. This included all the industrial and BRICS economies and roughly two-thirds of the developing nations. Working at the start of this decade, their figures relate to the end of last century, contextualising the figures with an approximation of world population at about six billion.

One of the biggest innovations of their work was that by using production and trade datasets – instead of trying to estimate the water use of the various economic sectors – they automatically took into account green water as well as blue water. Remember, green water is soil water and is the Great Ignored in our narrative. Though vital to the running of our world and the production of our food, it is often excluded from studies as it is economically invisible. As no one pumps it, markets it, moves it around, it gets (wrongly) labelled as a public good or (worse) disregarded entirely. That economists should decide to turn a wilful blind eye to one of the most important determinants of human life and national security purely because they can't work out a way to stick a price tag on it might serve to confirm some of our less generous prejudices about the wisdom of economists. That other scientists and geographers should do the same is beyond belief. Yet Arjen's modelling in 2000 was the first to include green water and to give anything like an accurate image of our genuine global water use.

Which they calculated at 7500 cubic kilometres a year.

It's hard to know what to do with a number that size. Most of us can estimate the distance of a kilometre or 100 kilometres, or guess at the size of hectare. But when I say 17 million square kilometres, is that the size of the Grand Canyon, Russia or the Moon? (Russia, as it happens.) Past a certain size an evolutionary blindness sets in. It wasn't important for us to see the woods, just the trees. We are small and slow-moving creatures on a planet of blue whales, African elephants, towering mountains. Not to mention giant rivers.

Take the Amazon. Most of us know that the Amazon is the largest river in the world. Its annual flow is estimated at 8000 cubic kilometres. Roughly then, we're using an Amazon a year. To be clear, the Amazon is not just the largest river in the world. It is the largest by a considerable margin. In terms of flow, it is five times the size of its nearest rivals, the African Congo and fellow-South American Orinoco. It is eight times the size of the Indian Ganges and the Chinese Yangtse, and ten times as big as the old man of the south, the Mississippi. While the Nile is by most estimations the world's longest river, it's a small river next to the Amazon in terms of flow, with only 100 cubic kilometres a year.

Interestingly, a quick look at river flows tells us something else about man's relationship with ever-important freshwater. We don't like anything too big. Famously, there is not a single bridge across the Amazon. This is not – as most think – because it is unbridgeable (though the task would certainly prove tricky in many places). Rather, no one needs a bridge over the Amazon as there are no really major urban centres built on it. Similarly, with few

66

SHOULD I HAVE THE PASTA OR THE STEAK?
The water cost of our food is nearly always invisible. A tonne of grain needs at least 1000 tonnes of water to produce it. That might seem a lot, but it takes sixteen times as much water to raise a tonne of beef. If that difference were reflected in a market price that fairly passed on the full environmental costs of your food, how often would you be eating steak?

exceptions, man has declined to locate himself beside the world's giant rivers, either in antiquity or since. We've always instinctively favoured those rivers with flows beneath the 100-cubic-kilometres-per-year mark. These minnows have drawn human settlements and supported most of the greatest cities in human history.

Now, turn to Europe. The largest river on the continent is the Danube. A beautiful, majestic river, rich with history. But, truthfully, on the small side in global terms. You could very easily lose it in the Amazon, which is around 33 times larger. However, the Danube Basin is not the most populous basin in Europe. Historically, the bigger populations have gravitated towards those rivers with small but reliable annual flows, such as the Rhine, Loire and Rhone, all of which have flows of about 6 cubic kilometres a year. Or the tiny rivers such as the Seine, or the very tiny such as the Thames, with its flow of only 2 cubic kilometres per year. Let's quickly throw those two figures into powerful juxtaposition: the Amazon has a flow of 8000 cubic kilometres per year, the Thames just 2. Now hold those figures in your head under the umbrella of a third: our annual global water use is 7500 cubic kilometres.

This isn't simply an exercise in showing off how large the Amazon is. It's important to understand that these water resources are renewable, not infinite. Rivers can run dry. Even the ones that have major economic significance in Asia and the Middle East. Diversion and over-use are causing irreparable damage to the rivers of semi-arid regions. The Colorado, the Nile, the Indus and the Yellow are all drying up. Amazingly, these river-flow statistics are hard to come by. For some reason, the differing schools of politics, economics and geography have deemed river lengths and water-basin sizes important and valuable without ever giving much time or energy to disseminating information about river flow. This is foolhardy in the extreme. No other figure is more valuable in understanding how much water is available for an economy. Yet these numbers remain the closely guarded secrets of hydrologists.

Understanding and using the numbers

We can all accept the very apparent truth that 7500 cubic kilometres is a lot of water. How does that break down by usage? Arjen and his team calculated that roughly 5 per cent goes towards domestic use. Another 16 is used by industry. And the remainder, at nearly 80, is used in raising crops and livestock for food, and also for making fibres such as cotton. All the water used in homes across the world is blue water. So too is most of the water used in industry. In agriculture, it is the hitherto unmeasured green water that dominates, accounting for about 70 per cent of the water used in this sector. Here is but one of Arjen's important contributions: an estimation of total blue- and green-water use.

68

Through their modelling, we are able to see the 'flows' of virtual water. We can identify the net 'exporters' and 'importers'. Most importantly, the modelling illustrates how the national economies are dependent on the global trading system for their water and food security. In terms of pure volume, the industrialised countries are the main 'traders' in virtual water. They use their wealth to ensure that, through trade, any inherent water insecurity is hidden. BRICS also participate actively in this trade. The system does not serve everyone. The developing economies scarcely participate. Even those with considerable populations, such as Bangladesh, barely engage in commodity trade. The per-capita figures for trade reveal a stunning global asymmetry. The wealthy nations and BRICS are making themselves food- and water-secure through trade. In this, as in so many areas, the poorer nations are being left behind.

The water footprint

It's testament to the age that you probably already have a reasonable idea of what I mean by the phrase 'water footprint'. The trail has been well and truly blazed by the 'ecological footprint' of Wackernagel and Rees and the energy footprint – terms that gained much currency towards the close of the 1990s as ways of discussing the environmental impact of humans on an individual, national and global level. In the last century, few outside that science community would have been familiar with the term 'carbon footprint'. Today we encounter it perpetually. Most often, we are being offered opportunities to reduce it. The carbon footprint is conceptually ingrained from the classroom to the car showroom. From supermarket checkout to airport check-in.

A remarkable achievement. What satisfaction when an idea enters the common discourse. Especially such an important one.

So, tracing a well-trodden path, comes the water footprint. If anything, it should be an easier concept to grasp than its forebears. We all know what water looks like and, as discussed throughout this chapter, have some (albeit vague and differing) ideas about how to quantify it. Ecological and energy footprints have a range of complex and diverse inputs. These are quite simple for science to get a handle on, but less straightforward for the layman's imagination. Water is water, and so all products, goods and services translate, via the water footprint, into a language we already understand. When I tell you that Arjen and his team of modellers discovered that the water footprint of a cup of coffee is 140 litres, the statistic has a big impact because it relates to a too-frequent pleasure assumed to be environmentally innocent.

The first review and analysis of water footprints – of both nations and individuals – was produced by Arjen, working with Ashok Chapagain, at the time a researcher at the UNESCO-IHE Institute for Water Education in Delft. It is hard to overestimate the impact their work had on publication

69

and public discussion. Until that time, I had experienced considerable resistance from engineers and economists to the idea of virtual water. Of course no one denied the idea. But they disputed its usefulness. And they did so quite vociferously. The economists saw no point in going beyond an analysis of traded commodities. The engineers were philosophically sceptical of soil water and trade. Theirs is the world of the hydraulic mission. Of practical, physical, literal and highly visible problems. For them, water scarcity is real and never virtual. So they were never likely to be interested in a virtual solution.

70

But Arjen and Ashok's work changed that perception. Some hefty modelling meant that virtual water was no longer a soft and abstract daydream. It had the wondrous weight and significance of numbers behind it now. I should note that it is thanks to Arjen and Ashok that I was able to get your attention with the water footprint of your breakfast in the previous chapter. More usefully, it is thanks to their work that we can compare the water footprints of national diets across the world. This all contributes, slowly but vitally, to the accumulation of knowledge. From here, change. But there is still some way to go.

Water footprints and big business or how much water does it take to make a micro-chip?

There are many interesting things about my job. Being able to devote my time, energy and intellect to a subject that I consider to be massively important is, no doubt, the best aspect. The travel is also rather a lot of fun. But something else I enjoy is the peculiar diversity of the people I meet. As water slips up the political agenda, I spend less time with my fellow academics and more with that attractive collection of individuals who are out there in the world actually doing things.

So it was that I found myself recently seated around a table with some scientist peers, bright-eyed environmental activists from several NGOs – notably Waterwise and the WWF – and several senior managers from Intel, Nestlé, Unilever and Kimberley-Clark among others. We were all there building on the initiative and information service which Arjen called the Water Footprint Network (WFN).

Now, so often in the environmental discourse private companies and corporations are the villains. They are the Bad Other. At best, criminally negligent; at worst, deliberately evil until campaigned or legislated into serving society properly. You may be conjuring romantic images of us aged academics banding together under the leadership of a feisty eco-campaigner to deal some earnest and effective exposé deathblow to the wicked water wastefulness of a faceless international corporate. If so, prepare to be disappointed.

71

These senior managers and heads of research were there to share information, not to conceal it. In fact, in many ways they were significantly ahead of us in the worlds of academe and activism. Because if there is one thing that large companies with an eternal eye on the bottom line do really well, it's auditing. And these companies had brought together a massive amount of data on their water footprints. For several years, they had been evaluating both the effectiveness of their own in-house water management and that of the supply chains of their industries. And they were here to share their findings.

I've never liked the well-worn phrase about old dogs and new tricks. Less so now I am very much an old dog. There remains nothing I enjoy more than new tricks, or at least new info. And, as an early convert to the Apple Macintosh and still using a MacBook Air, I was amazed to learn from the Intel representatives that computer-chip manufacture is a very water-intensive process. Further, Intel has a considerable manufacturing and R&D facility in Israel, not a natural home for water-hungry industry. Undoubtedly, there was a corporate reputational scandal in the making here. A heavily polluting corporation misusing water in the water-scarce Middle East would make for unattractive copy. But instead, Intel's story borders on the inspirational. Once they were aware of the sheer quantities of water their process required, they cleaned up their act. Intel now treats and reuses its wastewater. Where once it might have been an enemy to water-vulnerable Israel, Intel now contributes positively to both its economy and water environment.

72

Of course, I don't intend to go unnecessarily doe-eyed over the benevolence of the corporate world. Private and public companies are motivated by only a handful of factors, and ecological do-gooding is not (directly) one of them. The profit imperative is naturally the golden rule of the business world, and sometimes water-management efficiency is yet another means of cutting costs and maximising profits. If there is nothing intrinsically good about this, there is certainly nothing bad. However, increasingly, due to a growing awareness and eco-activism in our civic society, companies are very alive to the peril of reputational risk. Much time, energy and ingenuity is spent developing corporate identities and reputations based around cherished core values. In an age where many companies are nothing but a brand, no one wants to jeopardise their good name. Instinctively, we take water scarcity seriously. It is certainly written deep in our genetic make-up. Thirst can make us panic. We've all tasted the very fringe of drought.

While Intel's anecdote was interesting in itself, it would hardly have been too reassuring a sign if it had been only an isolated incident. But it wasn't. Nestlé and Pepsi had identified that their biggest water consumption took place in their upstream processes, specifically the farming of cocoa beans, coffee beans and tea leaves, the core ingredients in their globally distributed, highly addictive products.

Conversely, Unilever had realised the potential for water-saving measures in its downstream activities, and was working on developing a new detergent for water-scarce India. At the risk of sounding like a commercial, their new powder promises to produce an impressive lather with less water and also to require less rinsing. Greater cleanliness per drop. Here is the contribution that industry can make in our drive to manage our water resources better. What was so rewarding to discover at this meeting was that all the companies present were taking the concept of the water footprint seriously. By seriously, I mean that they were taking it and were actively and practically applying it to their own water use. They were trying to see how they were using water, and how much they were using, and then looking to improve on both fronts. But the private sector suffers from the same problem faced by the world of science: the acquisition of usable data.

73

Data are unfortunately more slippery than water. Putting together relevant data on a company's water footprint is a highly daunting task. Because you are dealing with dynamic processes, not a static model. The inputs and outcomes are forever changing in quality, quantity and even in their very nature. Again, companies have got very competent at understanding the underlying economic fundamentals of their business, their industry, their individual processes and themselves. Many of these companies are able to account for their cash and spending down to the last dollar; incredible, given their multi-national size and scope. But the discipline and rigour does not (yet) exist in relation to the use of water resources. For most of human history, water has been considered free and plentiful. It would have been profoundly counter-intuitive to expend valuable time and money doing a heavy audit of such a bountiful (and financially irrelevant) resource. But the change has come to industry. And we need their help in changing everyone's behaviour.

74

Even better than the real thing

It seems that no major change in values can be accepted into the mainstream until an emblematic event has occurred. The damage that water mismanagement can do to corporate reputation enjoyed its emblematic moment in 2003, when the world's biggest brand ran adrift in a little-known corner of India. The brand in question was the mighty Coca-Cola. And playing David to its corporate Goliath was the panchayat (or local council) of a small village called Plachimada, in the province of Kerala. On 7 April, the panchayat declined to renew the operating licence for Coca-Cola's Indian bottling operation HCBL. Prior to the arrival of Coca-Cola in 1999, the local wells had supplied sufficient water for the village and several neighbouring areas. But within a few years of the soda giant's arrival, the wells were depleted and the remaining water severely compromised by industrial pollution. Most worrying of all were claims that the company had grossly over-extracted groundwater reserves.

In 2004, work at the bottling factory was halted, and the case continues to wind its way through the Indian legal system. I have not examined the case closely, but it would seem that natural drought also had a part to play in the water problems of Plachimada. But then, how bright is it to set up a water-intensive bottling plant in a drought-prone area? Whether or not Coca-Cola are true villains in this tale is, broadly, academic. The reputational damage was done. The narrative written. Now, Coca-Cola are keen to invest (and be seen to invest) in renewing and treating their wastewater in India. Water management will never again be considered economically irrelevant by the company. Thus, an emblematic event.

What we've learnt by staring at our feet...

There are 200 or so economies in the world. Each in its own way is testing the capacity of the global hydrological system to provide long-term water services to provide our food, our livelihoods and our water environments.

The industrialised economies have shown us that technology can yield incredible improvements in water productivity, both in industry and in rain-fed agriculture. Significantly, these economies have also tested to destruction the idea that irrigated farming is the panacea that will provide a solution to our ever-growing food needs. Most helpfully of all, it is the industrialised nations – through their unconscious behaviour rather than deliberate innovation – that have shown how the solutions to water problems may come from outside the water sector. These economies have alleviated real (and unrealisable) burdens on their local water supplies by diversifying into highly water-productive industries (and away from water-intensive agriculture) and by meeting this food shortfall through trade, and the 'importing' of virtual water. Putting aside our unsustainable dietary reliance on meat protein, there is a very real reason to feel positive about the progress of the industrialised economies. With stabilising or even shrinking populations and ever-decreasing per capita water consumption, these countries are using less water each year.

With water productivity, BRICS have achieved much, and have much yet to achieve. Brazil remains the world's water tower. China – through population control and water management – has done the world very considerable service in the area of global water security. As water productivity improves and as these economies come to understand better the strength of virtual-water 'trades', so they will play an even greater role in how our global water resource is managed. Perhaps the defining role.

75

And then, at the bottom of the pile, are the developing countries. Here is the challenge. Who will help them, and why? The virtuous circle of virtual 'trade' could be developed to circumnavigate the poor. The cash-rich and the water-rich economies can deal between themselves. Developing nations might benefit obliquely, through the dumping of cheap subsidised grain, for example. (Though that benefit in virtual-water 'imports' is counterbalanced by the damage to local rural economies.) But – if we are to construct a global solution to the allocation of our water resources – there exists no economic or scientific imperative to include these nations, short of the dollars required to secure water through either trade or infrastructure.

76

Of course, there is another imperative. That of compassion. The dictates of market economics and international trade, the forces that currently invisibly govern the world's virtual-water 'trade', may make no concession to compassion. But we as individuals, as voters, as global citizens most certainly can. That is why it is an idea in our heads and a capacity of our hands to ensure that our most precious resource is allocated efficiently, sustainably and equitably. That we can is why we must.

The wicked problem of water scarcity

What is a wicked problem? A problem so complex that we can neither properly quantify nor effectively model it. Complex problems are associated with high levels of uncertainty. They are also urgent. Remember, Uncertainty is the constant companion of politicians. They live alongside Uncertainty and have centuries of experience in deflecting, reconstructing and only facing the problems that Uncertainty brings once society supports them in doing so. In other words it is up to us. We have to send a message to the politicians that we are with them. We will hold their hand, on the condition that they guide us well.

We'll grant them the political capital, if they will exhibit the executive courage.

Global water management poses a wicked problem to us environmental scientists because it contains both the knowns, knowable unknowns and the unknowable unknowns. Essentially, the knowns are the current situation. In other words, the state of current technology, the current population size, the current levels of water consumption, the current ability to use water. The knowable unknowns are the unpredictable political and social processes. What twists and turns will international demographics take? Can African farmers lift their crop productivity?

77

Then there are the unknown unknowns. How best to illustrate this? I would not be the first to draw attention to the political-philosophical discourse of the 1990s, heralding the end of history and the unassailable triumph of liberal, free-market democracy, and how the opening events of this century so mocks the naivety of that discourse.

And here is where the wickedness really takes off.

Here is a shocking thought. Many of the most dangerous threats we face in the twenty-first century are unintended outcomes from interventions, confidently and optimistically taken in the latter half of the twentieth century. Climate change is the mega-example. We solved problems of mobility, of industry, of quality of life, of peace and prosperity. But we didn't have the crystal ball that allowed us to understand that this would give birth to the wicked problem of global warming. People might have been able to predict; indeed, with varying levels of precision, many did. But no one could have proved this outcome with *a priori* evidence. Similarly, water management, particularly the big water for irrigation, has left us with low flows to remedy and toxic environments with low food-production potential. These could not be accurately predicted. But we must now deal with these unknowns becoming reality.

The wickedness is this: we do not know what is really going to happen down the line as a result of what we are doing now. And the problem is that we can only know these unknowns retrospectively. Human beings are terrific at turning problems into their own solutions. But, with a wicked problem, the solutions then turn into wholly new and surprising problems.

So it has been with the industrialised nations.

The so-called solutions to our demands for energy, transport, food, goods and – of course – water have themselves in turn become problems as great as the initial scarcity. The solutions have become bigger problems than those we were attempting to escape. The unknowns proved wicked.

 78

The question of whether there will be sufficient water for a rapidly reproducing humanity with ever-greater water demands is a very urgent and very wicked problem. Wicked because we – as individuals, as societies, as nations – simply don't comprehend the natural systems. Science and technology have a track record in solving this problem which I might generously describe as mixed.

Even virtual water itself has a wicked side. It is this wickedness which we shall address at the beginning of the next chapter.

CHAPTER 3

Well-fed, well-watered and well-paid: water and the subsidised agriculture of the industrialised nations

Humankind cannot bear too much reality
T.S. ELIOT, 'BURNT NORTON' FROM FOUR QUARTETS

I have a nightmare

As an opening refrain, it does little to inspire. This observation has been made by many, and I am consciously borrowing from American environmentalist Michael Shellenberger. It is a strong point. Scaring people is not a sustainable way of ensuring support. We are resilient to bad news and shut our ears to it. A speech about having a nightmare would not have captured the ears, hearts and imaginations of two hundred thousand people gathered to hear Martin Luther King at the Lincoln Memorial. A speech about dreams did just that.

Consequently, I will try to inspire rather than frighten. To persuade, not badger. To reason, not lecture. I will do this not simply because it is – in some abstract, moral sense – the right way to go about things but because I believe that in adopting this approach I will find ears more open and imaginations more readily engaged.

However, there remains the problem of how to communicate bad news, for bad news I have. Virtual water – like markets, the environment and fruit machines – has no moral compass and feels no obligations to any one person or nation. Investments can go down as well as up. That disclaimer appended to all financial products serves as a description of virtual water. Virtual water has a light side. And a dark side. We must address both in our assessment.

The industrialised economies have been enjoying the light side of virtual water. On the light side, virtual water *brings* water security to the rich industrialised economies and many other economies as well, *helps* both the poor and rich in the world, and *saves* precious global water resources. Those are incredibly positive results, and I will demonstrate how this has already happened with examples drawn from three industrialised nations.

80

But industrialised economies have also been victim to the dark side of virtual water. On the dark side, virtual water *hides*. The invisibility of virtual water means that some very important underlying environmental and eco-nomic fundamentals are hidden from us. Knowing about these underlying fundamentals is vital to ensuring that the world's water resources are sustainably managed. But by hiding this knowledge, virtual-water 'trade' *deludes* water users, policy-makers and politicians. Because we can't see the problem, we (wrongly) think there isn't one. Which means that virtual-water 'trade' ultimately *slows down* the progress societies might make in learning to value and manage water properly.

In brief.

The light side: secures; helps; saves water.

The dark side: hides; deludes; slows reform.

A virtuous coalition of water scientists and activists is coming together, informally and haphazardly. We are trying to communicate the problem, but the allure of the dark side is very great. It seduces with its seeming benign ease. Many embrace the dark side, believing it to be the light. Politicians hear of this invisible economic force painlessly solving the problems of water scarcity. And that is all they hear. Their ears are open to the dream, but they remain closed to the nightmare. Hence they stay wilfully blind to the problems. Gradually, grudgingly, the industrialised nations are beginning to engage with the underlying fundamentals that cause resource scarcity and polluted environments. Slowly, politicians are struggling against their instincts. They are seeing beyond the easy solution of the dark side – a solution which hides, deludes and thereby slows reform – to face the uncomfortable truths of water management.

We enjoy being blind to risk, until that risk manifests itself as a reality. The great economic crisis of 2008 was born of a systematic fear in the financial sector of accepting the true cost of risk. This debt could be deferred for a time. It could be packaged up and passed on. But ultimately it had to be paid. After the event, once the risk has been realised, everyone is an expert. Everyone is aggrieved and wonders how such a fraud could have been perpetuated. Yet we were all unwitting participants. The financial sophistry of securitisation and massive leverage created the conditions in which we were all happy to be blind. The conditions were in place to encourage us as individuals and society to underestimate the risk and misjudge the impact of our decisions. Lenders and borrowers were mutually complicit. We hankered for impossible debt. Water-users borrow from the environment without precaution. Politicians who should be looking out for the environment and society's water-resource security are complicit. Virtual-water 'trade' certainly helps keep this blind and dangerous complicity in place.

81

Finance is not real, though the human misery and suffering endured in a recession most certainly is. Finance can recover. Ultimately, it is about numbers, and numbers are infinite.

Water is not infinite. We are wrong to assume that the atmosphere and water environment can give all we take. Or that it can take all we give. We are drawing too much in some places. We are over-polluting in others. Neither course of action is sustainable.

But virtual-water 'trade' – by enabling a calm, ordered and harmonious system – fools us into thinking that everything is progressing well. And can continue in the same way. As the frog in the slowly boiling water, we do not feel the need to jump. But jump we must.

As God is my witness, I'll never be hungry again

82

Two industrialised global players have been locked in a half-century-long dance; a very intense one with unintended consequences. It has affected global farm-trade systems and especially other exporters of wheat and the importers who depend on this water-intensive staple. The partners in this enduring global dance who have determined the behaviour of all those participating, whether competing exporters or importers, are the US and the EU.

In 1957 the signatories of the Treaty of Rome were accommodating themselves to the aftermath of two devastating bouts of the mechanised killing of modern European warfare. They were but a shadow of their imperial glories. These governments of industrialised economies feared not the passing of empires but the challenges of providing secure and violence-free lives for the peoples of Europe.

European experience of the chaos of war and of the associated dislocation of food-commodity trade as recently as the middle of the twentieth century showed that hunger and international starvation were real possibilities. Europe was dangerously exposed to food insecurity through its reliance on trade. As the continent began to heal, the attentions of its political classes (rightly) turned to ensuring that the people of Europe would never be hungry again. Yet the action they took laid the foundations for perhaps the greatest trade distortion in the history of humanity, doing untold damage to some environments, and to the economies of the developing world. Once Europe embarked on this course, the US had to respond, and the response was a process which competed down the global price of wheat.

But first, a helpful and quite astounding contextualising fact: the price of wheat has been falling for a thousand years. This is an extraordinary statement. How is such a thing possible? Continual improvements in farm inputs and farm-production systems, and in marketing and distribution, played a considerable role.

The trend has continued. The second half of the twentieth century saw remarkable agronomic and technological advances. Humanity has become particularly ingenious when it comes to fertiliser. The haphazard tradition of gently improving on nature's own casual muckspreading has given way to a field of bioscience that enjoys world-class intellectual and financial resources. But, as we will repeatedly discover, the cost of wheat is misleading. Economics fails to take into account environmental costs, unless translated into green taxes by governments. The very real financial and ecological cost of modern pesticides, herbicides, fertilisers and energy-hungry and water-hungry farming methods is not reflected in the price of wheat. It should be. Until such time, we are spending on an invisible credit card, running up debts in an account we do not know we have. If we wait until the red letters pile up and the bailiffs come knocking, we will suffer very greatly.

But it was not our wunder-chemicals or whizzy technology that pushed prices of wheat down even further over the past sixty years. It was politicians seeking food security in Europe and responsive subsidy policies in the US that together have kept the world over-supplied with half-cost wheat.

In (what would become) the EU, the Common Agricultural Policy (CAP) began subsidising staple foods, backed by

83

EU, EC AND EEC
The EU was established by the Treaty of Maastricht in 1993. It had been some time in development. Almost immediately after the end of the Second World War, the western and central European nations began moving towards political union and the establishment of a common market. The 1957 Treaty of Rome instituted the European Economic Community (EEC). Its signatories were Italy, France, West Germany, Belgium, Luxembourg and the Netherlands, which states comprised the six founder members of the EEC. At the time of writing, there are 27 members of the EU, with a post-credit-crunch Ireland knocking sheepishly at the door.

a guarantee to buy surplus product at a fixed price. Farmers had every incentive to become hyper-productive. They did just that. The famed butter mountains and milk lakes held in EU warehouses and sold at incredible losses and disruptions to foreign markets stands testament to the success of this drive for productivity at the cost of all else. In the 1950s, wheat production in the nascent EU (or EEC as was) stood at an impressively high 3 tonnes per hectare. By 1990, this figure had tripled to 9 tonnes. Similarly, the US saw productivity increase greatly under the guiding hand of federal subsidies for farmers. Not one ear of wheat has been produced in the US or member nations of the EEC/EU in the last fifty years unaffected by the shadow of the system of subsidies.

84

This has been a wonderful development for (most of) the stomachs in the world. But – as is an increasingly common refrain in this book – the cost and suffering has been borne by the farmers of the developing world. And the environment.

CAPPING COSTS AND COSTING THE CAP
Despite a series of reforms since the turn of the century, the CAP still accounts for just under half of the entire EU budget. In 2006, the figure was €49.8 billion, up from €48.5 billion in 2005.

What to expect from this chapter

In this chapter, I am going to take a hard look at three very different industrialised economies and their relationships with water and virtual water.

First at the US, an economy that has transformed from being a non-player to being a pivotal actor in the global drama of virtual-water 'trade' in only two centuries. Remember, virtual-water 'trade' has been in place since man's prehistory.

Second, the UK. This tiny, crowded island is of particular interest because of its long trading history. The UK has depended on virtual-water 'imports' in the form of a flexible grain trade ever since its population reached ten million, two hundred years ago. Its population is now a stunning 66 million. The dependence on trade is very great. It is also well managed, although there are losers.

Finally, Spain. Anyone who has enjoyed the Iberian peninsula's warm climate should be able to guess that Spain – of all the industrialised nations – has a problem with water. It is profoundly water-scarce by the standards of industrialised economies. Yet the taps stay on. The people of Spain are food-secure – also through trade. Along with Israel and Singapore, Spain is the industrialised nation most alive to the threat of water scarcity. Its government and its society understand the problem remarkably well. When I turn to Spain, the story will be one of increasingly progressive measures: this is an economy on the generally light side of virtual water, but with some very serious dark excesses in the south.

85

~~~~~~~~~~~~~~~~~~~~~ *PART 1* ~~~~~~~~~~~~~~~~~~~~~

The US: a pivotal global player in achieving sustainable water security

> The crisis of our diminishing water resources is just as severe as any wartime crisis we have ever faced. Our survival is just as much at stake as it was at the time of Pearl Harbor, or the Argonne, or Gettysburg, or Saratoga.
>
> Jim Wright, former US Congressman and Speaker of the House

The size and importance of the US is perhaps overplayed. But its water resources in relation to its modest population are globally pivotal. There is one category in which America is indisputably the biggest: consumption. Americans eat more food, buy more stuff and burn more fuel than any other nationality. They also use more water: the average American water footprint is twice the global average. There are other economies with high water footprints, most obviously the oil-rich nations of the Middle East. But these all have relatively small populations compared with 300 million Americans. Importantly, that 300 million is expected to rise to 450 million by 2050.

The reasons that each American on average consumes 2500 cubic metres per year are manifold. The average American is wealthy. The average American has a diet high in meat and other livestock products such as milk and cheese. The average American travels a lot, and predominantly by car or aeroplane. The average American consumes a vast array of goods and services, with greater variety and in greater numbers than other populations. Each and every one of these goods and services imposes a water cost.

86

Beyond the headlines

Let's dig deeper into the 2500 cubic metres per year figure for average individual consumption.

Approximately 19 per cent of the US water footprint derives from virtual-water 'imports'. This made up of 11 per cent for agricultural commodities, 8 per cent for industrial ones. The global importance of the US, however, lies in its

Figure 3.1 US water footprint. *Source:* A.K. Chapagain and A.Y. Hoekstra (2003), *Water Footprints of Nations,* Delft: IHE.

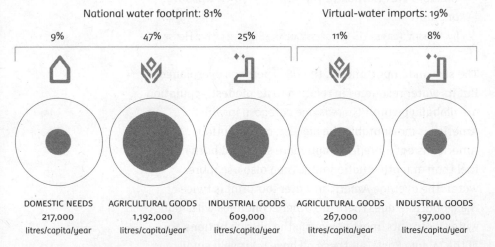

National water footprint: 81%   Virtual-water imports: 19%

| 9% | 47% | 25% | 11% | 8% |

DOMESTIC NEEDS	AGRICULTURAL GOODS	INDUSTRIAL GOODS	AGRICULTURAL GOODS	INDUSTRIAL GOODS
217,000 litres/capita/year	1,192,000 litres/capita/year	609,000 litres/capita/year	267,000 litres/capita/year	197,000 litres/capita/year

virtual-water 'exports'. It is an extremely important net 'exporter' with a positive annual virtual-water 'trade' balance of 53.5 cubic kilometres.

These are significant volumes of water. The US net virtual-water 'exports' are enough to meet the needs of all 43 sub-Saharan African nations combined, excluding Nigeria. Only Australia betters the US, 'exporting' 64 cubic kilometres a year. Australia's relatively tiny population of 20 million gives a stunning per-capita virtual-water 'export' figure of 336 cubic metres per head a year. Despite the extreme dryness of much of Australia, there is sufficient blue and green water in its vast territories for its own water needs and those of many other economies enduring water scarcity.

Table 3.1 Regions ranked in terms of their water related to trade, 1995–99. *Source:* A.K. Chapagain and A.Y. Hoekstra (2003), *Water Footprints of Nations*, Delft: IHE.

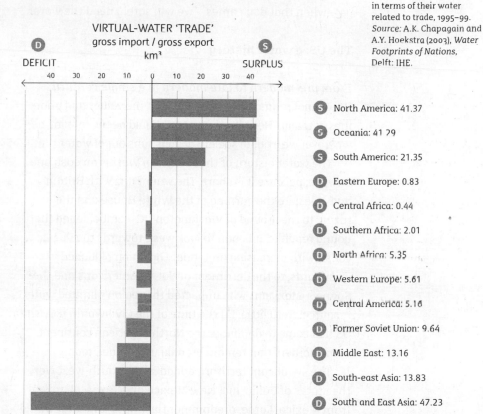

VIRTUAL-WATER 'TRADE'
gross import / gross export
km³

D DEFICIT   S SURPLUS

40 30 20 10 0 10 20 30 40

S North America: 41.37

S Oceania: 41.79

S South America: 21.35

D Eastern Europe: 0.83

D Central Africa: 0.44

D Southern Africa: 2.01

D North Africa: 5.35

D Western Europe: 5.61

D Central America: 5.18

D Former Soviet Union: 9.64

D Middle East: 13.16

D South-east Asia: 13.83

D South and East Asia: 47.23

Table 3.1 is a simple summary of virtual-water 'trade' surpluses and deficits, on a continental basis. North America, including both the US and Canada, and Australia, along with South America, are the continents upon which the rest of the world depends – via virtual-water 'trade' – for their water security. North America and Australia each provide around 40 per cent of the global water surplus. Currently South America only provides 20 per cent. I say 'only' as South America is the most water-rich continent by some considerable distance. It is our very great fortune that South America has not yet tapped its potential. One day, its surplus will become evident as it outstrips that of North America and Australia combined. Which is useful, as – when that day comes – we will sorely need the water.

The US: a water history

From pre-modern to late modern in a single century
We cannot re-imagine yesterday with the values and priorities of today. 'Hesitate to irrigate' should be the maxim, as wherever we irrigate society always runs out of water.

The water history of the American West is an easy one to write, because it is short. The war of 1812 with Britain had – despite the burning of the White House and the razing to the ground of Washington DC – emboldened the young republic. It began to look west, towards the Pacific coast, with increasing ambition. The union ploughed westwards, to the detriment of Native Americans and the Spanish-Mexicans who impacted the region's limited water resources very little. By the time of the Civil War in 1861, the US had come to dominate the North American continent along borders that remain broadly unchanged today.

The significant territory added in the south-west were the states of California, New Mexico and Texas, all taken from Mexico. Large, predominantly empty land that would later form the states of Arizona, Nevada, Colorado, Utah,

Nebraska and Dakota had the status of incorporated territories rather than states until at least the Civil War and,
in cases such as Arizona, until the start of the twentieth
century. The main point to take away from this brief pot-
ted history is that the American West is very youthful
indeed, and although the land itself was very consciously
and deliberately acquired, its future development was fit-
ful and haphazard, owing more to the individualism of gold
prospectors, pasture-seeking ranchers and homesteaders
than to any grand scheme.

The development of the farms and rangelands of the
West is a classic example of enterprising capitalism – blind
to the environmental value of natural resources – combining these resources, knowledge, technology, skill and
family labour to take advantage of private and public
investments in railways, ports, shipping and farm technology. As the web of capitalism spread westwards, it
transformed the land and created a new reality. Where
once was no infrastructure or economic development, now
stood wealth generating farmlands, which brought in tow
the cross-country migrants who transformed the western
US into one of the most powerful agricultural regions in
the world in just a few decades.

As money moved west, so did the demand for water.
The 1920s saw an unprecedented investment by the US
federal government in hydraulic works. Environmentally
and socially, the so-called hydraulic mission of the 1920s
and 1930s was certainly hazardous. The imperatives behind
it were economic not environmental. The objectives were
to drive the growth – in terms of both livelihoods and
profits – of these new farmlands. The concept of environmental sustainability and stewardship are anachronisms
in this period. It is most likely that it simply never occurred
to anyone that it was possible to over-dam. The clumsi-
ness of the expression over-dam reveals that we humans
have not conceptually caught up with reality. We lack a

89

clear, designated word for what the US government did to rivers through its hydraulic mission of the early twentieth century. Too often we gather the words and concepts retrospectively. Only after the disaster do we have the linguistic and intellectual tools to discuss it effectively and clearly.

The over-damming between the 1920s and the late 1970s wounded the water environment, as well as causing mortal harm to Native American societies and much wildlife. The Native American communities had lived in a more balanced accord with nature. They were – to use a phrase coming back into vogue – custodians of their environment rather than its masters. But the hydraulic mission had no consideration for the delicate balance these ancient peoples had formed with the land. The natural world and its water were – under the arrogant dictates of modernist man, powered by industry and ideology – not conceived as partners. They were to be bent by human will; they were to manifest human ambition.

Native American communities crumbled as a result. Their lives and livelihoods were destroyed. Other parts of the living environment suffered almost terminally. A fifty-million-strong bison population was all but destroyed. The wealth-creation of the farmland revolution in the West looks more impressive than it truly is. If economics had a formula for costing the environmental and social damage of the over-ambitious damming of the 1920s, and if farmers and the US government had been forced to reflect this environmental impact in the prices of their traded commodities, the story would have progressed very differently. And the current elemental politics of reversing the over-allocated water rights would have been avoided. 'Hesitate to irrigate' should be the maxim, as wherever we irrigate, society always runs out of water.

However, we cannot re-imagine yesterday with the values and priorities of today. By the close of the twentieth century, most economies in the world had become

90

GET MORE VALUE FROM LESS WATER – THE PRODUCTIVITY OF WATER
Access to water incurs costs, even if society is unwilling to recognise them. Irrigation water is almost everywhere delivered at very low cost because farmers want and expect it to be free, like the water in the soil fed by rainfall. Users of domestic water are used to paying the costs for having running potable water. These costs can be ten to a thousand times more than a farmer pays. It is the water used on farms and in industry and services which can be used more or less productively. A cubic metre of water can produce a mugfull of wheat or ten mugfulls. A factory can reduce the water used to produce a car. Motor manufacturers proudly say so on their corporate-responsibility websites. A farmer is lucky to get $0.20 from using a cubic metre of green and/or blue water, and they use tens of thousands

dependent to some extent on virtual water from the Americas. The hydraulic mission of the 1920s played a great role in this. The federal government brought dams, pumps and other hydraulic works that diverted and pumped water to family farms and later to corporate farms that have become players in the global market. From there, through trade, the produce of these farms served to feed and water the global economy. This unchecked industrialisation of water in the US has proven internationally beneficial. It enabled the US economy to expand at historically unprecedented rates, and has greatly added to food and water security for the rest of the world. The Native Americans, the bison and the Colorado River lost; the water-scarce oil-rich economies won. The concept of virtual water illuminates this trade-off, previously hidden.

91

Wheat addiction

Since the middle of the nineteenth century, US farmers and the remarkable US family-managed agri-trade corporations have been able to deliver wheat anywhere in the world. This is an impressive globally strategic and impressively enduring example of virtual-water 'trade'. Remember, to produce a tonne of wheat requires about 1000 tonnes (or 1000 cubic metres) of water. To export wheat is therefore to 'export' massive volumes of virtual water. Most of the world economies have been dependent on US farmers and traders ever since. Globally, we are addicted to virtual-water 'trade'. Specifically, many nations have managed (peacefully) to become food- and water-secure as a result of US wheat exports.

of cubic metres in a year. A teacher uses only a few – 3–5 cubic metres of water annually – and produces services worth many thousands of dollars per cubic metre of blue water. Top bankers use as little water and are rewarded with pay of hundreds of thousands of dollars. An economist argues that when an input is scarce we need to re-allocate the use of that input – and the employment associated with it – as much as possible towards higher-value activities. Farmers and especially politicians who watch society carefully and are aware of what is comfortable and politically feasible have less imagination than economists about these underlying fundamentals. As we shall see, valuing water properly is an elemental issue, but it has been impossible, to date, to capture the value of water in markets and supply chains. We shall still be talking about it on the last page of the book.

Water productivity and the second half of the twentieth century

With much effort most of us could save half a cubic metre of water in a year at work. We could save as much in a day at home by eating sensibly and not throwing food away.

People are often very down on the 1950s, but whatever the successes and failures of that particular decade were, it is certainly the case that the productivity of water has increased significantly since that time. The productivity of water can most easily be defined as the amount of water required to produce a dollar of value. In the US, water productivity had been improving steadily and constantly throughout the western expansion and the hydraulic mission of the 1920s. However, from the mid-1970s, productivity improved dramatically, despite a continuing rise in population. What was behind this revolution in productivity?

First, the use of freshwater flattened out. Less water was used in irrigation. At the same time, the value of irrigated farm products rose. Second, the already very diverse and productive US industrial and service sectors increased the output and the value of their activities. Here is the important lesson that US water history teaches us: get more value from less water.

Essentially, US industry and agriculture have got a lot smarter with water. For industry, there is an obvious bottom-line incentive. Industry has shown that it is willing to address the costs of water inputs. It uses relatively expensive – one dollar a cubic metre – blue water. Although it still does not internalise – as the economists put it – all the environmental costs of their activities. They are not yet responsible for reinstating damaged water environments. Legislation is tending in that direction, but the full environmental costs are not yet included in the prices of agricultural and manufactured commodities. The record of industry is more impressive. In the last quarter of the twentieth century, most US industries managed roughly to halve their blue-water use. The pulp and paper industry drove its usage down very significantly, and enjoyed improved profitability as a result. Here, environmental and water-management gains were a happy side effect. More recently, the emergence of corporate

responsibility has inspired policies that reduce companies'
water footprints for ethical – rather than financial –
reasons. There is a buzz in the conference agenda of the
trans-national corporates, with sessions and whole conferences focusing on corporate responsibility, justice in the
supply chain and 'creating shared value'.

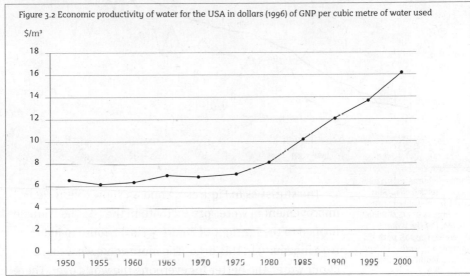

Figure 3.2 Economic productivity of water for the USA in dollars (1996) of GNP per cubic metre of water used

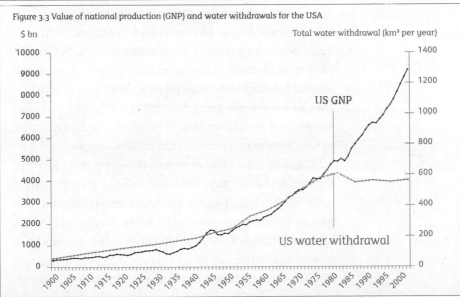

Figure 3.3 Value of national production (GNP) and water withdrawals for the USA

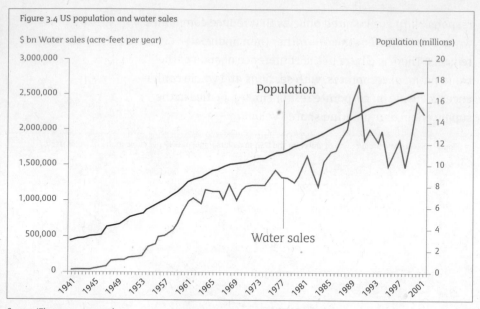

Figure 3.4 US population and water sales

Source (Figures 3.2, 3.3 and 3.4): P. Gleick (2009), 'Soft paths in the United States', in D. Brooks et al., *Making the Most of the Water We Have: The soft path approach to water management*, London: Earthscan.

The statistics in Figures 3.2 and 3.3 show a very clear improvement in water productivity in the US. The triangle formed to the far right of Figure 3.3 is a tribute to industry's ingenuity in this area. The more value we wring out of our water, the better for everyone the world over. There is a fundamental piece of good news here: economic advancement brings increased water efficiency. This fact could be the holy grail of water management. But first we have to get society to imagine this holy grail. Is your imagination turning? Unfortunately it is a universal tragedy that increased efficiency does not automatically remedy the original over-allocation of water to users with a sense of entitlement and none for the collective good.

Consider this: as an economy develops, more jobs are created in the private, public and voluntary sectors. In policing, teaching, healthcare, retail, entertainment and leisure, financial services, and the knowledge and the caring economies. All these wildly differing job sectors have one thing in common. They are incredibly water-efficient. They generate incomes of between $10,000 and $100,000

per annum and yet require only 2 or 3 cubic metres of
water per worker or volunteer per year. For context:
remember that a vegetarian diet uses 2.5 cubic metres
per day and a non-vegetarian 5 cubic metres per day.
Someone involved in these public, private and voluntary
activities needs less than these tiny volumes of water
in their employment in a year. There are 365 days in the
year. With much effort we could save half a cubic metre of
water in a year at work. We could save as much in a day at
home by eating sensibly and not throwing food away. An
interesting virtual-water 'exchange' is taking place in the
industrialised economies. In an economic system these
jobs with tiny virtual-water content enable families access
to daily necessities with very large virtual-water content.

95

   Water is deeply associated with economic processes,
and one of the outcomes is highly water-efficient sectors.

   Industrial jobs can be water-demanding. Yet the
average water per job per year is only 100 cubic metres.
Significantly less water than is consumed in one month of
the average non-vegetarian diet. Farming is the industry
where the water-consumption-to-wealth-generation ratio
becomes less favourable. Jobs in this sector can require up
to 100,000 cubic metres per year.

   My purpose here is to help water users – all of us consumers – to know our relationship with water. How much
we use in what. What kinds of water we use. And especially to help water users be comfortable about their water
security, which is achieved via job diversification and
trade. These processes are new to humankind. Our individual and collective imaginations have not caught up with
water-security realities. In industrialised societies we are
all unwittingly using water very efficiently in most industries and services. At the same time are also seriously
blind to the potential for the further gains in water productivity that can be achieved by our farmers and other
nations' farmers worldwide. We are very seriously blind to

the stupidity of bad diets and the tendency to buy more food than we need, which is then wasted. The productivity of water matters, and we must not undo miracles of productivity by not caring for human and environmental health. Seek more crop per drop. More jobs per drop. More care per drop. An understanding of these three dictums is nowhere more necessary than in the US. Throughout these chapters we are discovering that water-resource scarcity is solved outside the narrow world of local water resources by *economic processes* beyond the water sector.

96

The future: demand management

I might (prematurely) announce the demise of the hydraulic mission in industrialised economies. There has been an exciting shift. In these economies, we no longer expect the water industry to meet increased demands of society through building infrastructure. The days of bigger pumps, dams, storage and water carriers are over. Instead, the objective is to incentivise water users to use their water more efficiently. In other words, supply management has given way to demand management.

But how is demand managed?

The industrialised economies follow what are known as 'soft path' management approaches. The soft-path approach is to change water-consumer behaviour through a combination of regulation and incentives. These are soft path in contrast to the hard path of storing, conveying and pumping additional water. Hard-path management has been politically taboo in industrialised democracies since the 1970s. Only extreme disasters (environmental, social, medical or military) are likely to bring hard-path methods back in these economies.

There are several shortcomings to soft-path management approaches. Primarily, these approaches are incredibly organisationally intensive. Water supplies have to be reliably metered and accounted for. Regulators have to be appointed. Consumers have to be informed, cajoled and wooed. They require time and money, and expend political as well as financial capital. In the case of water use in the US, the soft-path management approaches also bring the federal government into direct conflict with one of the most powerful lobbying groups in the world: the US farm lobby.

The farm lobby is a many-headed hydra. There are the farmers, both the individual farmer-voters with their small, non-economically viable farmsteads, as well as the massive farm corporations. Farmers have consider-able political clout in the US for a variety of reasons. As well as the common-sense economic, social and polit-ical imperatives of keeping the farm industry happy and thriving, there are emotional and cultural reasons for the farmers' privileged position. They lay great claim to being the national backbone. The American dream, and particu-larly the manifest destiny of the expansion westwards, is rooted in the very soil and green water of the continent. And no one is closer to the soil and water than the farmers.

97

However, the farmers – big and small – are not alone. They have influential allies among the equipment manu-facturers, the seed and fertiliser industries and the major global food-commodity traders. Commodity trading on the recognisable contemporary global scale was born in the nineteenth century in the US. The first commodities traded were wheat, corn, cattle and pigs. This was concur-rent with the final, decisive push into the west, and the start of the great hydraulic mission of the first half of the twentieth century. It would be an exaggeration to say that modern global capitalism is built on the farming industry and the infrastructures put in place by global capitalism in the western US. But as with all exaggerations, the asser-tion contains more than a grain of truth.

Small wonder then that the farm lobby has such strength today. US politicians cannot afford to ignore the fabled special interests; the farm lobby is the first and the most special of all. Successive US administrations and legislatures have pursued policies that support the farm lobby, particularly during George W. Bush's two terms as president. There are many important reasons for doing so. This is an industry that has played a leading role in saving the world. Paradoxically, it is also leading it to ruin, damaging the environment and unwittingly wrecking the lives of poor farmers in the less developed economies.

America at the crossroads

98

The US is facing an historic choice in the way it uses its vast potential resources of land, water and solar energy. First, it can continue to meet most of its food needs. Second, it can continue to meet the water and food needs of the water-scarce economies of the globe, through virtual-water 'trade'. Third, it could switch even more to growing biofuels, a government-supported initiative to replace fossil fuels with energy for transportation from crops and other vegetation. But the down side of diverting crops from food to energy production is losing its attraction. It is seen to be unsustainable both environmentally as well as economically. This final option would, in my opinion, be a disaster. Environmentally, the supposed climate-change gains by switching to biofuels would be undermined by the extravagant use of land and water resources. The water footprint of bioethanol produced from food crops such as maize is so large as to undo any potential environmental benefit. Worrying too would be a US that pursued the first option without a concession to the second. We have come to rely on the US virtual-water 'exports'. If the US stopped feeding the world, ours would become a much less predictable and secure planet. Overnight. It's a chilling thought, and we might ask what does the US feel it owes us that it performs this heroic international duty?

The key points

If you absorb nothing else from this hurried water history
of the US, take with you these important facts. In the context of improving water productivity the world over, the
US has achieved some remarkable things since the end of
the 1939–45 so-called World War. The productivity of green
water on US farms has more than doubled. So too the productivity of blue water on irrigated land. Consequently, the
US manages to meet the swelling needs of its population
and continues to 'export' virtual water to three-quarters of
the world's nations.

However, statistics on water productivity have a
tendency to conceal other very important facts and processes. Diversifying an economy in one sense saves water.
Each progressive diversification creates more well-paying
jobs, making ever-smaller demands on the local water
environment. Wealth and water are performing a twirling,
arcing dance together. Each powers the other onwards,
forwards. Even when separated, the dance continues.

99

The US and the light side of virtual water

Securing

The US in the middle of the twentieth century had much of
which it could be proud. Undoubtedly, it had secured the
water and food needs of its own population, a trick managed
by few economies for any considerable period of time in the
history of the world. Further, the US was meeting the needs
of around fifty economies that were proving to be water-
and food-insecure. Through trade, the US was plugging the
gaps in these nations' diets, including those of almost all of
industrialised Europe and all of the Gulf economies.

Between 1950 and 2000, the number of economies
needing virtual-water 'imports' to top up their food and
water grew to 150. The US – with its subsidised agriculture,
underpinned by its unmatched hydraulic engineering

achievements – was only too happy to oblige. Here was a water-rich, diversified economy efficiently feeding other economies through virtual-water 'trade'. Indeed, it was the true realisation of the light side of virtual water. The US secured its food and those of other nations. It helped the rich and the poor. And all the while it contributed to saving water globally. Its trade officials can and do claim that by some measures the US is a responsible trading nation.

Helping the rich and the poor

Cheap food imports of staple grains have helped economies the world over, both rich and poor. Industrialised trading partners such as Japan benefited heavily, as did the oil-rich states of the Middle East and North Africa. Less fortunate were the poorer, resource-scarce sub-Saharan nations.

Egypt is an example of a big winner. Since the late 1960s, Egypt has been 'importing' ever-increasing amounts of virtual water in the form of cheap staple foods. By the end of the century, it was 'importing' almost 40 cubic kilometres per year; half of its total water needs. The majority of Egyptians enjoy relatively modest incomes; inexpensive food is a vital condition of life, and one that is protected fiercely by every sinew of the national government. US farm subsidies kept poor Egyptians fed and watered for three decades; an heroic – if mostly unintended – international endeavour. In recent years, Australian and South American producers have taken on part of the role of supplying wheat to Egypt. Australian and Argentinian farmers have to compete with the unfair prices offered by the EU and the US.

For the past decade the US has shifted its federal subsidies to bioethanol crops. Egypt has a very interesting story to tell, when it comes to virtual water, and I'll be returning to this later in the chapter and again in even greater detail in the chapter on three developing economies.

The US undoubtedly delivers cheap food to the poor of the world. Although this has not been done out of pure

100

THE USEFUL CONCEPT OF COMPARATIVE ADVANTAGE
Economic theory has lots of laws; to most of them, reality plays willing criminal. First, absolute advantage should be glossed. It's a very straight-forward concept. Having an absolute advantage in the production of a good means the ability to generate more output from the same input. Comparative advantage is slightly different. It is the ability to produce a good at a lower cost because the producer has some advantage in comparison to another producer. For example more abundant and cheaper – even free – water. Or more abundant and cheaper labour.

altruism, the US governmental departments and the private-sector trading houses like to project an image of the US as a responsible producer and exporter of food. That image – though partial and incomplete – is not too far from the truth.

The US is also a leading global provider of food aid. Whenever the world's poor face disasters (natural or political), often associated with water in the form of droughts or floods, the international community mobilises to deliver humanitarian aid, much of which takes the form of food handouts. Not surprisingly, a considerable amount of that food comes from the US. The amounts involved compared to the quantity of global food trade are like two grains of wheat hidden in two bushels of chaff: the volumes are tiny, almost to the point of insignificance. But timeliness of availability is vital, which is where the vast subsidised food surpluses of the US and EU become remarkably helpful. When disaster strikes, readily available cheap food saves lives. But there are negative economic consequences for farmers' incomes in developing economies.

101

Ameliorating global water scarcity: a US contribution
The experience of the US shows clearly how virtual-water 'trade' ameliorates water scarcity. It may be unintentional, invisible and virtual, but the amelioration is very real indeed.

The trade in water-intensive food 'moves' water from one economy to another. Speaking as an ecological scientist, the ideal trade is one that 'moves' water from those economies enjoying water surpluses to those that are water-scarce: for example, from the water-rich plains of the US to the sun-parched shores of Arabia. Or to the drought- and famine-prone developing nations of Africa. Or to the massively 'overpopulated' Singapore. There is no shortage of thirsty economies, desperate for any drop of virtual-water 'trade'. Here is what international virtual-water 'trade' can do. It can shift water (or rather its virtual benefit) suddenly, dramatically and efficiently to those economies that need it most, with a speed and in quantities impossible to rival through engineering and hydraulic processes. It is fast, flexible and highly effective.

An economist might have different priorities. It is economically sound to move precious water from water-scarce economies provided there are no negative environmental or social consequences. These consequences are widely evident where high-value commodities such as tomatoes and fruit, as well as dairy and livestock products, are being exported. It makes economic sense; but environmentally and socially it is madness. This trade drains water from poor farming communities in water environments often close to over-exploitation, living under the Damoclesean threat of drought. Markets cannot codify and incorporate these costs, so it treats them as non-existent. This is the rationale of the ostrich, thinking itself safe from all dangers unseen when its head is in the sand.

102

Given the sheer strength of its presence in international trade, the US is key to saving water globally. When 'moving' virtual water through traded food commodities to a water-scarce economy like Egypt, the US is ensuring that water is taken from a local environment in a water-efficient (US farmers get high returns to water) sustainable way, easing the water-scarcity problems of a less resilient water environment. This saves water globally and should provide the foundation for better water management in water-scarce economies, but this is not always the case.

In the world of traded food commodities, countries rich in natural resources (such as land and water) and with large pools of manual labourers should enjoy comparative advantage in farming. Unfortunately, here is where the reality of farming subsidies breaks the law of economic theory. Commodities ought to be produced where they get the highest returns on inputs, including water. Subsidies pervert this logic, and the farming industries of developing economies are crushed by cheap, subsidised exports, dumped on the local markets by industrialised economies which (often) would be better served concentrating their efforts in other economic sectors that offer stronger returns on water inputs.

Farming and water

The final frontier

Today we have few myths and fewer heroes. We doubt our religious leaders. We distrust our politicians. We cynically accept the partisanship of our media. Teachers, soldiers and doctors are less-respected professions in a political environment that often too closely associates them with financial burden and state inefficiency, or with cold-hearted capitalism when operating privately.

103

Perhaps the last great cultural myths are about our farmers, ranging from the romantic cowboys of the US to the dignified villagers on the frontline against famine in the developing world. Ultimately, no matter how the world restructures politically or economically, no matter which way the lines fall on the map or which flags are raised over parliament buildings and city halls, the people of the world must eat, and only the farmers can ensure that they are fed.

However, as heroes, they remain more unsung than sports celebrities, pop stars or Hollywood actors. Not for them the wealth, the glamour, the fame, the adoration. Farming is among the toughest professions in the world. Though methods and produce vary the world over, one thing is constant: uncertain times, bureaucracy and the uncertainties of the natural world combine to ensure that the job is unpredictable in its rewards and brutal in its disappointments. This varies little whether the farm in question is in the American West or on the Indian subcontinent. The suicide rates are shocking, and some of the highest internationally, regardless of geography. As ever, the plight of those in the world's poorer economies is more desperate, but in relative terms farmers are at the bottom of the professional pile.

A very important feature of industrialised economies such as the US is that they are able to extend protection to the farming industry from environmental and market risks; no such security nets exist for most of the world's farmers. Mother Nature is capricious to the point of vindictiveness. Too often she provides water in quantities too slight to be productive or too great to be anything but destructive. Poor farmers are subject to the whims of climatic variability. This disadvantage is compounded by the relative poor quality of their soil. For the farmers of the developing world, this is the complete story: they are reliant upon the generosity (or otherwise) of their environment. Their armoury consists merely of land, water and hard work. In the industrialised economies, things are very different indeed. The inputs available to a farmer in an industrialised economy are not just three. They can be a hundred and three.

The reason I am focusing on farmers, and farmers such as those in advanced economies like the US, is because of their essential role in achieving water security for the global population. They feed consumers in their own countries. Some of them send food to the international market which we have already shown is the invisible means by which most economies enjoy a version of water security.

I am also emphasising the difficulties faced by farmers as we food consumers depend on them for our food and water security. It is being argued that we should support policies that incentivise farmers and also protect them from the vagaries of Mother Nature and the market. A transition to global water security, which is certainly possible, will not be achieved by market forces. It will be achieved by a mix of water resources and intelligent policies that enable farmers to increase their water productivity at the same time as being stewards of those water resources.

Farmers in the US have waged a broadly successful struggle with the elements – including water – and the market. Unlike their impoverished counterparts in other hemispheres, their productivity ambitions are not so hampered by the inadequacies of the soil or the moods of nature. In the industrialised nations, the farmers have the great weight of science and industry behind them in their struggle to wring every last drop of productivity out of the earth. On the bio-chemical side, they have the amassed weaponry of industrial fertilisers, complex pesticides and engineered seeds. Similarly, farming mechanisation has advanced to the point where it would cripple any living Luddites with a cold terror. Further, all this is underpinned by the existence of well-organised and regulated markets for farm produce, a vast array of food-processing facilities and breathtaking transport and communication infrastructures. As would be expected, very little is left to chance in the farming of the industrial world. The process is mechanised, structured and highly efficient. Where the poor face the dual disruptions of non-compliant nature and social unrest, in the form of civil war and lawlessness, the rich function in an environment of subsidies, guaranteed prices and relatively stable markets.

105

Farmers in the US, like farmers in all advanced OECD economies, have been able to save water in that they get much higher levels of water productivity. Today's farmers get over five times the tonnage they used to. The economic/political processes that made all this possible have taken a century and a half of unprecedented big-farm politics to put in place. The consequences for the farmer have been important without making farming easy. For the US economy they are quite hard to fathom. For the global economy and food security, they have been essential and generally very favourable, with downsides for poor farmers in sub-Saharan Africa. For the US environment they have been tough – the intensification has not always been sustainable. But for the global environment they have been very important: the 150 or so economies in regions less well endowed with water have been able to conserve rather than over-exploit that local water.

Water is never still

106

This is nowhere truer than in the dynamics of virtual-water 'trade'. This is not a static situation. Currently, the water-rich industrialised economies 'export' to the water-scarce. Also, the industrialised economies trade extensively between themselves. Because they can. The remarkable strides in productivity seen in the industrialised and (more recently) in the BRICS economies since the middle of the twentieth century will be replicated in the developing economies. These economies will, as their populations grow and become more affluent, experience an increase in water demand. At the same time, efforts at environmental protection will start to divert water from agriculture. This is already happening in the industrialised economies.

Why are numbers like boiled eggs at picnics?
Because they are far better hard than soft. Shell a soft-boiled egg at a picnic and you could find yourself with an unattractive yellow mess on your hands. Rely too heavily on soft numbers and you may have a similar mess to deal with. Like boiled eggs, numbers come soft or hard. Hard numbers are the verified, the proven. In our world of flux, hard numbers are probably the closest thing we have to existential truth. Soft numbers are what we use when no hard numbers are to hand, or they serve the interests of the powerful. Remember constructed knowledge can be based on soft or hard numbers and such knowledge easily overwhelms observed science that does not have the option to use soft numbers.

Soft numbers are based on a cocktail of heroic assumptions, common sense and reliable but unverified data. At the time of writing, many of the virtual-water statistics are based on soft numbers. Virtual water is a fledgling concept, still a flighty teenager, and there has not been the time and resource to generate hard numbers. Given the wildly varying environmental and socio-economic circumstances across the world's 200 economies, soft numbers are inevitable. It will take many scientists and many modellers many lifetimes of research to produce hard numbers. Even then, they will be partially out of date by the time they are collated. The world spins faster in practice than in science.

Soft numbers have nevertheless been useful. They have illuminated the concept of virtual water and made the just as useful concept of water footprints more accessible. They help quantify the scale of major 'movements' and 'savings' achieved through virtual-water 'flows'. For the purposes of our engagement with the urgent issue of global and regional water security they will suffice, though I admit that I would feel more secure if more modellers had deployed better statistics to quantify levels of virtual-water 'trade' in the literature.

107

A land of milk and honey: growing oranges in the Californian desert

Scarcely anyone lived in California when it became the thirty-first state in the union in 1850. The discovery of gold changed that dramatically. The state is now the most populous in the US, and home to nearly 37 million people. As is so often the case with human development, little or nothing about the growth of California was sensible, co-ordinated or planned. Its eruption and ongoing affluence is a tribute to that reckless, unruly entity – the human spirit.

By the end of the first decade of the twentieth century, southern California had run out of water. At the time of writing, a hundred years later, it is the main agricultural base of the entire country. To call this turn of events counter-intuitive would be a monumental understatement. Nationally, the US has a very healthy water surplus. Most regions in this capacious and bountiful land are well or reasonably well endowed with water. Yet a series of unusual decisions and coincidences have led much of the nation's agriculture to develop in the water-scarce southwestern states of California and Arizona.

108

The farmers followed the sun, and the money. And water was forced to catch up. Within the state of California, much engineering expertise and many tax dollars were expended in drawing water from the north and east to the sunny south-west. Vast dams and pipelines brought and stored water in this arid land. From there, the farmers and agricultural companies produced their unprecedented miracle of land and water productivity.

An environmental determinist would naturally find Californian farming an awe-inspiring puzzle. This water-scarce region produces around four hundred different food commodities, including a stunning 22 per cent of all US milk and about half of all farm-produced fruits, nuts and vegetables. Most of this comes from the arid south. The state's top 20 crop and livestock commodities alone account for more than $30 billion of revenue each year. This is 12.8 per cent of the total US agricultural production by value. If California's 75,000 farms, ranches and food-processing companies declared themselves an independent nation state, they would have GDP greater than the majority of the world's economies. Impossible agriculture in the desert is generating more economic value than a hundred countries.

Much of this food goes abroad, and to many different economies. In 2007, 16 per cent of the state's production was exported to 156 of the 200 economies in the world, generating $10.9 billion. The markets of the EU, Canada and

Japan accounted for nearly 57 per cent of these exports; Europe, Canada and Japan all have far richer natural water environments. The story of California defies logic. It is an arid region of the world which exports roughly 10 cubic kilometres of virtual water per annum.

The small print

If this all seems too good to be true, that's because it is. 'Unsustainable' is, bluntly, too slight a term to describe California's use of water. Water certainly follows the money, as the mass of the celestial bodies pulls smaller masses into their orbits. As stars suffer gravitational collapse and turn inwards into black holes, so might the powerful Californian agricultural industry collapse under the weight of its own vigour. Never in human history have water and energy been harvested with such intensity, with such speed and in such quantities. Technical ingenuity, managerial capacity, fuelled by sheer wealth and willpower have allowed our ability to outstrip our reason. The story of Californian agriculture might be summarised thus: we could, therefore we did, never asking whether we should

109

California's residents have domestic water footprints double the global average, with a per-capita annual figure of 2400 cubic metres. It is correspondingly energy-hungry, with a per-capita energy footprint that is the fifth highest of all the US states. Bear in mind that the US average energy footprint is almost 30 tonnes of carbon per year. That is a stunning 14 times the international average. California is 37 million people vastly over-consuming energy and water. It has the potential to become a natural-resource black hole.

A very brief look at water in California

How can you buy or sell the sky, the warmth of the land? The idea is strange to us. If we do not own the freshness of the air and the sparkle of the water, how can you buy them? Every part of the earth is sacred to my people.
CHIEF SEATTLE

110

This history of the Native North Americans is perhaps the most tragic subplot in the story of North America. Here was a people who lived in accord with their environment. As noted earlier, they acted as custodians of the planet. Nor did this occur in some distant prehistory. They were performing their ecological balancing act until the start of the twentieth century.

I don't intend naively to eulogise Native American attitudes to the environment. Suffice to say – from the perspective of water – they were a great success. In California, they probably numbered only a few tens of thousands until the arrival of the Spanish via Mexico. After joining the union with only 93,000 inhabitants in 1850, California's population reached 1.4 million in 1900, jumping to 10 million by the middle of the last century, before slowing in growth to its current 37 million. It might not surprise you that two-thirds of this population choose – counter-intuitively – to live in the very water-scarce south of the state.

The gold mines, the vast irrigated farms, the thirsty green lawns and temperature-maintained swimming pools in every backyard have devastated meagre Californian water resources and those of the surrounding states with a rapacity that seems too intense to be anything but deliberate. Groundwater, which cannot be regulated, has been over-pumped. The water environment has been stretched beyond reason.

A very brief look at the future

But there is also hope. Symptomatic of the glorious contra-
dictions of this most exceptional of American exceptions,
precautionary ideas have appeared in parallel with preda-
tory forces. Since the end of the late twentieth century,
California has also been the global capital of green activism. While still over-consuming, water usage has fallen
in the state since 1980 and efficiency has been increasing
significantly since the 1970s. There are rays of light, but
they are not yet sufficient to pin anything other than the
most insubstantial of hopes upon.

111

California is remarkable, a true political-economy
phenomenon. Through a combination of private-sector
farmers, state and federal hydraulic prowess and tax
dollars, a broad labour market (including a steady flow of
immigrant workers), world-leading food-processing and
marketing systems, and a context of social and environmental activists, southern California has been transformed
from near-desert to a powerful global economy and a
major component of world agriculture. Water has been
managed to secure local needs and those of other economies around the world. The rich and the poor have been
helped. Internationally, water has been saved. All the criteria for the light side of virtual water are present.

But there is a fundamental problem.

In no sense is this miracle sustainable. The water
California so successfully and profitably exported was
subsidised. Its supposed cost is a happy fiction that con-
ceals unpleasant truths. Aside from the direct agricultural
subsidies, the water brought to southern California was the
result of a massive, expensive and over-hyped hydraulic
mission, pursued at both state and federal level. These systems for supplying and containing water are unviable and
cannot be replicated easily. The costs of these investments,
and the environmental costs of over-pumping groundwater

and draining water from surrounding areas are nowhere reflected in the market price of California's exports.

Reform is taking place, but at a politically determined pace. The powerful corporate-farming system has unrivalled clout in both Washington and Sacramento, the state capital. The true cost of Californian water use is hidden, the considerable profits from international trade delude us into believing that water is being managed sensibly and efficiently. Consequently, reform, urgently needed, is slowed. All the criteria for the dark side of virtual water are met in California.

112

The Californian water miracle is paradoxically apparently effective and a snake-oil fraud in equal measures. Curing as it harms; harming as it cures. Greater understanding of the invisible forces at play in virtual-water 'trade' and a developed and realistic approach to the limits of the water environment can bring the state from the dark side to the light. We have the technology. We have the insight. We need only the honesty and the inclination.

~~~~~~~~~~~~~~~~~~~ *PART 2* ~~~~~~~~~~~~~~~~~~~
The UK: a microcosm of capitalist crisis management

> *History is just one damned thing after another.*
> ARNOLD TOYNBEE

The purpose of this section is two-fold. First, I want to get the attention of readers in the UK, to help them understand water and how we have coped with water scarcity. Second, I want to use the UK experience to show readers coping with urgent water problems elsewhere – of quality as well as quantity – how these problems have been effectively solved outside the water sector. Water problems are solvable when we have strong economies that let us have allocative and management options. Water problems become human tragedies when they occur in non-diverse and weak economies. In addition, virtual-water 'trade' will be shown to have played a major role in bringing water security to the UK economy. From the arguments in the previous chapters it will come as no surprise that people in the UK have been blinded to the nature of their water security by the invisibility and silence of virtual-water 'trade'. The section will end with a reminder that the people of the UK are still ignorant regarding the worth of water, and are unwilling to pay all the costs of providing water services in systems that protect the water environment. They are totally ignorant of the basis of their food and water security.

113

Begin at the beginning

So goes the advice of the King of Hearts in Lewis Carroll's *Alice in Wonderland*. Yet for an analysis of the UK's relationship with water and virtual water, the most illuminating place to start is at the end. Or at least in the present.

The UK represents an unlikely, accidental, haphazard and highly fragile success story of water usage. As with so many things on this tiny, crowded island, there were no clear goals and no deliberate co-ordinated efforts. There is something in the British mentality that regards planning as very unsporting; it's almost like cheating. The Anglo-Saxon elite is proud of its pragmatism – especially market pragmatism – despite a number of encounters with the grave consequences of near market failure.

But the achievements are very real in the management of both big water on farms and of small water used by people and industry. The water efficiency of farming in the UK has increased by a factor of ten since the signing of the Act of Union in 1801. This means that despite the population growing by an incredible 600 per cent in the same period, the UK is in a better position in terms of water security than it was two hundred years ago with a population of fewer than ten million. If this seems counter-intuitive, it must appear even less explicable when we consider that these statistics sit against the backdrop of massive urbanisation. Urban populations are never food and water self-sufficient; rural populations historically can be and in some places are.

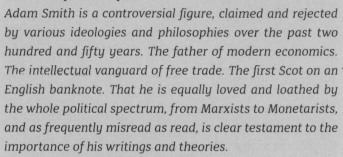

When is a pin not a pin?

Adam Smith is a controversial figure, claimed and rejected by various ideologies and philosophies over the past two hundred and fifty years. The father of modern economics. The intellectual vanguard of free trade. The first Scot on an English banknote. That he is equally loved and loathed by the whole political spectrum, from Marxists to Monetarists, and as frequently misread as read, is clear testament to the importance of his writings and theories.

His seminal text The Wealth of Nations (1776) is arguably the single most influential tome in the corpus of economic theory. The concepts of the division of labour, the invisible hand and the labour theory of value are happily and frequently bandied about by many who have never bothered to turn a single page of this sprawling five-book opus. Significant for our history of water in the British Isles is Smith's assertion that self-interest and competition can – if allowed to flower – bear forth the fruit of economic prosperity and social wellbeing. So profoundly and deeply did this ethos chime with the personality and tendencies of the populace of the UK that it has become the theoretical sine qua non of much political, social and economic decision and initiative ever since.

This idea is the seed from which the neo-liberal project, the dominant political and economic ideology of the UK, would grow. Within its densely packed pages, The Wealth of Nations carried the subtle fatal goodnight kiss to British mercantilism. Modern market capitalism was born.

The neo-liberal project

The UK was the first economy to industrialise. It did this at a point in its history when it had imperial ambitions and was a leading global trading power. My argument runs that as a consequence it was able to cope with water resources that were inadequate to meet its rapidly increasing needs of big water for food. It did not have the agricultural technology to increase the productivity of water to meet the needs of the growing population. But it did have the capacity to 'reach out' for virtual water in the Americas and elsewhere. No one noticed the progressive dependence on global water that was integral to the food-commodity trade.

115

The rapid diversification of the nineteenth-century UK economy also enabled its municipal governments to have a tax base that could raise funds to provide water and sewage services. The small-water challenge could also be successfully addressed.

The crises of capitalism

The UK political economy survived the pressures of demography, rapid economic change and social trans-formation but very nearly failed. The first failure of capitalism was highlighted by Marx in the middle of the nineteenth century. It was not over water – that would only become an issue a century later. Capitalism seemed destined to fail in handling a prime factor of production

labour. In the event it adapted. It improved the lot of working people and realised that healthy workers were more useful and more productive, and that health was closely related to safe water provision and disposal.

There have never been enough of us in the UK to wish the wheels to come off the neo-liberal project. Ardent revolutionaries aside, we are agreed it is in our mutual interest to muddle through. This muddling through has

THE FACTORS OF PRODUCTION
Essentially, these are the elements required to pro-duce goods and services. In the nineteenth century, these were simply labour (the ability to work), capital goods (the tools required) and land (the natural resources exploited). In the twentieth century, the quasi-mythological fourth factor of entrepreneurship was added to the formula-tion. Importantly, land as a factor of production includes *the exploitation of water resources*. It was not until long after Adam Smith – just a few decades ago – that protecting nat-ural resources got a place in the story.

116

often required a hefty dose of self-delusion. Delusion is a common human addiction. We have seen already – and it will be a recurring theme – that people everywhere are deeply deluded in their relationship with water.

The neo-liberal project has ridden the storm of the first potentially fatal failure in handling labour. It is in the midst of coping with the second – our failure to restrain our thoughtless demands on the environment, including water. This failure is evident in the way we have damaged our freshwater and soil water resources by dumping indus-trial waste and chemically loaded agricultural water into our streams, soil and aquifers.

However, the environmental failure of capitalism has – over the course of the past twenty years – been successfully pushed onto the agenda by environmental activists. They have confronted society's assumptions that natural resources are limitless. They insist that water and other natural resources have a value. Water is not free and should not be cheap. The planet cannot continue to function as both canteen and latrine when it comes to our industrial needs. Against all dictates of reason, against the very evidence of our eyes, corporations and consum-ers force the earth to be an uncomplaining sink for the pollution of intensive agriculture and dirty industry and farms. But through persistence, such activists have forced environmental issues to the forefront of our collective consciousness. In 2010, the environment receives almost as much political attention as troublesome collective labour in the late nineteenth century or the shortcomings of Wall Street and other national bourses in the twentieth century.

Not out just yet...

With these two elemental failures – relating to labour and the environment – the prevalent globalising project of neo-liberalism has been deeply involved, both nation-ally and internationally. Labour, international finance and trade, and the environment: all are active problems. The wheels are still turning. The lights are still on. The world hasn't ground to a halt, or poisoned itself out of existence. At least not yet. Progress in understanding and responding to the problems is slow. We have to view coping with our excesses as work in progress.

A very brief history of water use in the UK

The rain it raineth every day

The UK has managed to get the best out of its water. In the British Isles, you are rarely any significant distance from an evident body of water. In both a literal and a metaphorical sense, the UK is – more than most – defined by water. Few realise that the UK has been living beyond its water means for longer than most.

117

The early nineteenth century was a time of important triumphs over water problems. Technological innovations brought great improvements in water supply and sanitation. Rapid urbanisation brought squalor, with the concomitant horrors of typhoid and cholera, but the impetus and ambition to fix the urban water supply and sewage systems meant that these difficulties were ultimately surmounted. With universal, reliable drinking water and sewage systems, the battle of small water – the supply of high-quality running water in homes and factories – once addressed was quickly won. But it was won while ignoring the need for big water for food security. This was because the food consumers of the UK had been mainly fed by crops grown with green water. Green water remains the main source of water by volume – about 80 per cent – in the economy of the UK. It comes free and is not accounted. But the crops raised with the UK's green water are just as valuable as those raised with blue water overseas.

A case in point is the Thames basin. The basin has sufficient water resources to feed and provide water services for perhaps two million people. Yet by 2000, the basin was supporting 17.5 million. How was this achieved? The answer is by virtual-water 'trade'. London's big-water shortage is met through commodity trade. Leaving the Thames basin to meet quite easily the modest demands of domestic households and the region's highly water-efficient industries of financial services, retail, the media plus education and public services.

118

Aside from urbanisation, low industrial water demands and a well-established trade network, another factor has ensured that the UK enjoys a particular blissful ignorance regarding water insecurity. This factor is the weather, more often referred to in the UK as the *bloody* weather. It rains. A lot. If this is a green and pleasant land, it is down to the rain rather than the imagination of our poets and artists. Consequently, there was no irrigation in the UK during the nineteenth century, and only limited use of it even today. Less than 5 per cent of all arable land is equipped with irrigation equipment. The British bounty of rain and soil water was very easily taken for granted. It became ingrained in the national psyche as an inviolable fact of life. It needed no more policy consideration than the daily rise and fall of the sun over the horizon. For the UK government of the nineteenth century to consider the economic importance of green water would have been as anachronistic and unlikely as Alexander Graham Bell sending a text message.

There's no blue in the traffic light

I hope I have been clear so far. We don't think about water. It is the great ignored. This is strange, as high-quality water is – along with air – a tangible, finite resource that is wholly necessary and irreplaceable for life. Perhaps our minds simply cannot contemplate the horror of its absence. Our media and our environs are rich in water and water imagery, in advertising, in urban water features and

calming workplace fish tanks. We understand intuitively
(and, more recently, scientifically) that water is perfect
shorthand for life. When we send exploratory devices to
Mars or the moon or across the cosmos, it is water for
which we search. There is a simple equation in our mind. If
water, then life. And if not...

Since the turn of the century, consumers in the UK
have become increasingly keen on information. Products
on supermarket shelves give country of origin, estimated
expiry dates, a detailed breakdown of sugars, fats, salts,
a packaging history, serving suggestions. Sometimes,
as on a pint of milk I recently purchased from a leading
supermarket, you even get a friendly photo portrait of
the farmer, complete with micro-interview. If we eat a
chicken, its quality of life is often assured by an animal-
rights body. If we eat beef, we will get information about
the breed of cow. Rarely will you buy an apple on the high
street without being offered details of the county in which
it was grown.

119

Yet nowhere is the water cost noted, although the issue
is being closely considered by the food corporations and
supermarkets. In the much-debated traffic-light labelling
recommended by the UK Food Standards Agency, there
is red, amber and green. There is no blue. There exists no
mechanism for informing the consumer of how water-
intensive her or his basket of goods is. Possibly, there is no
space in our hypothetical consumer's head for the information, stuffed as it is with the specifics of weight, cost,
nationality, E-numbers and saturated-fat content. If the
label is so overcrowded, so too is the mind of the shopper?

Meanwhile the international food-commodity manufacturers and supermarkets are deeply engaged in
researching the water footprints of their supply chains.
The position at the time of writing is that the numbers
are not reliable enough and the labels are already too
crowded. But those that are close to consumers, such as

Nestlé, Unilever, Coke, Pepsi and Walmart are certainly willing to adopt any approach that will be credible and reduce corporate reputational risk. Other even mightier players in terms of the volumes of virtual water that they 'handle' – such as ADM, Bunge, Cargill and Dreyfus have so far resisted all persuasion that they recognise that they handle a pivotal proportion of global virtual-water 'trade'. They are private companies with no duties to shareholders, nor to consumers, who know neither them nor their strategic market power.

In addition, farmers – who do more water managing than any other profession – are not used to conceptualising water security as we are in this analysis. Imagine explaining to a farmer at your local farmers' market that he or she is playing a vital role in ensuring the UK suffers no water crisis. You might as well tell them that they are a fireman or doctor; farmers don't associate their vastly improved yields with water conservation. Why would they? The water is free. It falls from the sky with a frequency that – for all non-farmers – is tediously reliable. Here then are those working directly with water, yet they are under-informed of its importance, ignorant of its global scarcity and their strategic role in addressing this scarcity crisis. They are blind to their vital individual role in the collective management of water. They know that yields have improved, but they do not translate the ten-fold increase into a water-security miracle with major global as well as national significance.

Figure 3.5 clearly shows the remarkable success in improving the productivity and water efficiency of farming in the UK. The Malthusian gap, which yawns menacingly on the left of the graph, was closed down and inverted in the second half of the last century. Population clearly increased dramatically, more than tripling from nine million in 1800 to thirty million by 1900. From there it has doubled. The land area cultivated grew by 25 per cent in

the nineteenth century, only to decline again by a similar proportion in the latter half of the twentieth. But the
important and (outside these pages) unsung trend is the
exponential increase in water efficiency of UK farming.
Between 1800 and 1950 the water productivity of rain-fed
land tripled; it tripled *again* between 1950 and 2000.

Figure 3.5 UK popula-
tion and the increase in
farm-water productivity,
1800–2050. *Source:* UK
national and agricultural
statistics.

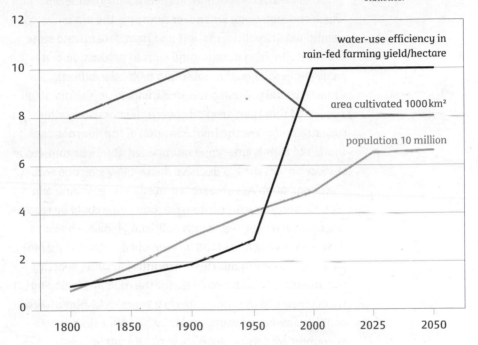

The politics of farm productivity

Corn isn't chicken feed
The UK has a habit of being ever-so-slightly out of step
with history. Sometimes it runs behind: it certainly got
both the Renaissance and the Reformation a little late. On
other occasions, it runs ahead. The UK finally exhausted
its thirst for civil war in the seventeenth century, a century
in which it also dabbled with both republicanism and revolution. British constitutional crises were a thing of the past

by the time the Bastille was stormed in 1789, the UK barely felt a ripple from the European revolutions of 1830 and 1848, and as the Bolsheviks and Mensheviks climbed the gates of the Winter Palace in 1917, the UK wondered why other countries hadn't already got all this unpleasantness out of their systems decades or even centuries ago.

So too with the death of protectionism. The French wince and look away whenever reform of the CAP is mentioned. US politicians, left and right, federal and state, are comfortable in decrying subsidised production and trade (while vigorously promoting their own exports). The Chinese would politely smile and imagine you insane if you suggested that they drop all government assistance for industry and allow the invisible hand of the international market to calmly intervene unimpeded. But in Britain, trade restriction was dealt a decisive death-blow long ago with the Importation Act of 1846. It proved to be economically feasible because water-intensive food crops could be readily imported at low prices. It was politically feasible because labour was weak and could be employed – albeit in dismal jobs – in the new industries. Encountering water scarcity was unnoticed and no problem for the rapidly developing UK economy. In the contemporary world, poor non-diverse economies, such as many in Africa and Asia, find the encounter with water scarcity very difficult indeed.

The Corn Laws of 1815 were the last gasp of the British landed gentry's attempt to preserve its wealth and power in the face of strengthening international trade in the early nineteenth century. Formally known as the Importation Act of 1815, the Corn Laws protected domestic prices by levying punitive duties on all foreign imports. They provided an invaluable sense of financial security and protection for the British farming industry at the time. But the Corn Laws were profoundly out of step with the contemporary political philosophy in the UK. Free trade was on balance hugely advantageous for Britain in imperial mode.

It is impossible to understand and follow the role of virtual water in the UK without an understanding of British farming since the start of the nineteenth century, and it is impossible to have anything even approximating an understanding of British farming in the period without a sense of the significance of the Corn Laws. Politically, the Corn Laws were the great contentious issue of the day. The repeal of the Corn Laws split the ruling Tory Party in 1846, with the free-market Peelites following their displaced Prime Minister Sir Robert Peel into the arms of the Whigs and the Radicals, leading to the formation of the Liberal Party.

In post-Napoleonic Europe, with British pre-eminence an ever-more-apparent reality, attention naturally turned to internal reform and restructuring. That said, the repeal of the Corn Laws in 1846 did not bring British capitalism crashing to its knees. Though there were dire implications for the wealthy landowning class and for the rural poor who had to migrate to the satanic mills of the expanding urban centres. They followed the money, as Adam Smith might have predicted. The labour crises in mining and manufacturing in the latter half of the century were more palpable than the dispute over the Corn Laws, and gave the violent nudge to capitalism, pushing it to reform. It was easier for labour to organise in the industrial heartlands than in dispersed rural villages. Peasant revolts have never been very successful in Britain, unlike China.

123

To re-CAP

That food productivity and water-use efficiency should continue to gather momentum in the UK after the repeal of the Corn Laws is certainly contrary to the assumptions of common sense. However, it makes perfect sense that both food productivity and water-use efficiency should suddenly spike after the military excesses and economic crises of the first half of the twentieth century. As mentioned earlier, the CAP of the EU (at the time the

EEC) provided trade protection and production incentives, including guaranteed purchases at a guaranteed price. In terms of market intervention, the CAP dwarfs the Corn Laws in much the same way as the slaughter of the 'world' wars dwarfed the destruction of Napoleon's European ambitions. By the middle of the twentieth century Europe no longer had a stomach for industrial slaughter. Reform and co-operation appeared to be more promising.

For any who claim that competition always brings the greatest efficiencies, or that national comparative advantage must always trump international collectivism, the empiricism of recent history gives the lie very clearly. The CAP experiment tested Europe's farming productivity potential to the full and revealed two things. First, it brought to light the incredible returns on water that can be achieved with a high-input and high-output farming regime. Water responds to money that buys technology and focuses science very well indeed. Second, the CAP clearly demonstrated the negative economic and environmental consequences of very high levels of price protection and other incentives.

Many commentators wish to write the CAP off as a folly. They are frequently – though not exclusively – on the political right. A large number are what I like to term fundamentalist economists. They refuse to discover anything of use or value in something that stains their theoretical purity. Such is the enviable position of the ideologue. That which chimes with your ideology is QED correct. It is empirical reality that has to play catch-up.

Opponents of the CAP have plenty at which it is possible to poke the finger of blame. The fabled butter mountains and milk lakes of the 1970s and 1980s were real. Perishable monuments to the excesses of subsidised farming. The impact of such over-production is slight in the CAP economies. Farmers have been rewarded for their efforts, some might say disproportionately. The impact on other economies, the recipients of the dumped, subsidised goods, is altogether different. Economically, these goods are a near-fatal opiate for a poor developing economy with rapidly expanding coastal cities. Developing economies become dependent on the cheap food, which concurrently weakens their indigenous farming industry, increasing poverty and the reliance on imports. Subsidised half-cost food can be shipped to coastal cities in poor economies more easily than it can be trucked from distant farms on poor roads. And so progresses the vicious circle of economic atrophy and poverty.

125

But for water specialists, there is something highly valuable about experiments like the CAP and US farming subsidies and the massive US investment in hydraulic infrastructure detailed earlier. These experiments demonstrate the potential productivity of scarce water. And the story is – broadly – very good. The UK shows that we are getting better at working our water resources – especially green-water resources – in farming. It's natural that economies become more water-efficient as they diversify and move to the water-light financial and service sectors. What is more interesting to note is how farming itself becomes more water-efficient as the wealth of an economy increases. Here's the important point: the context of incentives, subsidies and price guarantees may be highly artificial but the increased yields are utterly real. Therefore, there is no physical, geographical or environmental reason why such levels of productivity cannot be achieved in the 'real world' of messy political economies and the much-less-than-perfect market. We can consider the CAP as a *massive experiment* in an attempt to answer the question: how water-productive can farming be? Now we have our answer. The next question: how to duplicate this alongside the stewardship of the water environment without the unsustainable and irresponsible subsidies?

From the CAP, we have a fixed piece of knowledge. One variable from the legion of uncertainties we face has been eliminated. This is more than fortunate. Perhaps it is worth the cost in European taxation but not the negative impacts on poor developing economies. Things have been done with water and other natural resources that would never have been attempted in a farming economy determined by free-market principles, especially one that is blind to environmental fundamentals. Farm livelihoods have been kept in place and rural communities have been helped to cope with the new challenges of intensification of crop and livestock production. The transitions have often been tough, but they would have been much tougher without the protection of the CAP. Its supporters still have strong voices in France and other EU economies with large farming communities. They slow the rate of rural transformation to a human pace.

126

Competition might well encourage careful innovation; absolute financial security encourages innovation that is reckless, imaginative and sometimes – as in the improvements in water productivity – downright revolutionary. The information we now hold about water productivity as a consequence of the CAP is very valuable. Would that we had equivalent experimental knowledge about climate change.

The whole world, Hollywood style
You will notice that I tend, wherever possible, to steer away from referring to the industrialised massacres of the first half of the twentieth century as the First and Second World Wars. This is not some scholarly eccentricity. Though useful labels for an informal discussion, the names are inaccurate at best, arrogantly misleading at worst. I am not writing a political history, nor would I presume to, but I find the continuity of violence in the twentieth century too compelling to be happy with some violence being called 'world wars' because they involved Europe and the US.

Pulling the ladder up after ourselves

Compare and contrast
Cultural and financial globalisation are great levellers.
So goes the theory. The bar for wealth, quality and duration of life has been set by the industrialised nations.
In the international economic race, the other economies
are playing catch-up. National wealth, military might or
resource advantage have allowed some to enjoy what we
in the West hubristically call accelerated developed, which
translates as merely becoming more like us more quickly
than others. Japan showed how an economy can leap-frog
formerly more successful ones. Other economies – by
some metrics – continue to languish.

127

It is no exaggeration to say that to be a farmer in a
poor developing economy today – particularly in Africa
– is to be a contemporary of Britain at the start of the
nineteenth century. The experiences and contexts are
highly analogous. The big difference is that today's farmers in the developing economies have it just that little bit
tougher. UK farming interests between 1815 and 1846 were
enjoying a last desperate fling of mercantilism and protectionism. Trade with Europe was, in happy accord with
the views of Adam Smith, driving down the price of staple
goods in the UK. Why should people buy expensive domestic produce when cheaper imports from elsewhere were
abundantly available? Unwilling to pass quietly into the
night and dismantle their industry and historic economic
advantage, the British landowners fought back. And lost.
Quite comprehensively.

At first glance, the comparison with today's developing-
world farmer is striking. The industrialised economies
flood the developing world with their cheap (and often
subsidised) produce. There is no parity between the competitors in this bout of economic war; it makes David and
Goliath appear as balanced as the elephant and the fly.

Daily, the industrialised economies brutally confront and subjugate developing economies in their local market-places. Formally, part of the battle is conducted through the World Trade Organisation (WTO). Developing economies are ordered to liberalise their markets and forbidden from levying import tariffs or subsidising their own output. Industrialised economies are advised to reconsider their own protectionist measures, and are urged to temper the recklessness of their own agribusinesses. As ever, diktats for the weak; guidance for the strong. Occasionally, but only after decades of contention, the worst excesses in cotton and sugar have been addressed.

128

If the comparison is enlightening, the contrast is disturbing. There have been no triumphs for the weak. The weak do not have rapidly industrialising and diversifying economies, as the UK enjoyed two hundred years ago. The alternative livelihoods awaiting the British peasant heading to the big industrial towns and cities of early-Victorian Britain have no present-day counterpart in sub-Saharan Africa. The Victorian dream of the urban migrant is little more than a cruel torment for tens of millions of impoverished sub-Saharan African farming families. They are trapped in a cycle of low (and declining) crop productivity and very, very low water productivity. Their economic context is un-diversified. Expectations are low. Alternative employment is rare. The rural dispossessed of Britain in 1846 could console themselves with the opportunities for transition into the proletariat of the world's imperial hegemon, the British empire. They might have been but cogs in an unparalleled economic machine, but cogs they were. Cogs ate. There is no powerhouse industrialising imperial economy for the farmers of sub-Saharan Africa.

The exception in this comparison is South Africa, the 'S' in the BRICS acronym. Unlike other sub-Saharan economies, it has a relatively diversified and advanced economy. Agriculturally, South Africa has been enjoying

significant improvements in productivity and returns to
water. These increases pale next to those nurtured in
the highly incentivised, protected and financially secure
industrialised economies. But they are not too dissimilar
from those seen in Britain after the repeal of the Corn Laws.

One world: just add water

Water is the constraining environmental resource in agriculture. Without it, we are nowhere. We have the human
resources. We have farming technology. We have even
gained a form of mastery over the genetics of grains, fruit
and vegetables. And we have land. Plenty of land. Neither the
peasant farmer nor the global investor is interested in land
that is desert, of which there is too much. It is rain-fed land
that is useful. Or land to which engineers can bring water.

129

    Water availability is largely determined by the
environment. But water productivity is not. Water
productivity is determined by the twenty or more other
inputs accessible, or not, to the farmer, and how they are
combined. Forced into increasing poverty, barred from
lifting themselves out through government intervention,
the farmers of the developing economies are in no position
to increase their water productivity, let alone make the
phenomenal advances seen in the UK in the industrialising
era of the nineteenth century nor those brought about by
the introduction of the CAP.

    There are many reasons why you should petition your
politicians, adjust your purchasing behaviour and even
– should it ever help – march in the streets against the
depths of rural poverty in the world's developing economies. It is degrading to humanity, ours and theirs. It
leads to millions of unnecessary deaths – especially of
children – each and every year. It destabilises local politics
and foments armed conflict over other issues, regionally, nationally and internationally. Now you have a new
reason: water. Anything that tends to perpetuate rural

poverty directly impacts on local and global water productivity, with the corresponding knock-on effect on global
water security. Poverty is bad for water.

The politics of water efficiency

Water needs money and politics as much as technology on its side. The UK farmers of the nineteenth and the
first half of the twentieth centuries achieved a trebling of
water productivity using a relatively low-input and low-
output mode of production. Little had changed in terms
of farming technology or water availability between the
close of the nineteenth century and the second half of
the twentieth in the UK. Yet farmers were able to achieve
self-sufficiency (and beyond) in temperate crops after 1950.
What was different? The politics.

130

Imagine the potential to be unlocked across the world
in the BRICS and developing economies with the political
will in place to incentivise farmers. India gives us a tan-
talising insight into this brave new world of possibility.
In the second half of the twentieth century, despite a
demographic profile that might be fairly described as
challenging, India managed four- and five-fold increases in
water productivity and crop production respectively. Yes,
it required access to new technology, including new seeds.
But more so, it required market protection and financial
incentives for producers, including some dangerous energy
subsidies. And water plus gains in water-use efficiency. It
particularly required the political determination to push
these innovations through.

In the nineteenth century the UK was doing what
a hundred and ninety of the world's two hundred or so
national economies do today. Sit back, relax and let
virtual-water 'trade' take the strain. All this, without even
formally engaging with the concept. Where in the world
are departments of state applying the idea of virtual water
to their water-management strategy? Nowhere. But things

are changing, and the UK, with its long history of benefiting from virtual-water 'trade', is well placed to form the
theoretical vanguard. The UK may prove to be on the right
side of history this time.

An island afloat on virtual water

What has virtual water ever done for us?
What has virtual water ever done for the UK? The list is
comprehensive. Without virtual-water 'trade', the history of the British Isles over the last two centuries would
have been dramatically different. In the nineteenth
century, 'imported' virtual water from the New World in
cheap staples such as wheat allowed the UK economy to
remain stable as it moved further and further from food
self-sufficiency and water security.

131

By the middle of the twentieth century the tiny island
state of the UK, with its steadily crumbling empire, was
only about 40 per cent self-sufficient in food. Virtual-water
'imports' had been making up the shortfall for more than a
century. Suffering from the aftershock of two devastating
conflicts, and especially the fearful isolation of standing
alone in 1940, it was politically and emotionally untenable
to be so reliant on other economies for food and water
security. The stark discomfort of the war years brought
forth the protectionist panacea of the 1947 Agriculture Act.

The 1947 Agriculture Act captures the mood of the late
1940s in the UK and its governing classes. Its aim was to
secure efficient agricultural production and proper agricultural conditions.

Let's take a quick peek at it, with some key sections and
approaches emphasised:

> The...Act shall have effect for the *purpose of promoting
> and maintaining, by the provision of guaranteed prices
> and assured markets* for the produce...*a stable and effi-
> cient agricultural industry capable of producing such*

*part of the nation's food and other agricultural produce
as in the national interest it is desirable to produce in
the United Kingdom, and of producing it at minimum
prices consistently with proper remuneration and living
conditions for farmers and workers in agriculture and
an adequate return on capital invested in the industry.*
(No mention of the environment or the stewardship of
water services!)

So, if it seems familiar, that's because it is. Here are
the Corn Laws filtered through the strainer of socialism
with minds concentrated by a frightening war. Protecting
'proper remuneration and living conditions' rather than
landed interests, but otherwise scant difference.

132

The effect was immense. There was an explosion in
crop and livestock productivity on rain-fed farms. There
was a revolution in water productivity. By the 1970s, the
UK was once again self-sufficient in temperate crops and
had ceased to be a net importer of wheat. Reliance on
virtual-water 'imports' dropped from 60 per cent to 40 per
cent. Importantly, much of that 40 per cent consists of
produce that could never be produced in the UK, barring
any fortuitous side effects from the coming cataclysm of
climate change.

Keeping it in the family

The European common market created what might with
only mild exaggeration be termed a food-trading frenzy
in the latter half of the twentieth century. The UK was not
modest in participating. Its contribution increased further
after joining the EEC in 1973.

A phenomenal proportion of global virtual-water 'trade'
takes place between the member states of the EU. At the
close of the last century, the EU was trading on average
69 cubic kilometres per year internally. To put that into
context, global virtual-water 'trade' between all 13 regions
of the world, according to UN agencies, averaged 210 cubic

kilometres. Roughly a third of all trade was accounted for by the EU. That statistic is made all the more remarkable when you remember that a mere three hundred million people lived within the EU. The population is now close to five hundred million as a consequence of recent enlargement. By way of a contrast, the North American economies of Canada, Mexico and the US, with a combined population of around 450 million, only trade 19 cubic kilometres per year in their region. Clearly if the US were to be counted as 49 sub-economies, the internal virtual-water 'trade' would be as high, or higher, than that within the EU. In contrast, the 2.6 billion people of East and South Asia – one third of the world's population – account for a tiny proportion of the international 'trade' in virtual water: approximately 10.5 cubic kilometres.

133

There are many interesting conclusions we might draw from that flurry of statistics. Importantly, we can see that trade remains the preserve of the wealthier economies. The rich trade a lot; the poor trade relatively little. We shall return to this theme once we turn our attention to the BRICS and developing economies in Chapters 4 and 5. Of course, what is more eye-grabbing is that the EU accounts for a disproportionate amount of virtual-water 'trade'.

The WTO and taking on board the stewardship of the environment

The WTO: an elephant in the room

The negotiations of the WTO – and its predecessor the Uruguay Round – are grindingly slow. The lunacy and lethargy of the WTO is well demonstrated by its approach to sugar subsidies. Pure common sense argues that a well-co-ordinated global order would facilitate the production of sugar cane in economies with high rainfall. Econom-ically, this works. These economies are, almost without exception, poor. Labour is cheap and the climate is suited to producing a narrow band of food produce. Combined with the glut of soil water, it is clear these economies enjoy a simple comparative advantage. Impoverished farmers in these economies would benefit from the strong global demand for their product: everyone needs sugar.

And yet here is a clear example of the free market only being good for the goose of the industrialised economies. And the producers in poor tropical economies must feel as though they are being rudely treated. The industrialised nations have no philosophical or ideological objection (at least none that is fiercely and unequivocally expressed by policy-makers themselves) to heavily subsidising their own production of sugar beet. Politically, the architects of CAP decided that sugar self-sufficiency was a necessity. So too did the law-makers in the US. Once enshrined in law, the thorn of protectionism requires great effort to extract from the body politic. The weight and influence of farming and industrial interests in the US and EU is immense; reform can be immediately stifled. No industry will argue against its own financial benefit; no national economy will willingly cede valuable GDP to another.

134

Hence in the farm politics of the UK, EU and US it is entirely possible to ignore economics, common sense and justice. And behind all this lies water efficiency. Not only would it be economically prudent and socially just to allow rain-rich, cash-poor economies to compete fairly in the sugar market, it would also lead to far greater efficiency in our global use of water. Water knows no national boundaries. It cares not for subsidies or GDP. Very few economies have sovereignty over water. The ideology of ruthless competition makes no sense when trying to co-ordinate the use of a globally shared, increasingly scarce resource. The political brownie points earned by the policy-makers in industrialised economies by maintaining subsidised sugar-beet production will prove worthless in a world with a devastated water supply for food production. Again, we see that the key factor determining water (in)efficiency is not the almighty market or environmental precaution, but instead self-interested national and market politics.

Environmental stewardship and its impact on water management

But if we in the industrialised economies are blind, at least we are learning how to see. Environmentalism, once the preserve of the tree-hugging activist or the sneered-at dusty intellectual, has been embraced by the mainstream. The environmental activists were there first. Academia adopted the message which it should have coined and launched. By the 1970s scientists had joined the campaign arguing that society was dangerously misguided in treating the world's ability to provide resources and absorb pollution as infinite.

135

Activists had been developing their case since the 1950s. Culturally, things changed in the 1980s. The number of voices arguing for considerations of sustainability – a new word and concept – in our approach to the environment and natural resources, including water, grew. Despite the strong contrary tendency to reduce the role of the state and the lauding of privatisation, politicians increasingly listened. Remember, politicians are reactive to the will of the electorate, but their responses are gradual and uneven. The comparison is with turning around a tanker rather than steering a car. Over the past three decades, solid and irreversible progress has been made in advancing policies that protect the water environment. The US got there first. It installed the *Environmental* Protection Agency in 1971. The UK has experimented with various institutions. By now it has an *Environment* Agency in the Department for *Environment*, Food and Rural Affairs. Here, at the close of the first decade of the twenty-first century, much has been achieved in environmental legislation – making the environmental rules, as well as applying them.

Though the political resistance exerted by the ancient and powerful farming lobby, and the younger vibrant upstarts of the seed, fertiliser and pesticide corporations, makes progress slower than desired, we shan't be going backwards. Environment is one of the issues addressed by the political machine, and the farmers increasingly see themselves as stewards of the environment – including of the water environment. And society is beginning to value them as stewards as well as producers.

136

Leading the world, or not

The privatisation of water in the UK in 1989 was trumpeted as a great example through which Britain would lead the world, much praised by privatisation-addict Margaret Thatcher. What would become known informally as the British model of water privatisation entailed the sale of both concessions to supply water and the actual mainly locally owned assets and infrastructures. By contrast, under the French model of privatisation, the state retains ownership of the assets while local-government agencies as well as private companies can handle distribution.

The French model, itself similar to that which has existed in Germany for over a century, has been replicated across Europe. The British model is not copied anywhere. Assertions that the British model led to improvements in water quality probably say more about the parlous state of UK drinking water in 1989 than the efficacy of wholesale privatisation. Still, at the time of writing, approximately 90 per cent of all drinking-water and sanitation systems across the world remain unprivatised. Margaret Thatcher's experiment of 1989 – and its social fallout of water poverty, hosepipe bans and piecemeal investment in infrastructure – has certainly proved an instructive example to the rest of the world. Though with an effect contrary to that which she intended. UK water privatisation has been made to work, but its sustainability is not yet proven. Meanwhile privatisation of water services to households is resisted in the heart of capitalism – in New York City and in the heartlands of Republican Texas.

And note. The privatisation of blue water in the UK addressed water services for householders and industry. The small water. Very little blue water is used in the UK in farming.

Britain and the law of blue water

It's a simple law: wherever you irrigate, you always run out of water. No exceptions. The history of blue water in the UK is incredibly short. As anyone who has lived in these islands will agree, rain-fed farming predominates. By 1950, only 1.5 per cent of the UK's arable land was equipped for irrigation. By 2000, this figure was still only 5 per cent. Those areas of the UK that would benefit from irrigation for farming are precisely those areas that are blue-water-scarce. For example, East Anglia gets the least rainfall in the country; it is almost semi-arid. Much of the land farmed was very grudgingly yielded up by the North Sea in the first place. Climate-change predictions bring no good news on this water front. If rainfall decreases in summer, the need for irrigation will rise but the potential to irrigate will drop. Agriculture will have to adapt by reverting to making the best of its green water.

137

The inevitable future

The River Thames meanders its way through London. It flows slowly. Nothing is hurried. Urgency is forever elsewhere. So it is with the discourse on household water efficiency in the UK. It is moving, but slowly.

From farms to food...

The Department for Environment, Food and Rural Affairs (DEFRA) rose from the ashes of the politically discredited Ministry of Agriculture, Fisheries and Food in the wake of the 2001 foot-and-mouth crisis. Many (too cynically) wrote this change off as mere brand detoxification. Foot-and-mouth had been but the latest of a series of disasters, including – most famously – the long-running hysteria over BSE. But the change in titles, and the re-ordering of priorities it represents, is significant and illuminating.

The words agriculture and fisheries have vanished, swallowed up into their former colleague, food. Words are powerful but not omnipotent. I do not want to make too much of the semantics here, but the shift in emphasis from agriculture to food perhaps marks the point when a political tide turned against the farming lobby. Focus moved from the input to the output, from the supply side to demand and the role of consumers. Food is important; farming, only insofar as it provides food.

138

In August 2009, DEFRA launched its Food 2030 Forum, to which I was invited to make a minor contribution. In many ways, this is the contemporary corollary of the Agriculture Act of 1947. Here is a glimpse of the forum's mission statement (emphasis added):

> A number of challenges are facing the *food system* – rising population, diminishing natural resources and climate change. Alongside these, *diet-related ill health* continues to put a burden on the economy and society. These web pages provide an opportunity to discuss the challenges and other issues affecting the *food system*. They also provide a place to discuss the shape of the future food system. Food 2030 looks both at the food we *produce and consume* in the UK, and how *global food production can be increased in a sustainable way.*
> http://sandbox.defra.gov.uk/food2030/

There are some strong contrasts with 1947. The 1947 Act had a simple and uncomplicated aim: to increase food production and productivity with incentives that secured the livelihoods of farmers. It was a response to the lethal hostilities of the preceding decades. The policy-makers were facing the fight of tomorrow as though it were the battle of yesterday. The environment was not a concern; water resources were not even paid lip service. Health was not mentioned. Climate change was off the conceptual map. Nor was there any sense that the UK's high-input and high-output approach might impact on partner economies in other parts of the world, such as Africa.

Fast forward to 2009. We understand now that the threat of tomorrow is not about lethal hostilities that interrupt trade. The future threat is international, not national. Chronic, not acute. The terror of food insecurity in 1947 was a wicked problem – one that is urgent but full of uncertainty. Society tends to lunge at a solution which in turn brings on another – unintended – wicked problem. The apparent solution to food insecurity contributed to the contemporary wicked problems of climate change and water pollution. Again, if we face the challenge of the future with the weapons of the past, we will not only lose but worsen the outcome.

139

Today, the government has a broader approach, focusing on the much wider spectrum of natural resources, food production, consumption and waste. Seemingly, policy will be output- rather than input-led. In other words, it will be about food, rather than farms. The process seems informed by the dire consequences of rising populations and their dangerous levels of food consumption from already-stressed and stretched soil and water resources. Possibly some mandarin has been reading Malthus. The global impacts of UK food production and trade are also noted.

The water–food–trade nexus is globalised; so must government policy be. Further, DEFRA acknowledges the financial and social burden of ill-health, an increasing consequence of our ill-informed consumption preferences. There are no doubt legal reasons inhibiting the mention of the unstoppable ascendancy of supermarket ready meals and the ubiquity of fast-food restaurants when governments talk of historic highs of heart disease, diabetes and bowel cancer. Most probably, the same legal constraints that prevent the government from mentioning such illnesses in the same sentence as fast-food and supermarket brands are equally applicable to a popular-science book such as this.

A note of warning though. Politics has deliberately been pushed into the background in the expressed objectives of the Food 2030 Forum. Ever the same story. There is no policy without politics. Those engaging with DEFRA would do well to remember that the farm lobby and associated agriculture corporations will be highly political in the ways they operate and pressure. To ignore this fact would be to doom oneself to being politically outmanoeuvred by these very experienced and established players. There is no escaping the reality that any future food policy must engage with UK food producers. We are process-bound to accommodate their interests. The tail never truly wags the dog; water productivity will not lead the food-production industry in the UK, much as I might wish it to. Pragmatically, I can hope for two things. First, that the correct package of incentives and regulation can be devised to ensure we have a sensible, sustainable approach to food production, and that water management will be integral to it. Second, that millions of informed consumers on this tiny island embark on diets that are good for their own health and for the health of the water environment.

Ambitions of self-sufficiency are dangerous pipe dreams. They are dangerous for economies and very dangerous for the water environment. Subsidising crop and livestock production of commodities that we can gain easily and painlessly through trade from non-water-stressed places are a morally and financially costly folly. Yet financial incentives have a real role to play in our farming futures everywhere. By providing security for producers, they can underpin greater water efficiencies and better environmental stewardship. Hopefully, we are about to embark on an era of even-greater green-water efficiency; I believe there is still room for improvement in the UK, despite the monumental increases of the past seventy years. The trick is ensuring that the basket of incentives steer farmers – who are the UK's *de facto* water managers and stewards – to produce food effectively and safely. The mix of crop and livestock production must be both economically and environmentally sound. An example: incentivising the production of legumes would have the handy environmental side effect of eliminating toxic levels of nitrates, which have mighty carbon footprints. The solutions are out there. Some are known. Others are patiently waiting for a light to be shone upon them. In order to lead them out of the dark, we ourselves must be in the light.

141

The UK has run ahead of history at many important junctures. Perhaps water efficiency might be that small island's next useful innovation. Only the future will tell. There are some worrying features. First, the farmers who manage the big – green – water on UK farms are unaware of their impressive contribution to the water security of the UK. They are unaware of the ten-fold increase in water productivity since 1800. Second, UK consumers have no idea of their water footprints and of the role of dietary choice on these footprints. Third, agri-trade, agribusiness and supermarkets are very uncertain on how they might influence the growers to operate in water-efficient ways and in ways that are considerate of the water environment. The messages here are clear, but UK individuals and society remain in deep ignorance about the nature of their water security.

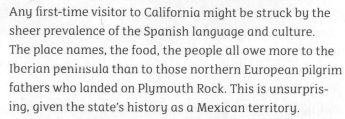

PART 3
Spain: turning the oil tanker

He who pours water hastily into a bottle spills more than goes in.
SPANISH PROVERB

There's no place like California...except perhaps Spain

142

Any first-time visitor to California might be struck by the sheer prevalence of the Spanish language and culture. The place names, the food, the people all owe more to the Iberian peninsula than to those northern European pilgrim fathers who landed on Plymouth Rock. This is unsurprising, given the state's history as a Mexican territory.

What is more surprising is that California also seems to have inherited Spain's geography. Spain is roughly 20 per cent larger, at 504,000 square kilometres, than California's 414,000. It's proportionately more populous: Spain houses 43 million souls to California's 37 million. But their population densities are identical. Both have lush and verdant mountainous coastal areas. Both have broad stretches of desert. Roughly, the two states divide into a water-rich north and a water-stressed south.

Importantly, both have a climate in the south that is ideal for year-round crop growing. What they lack is water. Historically, this has been a big problem for the farmers of southern Spain. For youthful southern California, history is what happened this morning. The problem of water scarcity in the south of the state was no sooner identified than rectified – albeit temporarily and at great cost – by the heroic hydraulic mission detailed earlier in this chapter.

But a lack of water doesn't matter for economies such as California and Spain. Because they are highly diversified and industrialised nations. Or, to put it more bluntly, they have money. And if you have money, then you will get water. California and Spain have drawn water from the local supplies, from other water basins and – through virtual-water 'trade' – from other economies to meet their water needs. No one who has been to either Spain or California could fail to notice that the climate isn't just pleasant for crops; it also suits people rather well. Neither economy has difficulty attracting plenty of skilled human capital. Both are famed for offering comfortable lifestyles. All such factors help greatly when faced with a lack of water. As shall become increasingly apparent during our discussion here, there are plenty of ways to make up for a shortage of water. A skilled professional workforce, plenty of finance and a little bit of ingenuity mean that both southern California and Spain have implausibly robust agricultural sectors, despite being heavily water-scarce.

143

Of course, there are some differences. Southern California, as we have seen, imports real water. In fact, the incredibly potent US hydraulic victories of the early twentieth century now deliver more than 20 cubic kilometres to the region annually. The region then 'exports' at least the same volume as virtual water. Spain, however, uses virtual-water 'imports' to meet its needs. It 'imports' around 27 cubic kilometres in agricultural products. These are low-value crops. Doing this enables Spain's farmers to allocate their scarce water to the production of high-value products: meat, dairy and luxury fruit and veg. Over the past ten years there has been a fundamental shift in the sources of Spanish virtual-water 'imports'. In 1997 the country was very reliant on US imports; by the middle of the last decade, Brazil and Argentina were meeting the majority of its virtual-water needs. Store that fact in some easily accessible chamber of your brain: its relevance will become clearer in our next chapter, when we start to look at Brazil's ascendance in international food trade.

> ### Jamón ibérico
>
> *Jamón ibérico, as the name suggests, comes only from Spain. Specifically, from the black Iberian pig. Production is strictly controlled and regulated. The purity of the breed, the nature of the pig's diet and the quality of the curing are all fanatically defended. It tastes amazing. Soft, fatty, delicate and strangely smooth in the mouth. But what makes jamón ibérico relevant to our study is the price. Because it is the most expensive ham in the world. And in water terms, represents a fantastic financial return to the water used.*

144

Although still a net 'importer' of virtual water, Spain's exports are increasing dramatically. In the past decade, the virtual water 'exported' in livestock products alone surged from 6 to 10 cubic kilometres. This has been achieved while the quantity of virtual-water 'imports' into the industry – in the form of imported animal feed – has risen more modestly, from 3 to 4 cubic kilometres. These figures represent a significant improvement in the economic productivity of Spanish agriculture. By taking relatively cheap virtual-water 'imports' and using them as an increasingly efficient input into the production of high-value livestock products, Spanish farmers are managing to wring more money from the same amount of water. By producing more and more, with similar amounts of imports, the Spanish livestock-export industry has grown in value from just over €1.5 billion in 1997 to €3.5 billion in 2006.

And that's a lot of ham.

The rain in Spain falls mainly...well, nowhere

While the north-western corner of Spain and its hilly border with France have enough soil water during the summer to keep vegetation and crops alive, the rest of the country is basically barren. There are a few woodlands and forests in the mountains of the south, but mostly the rest of the country is entirely without crops and vegetation. There are, however, some small areas of irrigated agriculture in the south, covered by either fabric or glass. What is significant about these irrigated lands is that they produce a considerable amount of economic value. Here is the very essence of Spain's story: a country making extremely profitable economic use of its scarce water resources.

As I've said, Spain doesn't really belong in Europe. Most of it is more like North Africa in terms of available water. So it is that Spain's water story is profoundly different from that of the rest of Europe. Its hydraulic mission and water-management approaches have little in common with its European neighbours. Despite enjoying the industrialised economy of a nation of temperate Europe, Spain wears a North African geography.

145

Three steps to heaven

Getting better at getting better

As a species, we're great at solutions. Often, we hit on them swiftly and decisively, and then pursue them with the single-mindedness of a tiger stalking its prey. Only with reflection do we realise that our initial solution is perhaps not so viable in the long term. We humans definitely gravitate towards immediacy over sustainability. Possibly the most significant civic change of the past few decades has been that driven by environmentalists. Culturally, we are increasingly capable of analysing our impact from the perspective of the future rather than the present.

Approaches to water security have evolved in the same way.

The first new approach adopted is always one of supply management. We need more water. Therefore, we store, divert and pump more freshwater to meet these greater requirements. Here, in two sentences, is the history of the hydraulic mission. After supply management, the second approach is marginally more significant: demand management. Rather than getting more water, we try and change our water-use habits. Mainly, this consists of using less water, and also using it more efficiently.

. Then there is the third approach. Sustainable intensification. Perhaps, on the printed page, this doesn't seem like the most exciting or inspiring phrase in the world. But it means a lot to us water scientists. It's exciting to me because it shows that people have come to recognise the need to protect our water environment. It's exciting because there is an implicit shift from a human-centric approach to water – focusing on supply and demand – to a water-centric one.

146

Virtual-water 'imports' can play an important role in sustainable intensification. The imports silently plug any politically poisonous gaps in a nation's water supplies. And virtual-water 'trade' itself is underpinned by economic diversification. The more diversified an economy, the more opportunities for trade. And therefore the more likely it is that an economy can sensibly and strategically augment its indigenous water environment with virtual-water 'imports'.

A water history of Spain

Engineering its way out of water insecurity
One of the reasons why Spain is such an interesting example to use in this study is that it has progressed rapidly through these three approaches in a very short period of time: the second half of the twentieth century. In many ways – social, economical and cultural – the Spain of 2011 is unrecognisable from the war-affected, fractured, impoverished authoritarian state of the 1950s. And its approach to water security has changed equally profoundly.

Spain managed to get its bout of mechanised murder out of the way slightly earlier than most of continental Europe.

The bloody civil conflict of the 1930s was a down-payment on death. It meant Spain could bow out of the devastation of the next decade and get on with what populations do in times of stability: eat and reproduce. As the population grew, so the country needed to increase crop production.

First came the supply-side solution in the ever-familiar form of the hydraulic mission. Spain built reservoirs to supply irrigated farms, and hydro-electric plants and dams to generate power. But Spain has quite a profound problem with its surface water. It is deeply susceptible to drought. Spain's groundwater supplies are far more reliable, and can be pumped to supplement depleted surface-water levels. But this was in truth the second wave of Spain's hydraulic mission. The Iberian peninsula had actually leapt on the water-engineering bandwagon many years earlier...

When it comes to the hydraulic mission, a strange quirk of history meant that Spain stole a march on California by a couple of decades. The collapse of Spanish imperial influence in the Caribbean and Pacific at the end of the nineteenth century saw Spanish professionals beating a hasty retreat back to the motherland. Among those returning was a cadre of water engineers. The final death throes of Spain's colonial dream left the country's collective consciousness haunted and uncertain. There was a need for the nation to pursue something ambitious, improving and uncontroversial. At the same time, with the end of imperial wealth and resources came a very basic and mundane need for greater water and food self-sufficiency. All these different factors coming together meant that the nation turned its eye to a culturally reassuring and unifying engineering project as a solution to its bruised national ego and its weakened financial position.

147

Changing attitudes

But the supply-management approach rightly fell out of fashion in Spain during the 1970s. The death of General Franco, dictator for almost four decades, in 1975 and the consequent restructuring of the constitution and country three years later filtered down into attitudes towards water. As civic life became more pluralistic and open, there was public debate about how to manage water. There were still many who wanted to keep to the old orthodoxy. Their mantra was simple: mobilise more and more water, regardless of the damage to the environment or the financial cost. But those on the other side of the debate were becoming both more numerous and more vocal. People were demanding that water be used more efficiently, with greater environmental consideration and with a focus on sustainable intensification. Naturally, the battles between both sides were rarely fought where the water was actually being over-diverted and over-pumped in rural, irrigated areas. Rather, the fight was conducted on the national and regional political stages, in the science community and sometimes on the very streets of Spain's cities.

148

The Ebro River controversy

The political conflict over water use in Spain came to a head at an important crunch time in the economy's recent social history. Towards the end of the last century, a massive water-transfer project was proposed, and began to move slowly up the chain of executive action. It was a typically foolish and wrong-headed conceit. A difficult, costly and environmentally reckless hydro-engineering folly that belonged to a water-management ideology that was already fifty years out of date. The plan was to divert water from the Ebro River in the north of the country to the irrigated farmlands of the south in the provinces of Andalusia and Murcia. As with so many ideas that worm their way into the political discourse, this scheme endured not because of its inherent quality (it had none) but because of the influence and wealth of its backers. It was pushed heavily by an alliance of southern irrigation interests and the old champions of the dam-building hydraulic-mission era, both of which groups had the ear of the local legislators in both provinces. Again, we see that farmers and engineers can as often be a force for harm as for good.

But by 2004, when the project became a significant national-election issue, the farmers and engineers found themselves on the wrong side of history. The socialist government that took power in the wake of the Madrid train bombing stayed true to its manifesto pledge and threw the scheme off the national agenda. Coming after nearly a century of ever-more-aggressive hydraulic innovation, the Ebro River transfer was a water project too far for the people of Spain, especially in the humid north, from where the water was to be transferred. The sheer scale of the engineering ambitions of the south frightened those in the north: they were being forced to remedy the water scarcity of the south, a scarcity born of an historically environmentally blind approach to water management. Worse, the remedy was itself deeply environmentally blind and a water transfer of unprecedented scope for Spain. The rejection of the scheme was a clear and powerful signal to the deeply entrenched old interests: finally a new water politics dominated Spain. Significantly, this new politics was spearheaded by a multifaceted coalition of environmental activists, socialists, northern civil society and politicians. These fringe voices were now being heard, and loudly heard, in distant, south-facing Madrid. But we should remember that the narrative of politics is cyclical not linear. Rarely are outcomes permanent. The struggle continues and, at the time of writing, Spain is suffering more than most economies in the global downturn. Its real-estate bubble has burst ferociously, unemployment is endemic, and the socialist administration has scant

149

HOW TO DRINK SALTWATER
Well, you can't actually drink saltwater, obviously. But Spain has an ancient tradition of virtually augmenting its freshwater and soil water supplies with saltwater from the Mediterranean and Atlantic. How? By turning saltwater into protein and injecting it into the national diet. All you need is a boat, a rod and some hooks...

political capital left. Spain may yet again see proposals like the Ebro River transfer reach the political light of day.

An alternative to dams and water transfer

The history of water management in Spain during the twentieth century is a history characterised by poor levels of hydrological and economic information, of intransigence and the attenuation in passing and implementing regulatory legislation. Even where regulation has been introduced, it has proved to be of slight operational value. Certainly, the traditional hydraulic solutions are no longer the unthinking, automatic option that they once were. Spanish society is now able to bear environmental and social activists offering up voices of protest and dissent. Today, Spain is more in step with the mainstream of European thought than at any time since the end of the 1939–45 war. Environmentalism and the protection of water environments are the norm on the European continent, and are being progressively institutionalised in EU agreements. The days of great damming and water-transfer projects on the European mainland are over. At least for the time being. But this veneer of good sense can be scratched off by sudden crises. The Spanish drought of the last decade saw proposals for piping water from France to meet Barcelona's thirst. Barcelona is in the water-rich north of Spain. Still, the knee-jerk reaction of supply management proved to be more politically feasible than the demand-management response of regulating the use of water in the administrative districts neighbouring Barcelona in the Ebro basin.

When there is panic, the question that comes to the political mind is: where can we get more water? Rather, we need to ask: how can we use our water better? There is no way of getting the right answer with the wrong question.

Again, we see that the politics of water allocation are as complex as any allocative struggle. And when they are

150

THE DECEMBER 2000 EU WATER FRAMEWORK DIRECTIVE
This is the centrepiece of EU water-management legislation. The directive makes it incumbent upon members to identify each of its river basins and assign them to district authorities. Further, it sets a series of timetables for analyses of water use and productivity relating to each river basin. The law forces countries to set out plans for sustainable economic use of their water resources.

progressively more politicised, they become less access-ible. Water is of great economic importance in Spain. Many jobs depend on it. When water has such strategic signifi-cance, the powerful special interests are unlikely to want the debate held in public. They will save their most deter-mined and effective engagement for private meetings and encounters. Forcing the discourse into the open is vital in ensuring that better decisions are made. But, frustratingly, the more urgent the issue, and the higher the stakes, the more likely it is to be debated away from the public.

Water is more than its economic value. This vital message has filtered through into the Spanish political and social consciousness since the start of this century. It has also penetrated the EU legislative landscape, most prominently in the form of the December 2000 EU Water Framework Directive. Ideas, once out, might wax and wane in popularity and fashion but can never truly disappear again. Many disparate elements are brought together under the loose banner of Spanish water environmental-ism: the sunshine activists of the younger generation; those weary grey hairs of the science community; city-dwellers from the north. This coalition has proven powerful and influential, but the future is ever unwritten.

151

ALL CHANGE: 2004 Post-Franco, Spanish democracy has followed a pendulum-swing pattern, with power being handed back and forth between two major parties, one on the left, the other on the right. After eight years of the Partido Popular, José Luis Rodríguez Zapatero led the Spanish Social-ist Workers Party back to power in 2004. The election was widely seen as a fierce and sudden repudiation of the Partido Popular's recent tenure, especially its prominent participation in George W. Bush's Iraq adventure

Ground over surface

The water demands of the south are many. Irrigated agriculture is the most obvious, but the cities and the tourist industry both place huge demands on the scant resources. The Spanish weather, like the Californian sun, is a temptation too great for the farming industry. When you have temperatures in excess of 30 degrees centigrade in summer and very mild winters, all irrigators will want to divert and pump more and more water. As long as the only cost they directly face is the relatively cheap cost of blue water, then basic economics tells us that their demand and

consumption will rise steadily. But the water is not inexhaustible. In fact, it is the very opposite.

Both Spain and California saw the greatest advances
in water use after hydraulic developments allowed for the
storage of surface water in reservoirs. But actual improvements in water-use efficiency and crop and livestock
productivity came with the exploitation of groundwater.
Groundwater has special qualities. It is local, extremely
reliable and can be depended upon in times of drought.
There's drought on the land, but not beneath it. Better,
groundwater is a symbol of a farmer's independence.

 152 Armed with their own pumps, they can get water when,
how and to whatever extent they feel they need. And
with independence comes great danger. What chance has
the water environment against wealthy, thirsty farmers? None. Regulation of groundwater use is practically
impossible, even in rich and highly developed economies.
It would be like trying to regulate inhalation of air. With
groundwater pumping there exists no intermediary
between the water and the water-user. Without an intermediary, there is no structure off which to hang suitable
checks and balances. As for self-regulation...Well, the
entitlement to water is so hard-wired into the psyche of
farmers the world over that you might as well expect them
to stop breathing. Even the greater water efficiencies and
productivity do not save the water environment. Farmers,
driven by simple economic imperatives, choose to expand
their irrigated land rather than leave water in the environment. Economics pushes farmers to 'export' scarce water
recklessly in expensive food commodities rather than sensibly and sustainably to protect their own environment. So
will it be until a method is found to cost the environmental
impact of water use.

Drought is the eternal enemy of the farmer. Their battle
is ancient and never-ending. Even the mighty ingenuity
of the hydraulic mission is no game-changer. Hydraulic

engineers can construct surface-water storage systems of incredible magnitude. But even the greatest of these can only meet the water deficit of a single year of drought. And drought knows nothing of timetables. It has no compassion for human suffering. When it strikes, surface-water reservoirs are a useful short-term aid. From there, we turn to groundwater reservoirs. Often, these can provide two or more years of help. In drought-beaten southern Spain, groundwater has been essential to the agricultural industry. The ease of control and accessibility enjoyed by Spanish farmers has led to the most productive and profitable farming in the nation's history. Groundwater has made Spanish farming reliable and, most importantly, bankable. But there is a simple downside: it is wildly, ludicrously unsustainable. In Spain since the 1970s, we see a powerful, profitable industry being built on wanton environmental vandalism.

153

Andalusia's adventures underground

I highlight the 1970s, as it was only after the end of both Franco and then his authoritarian style of government that Spain's farmers and entrepreneurs were free to push their productivity and efficiency. Spain was late to shake off fascism, and then late to take its place at the EU table, finally joining in 1986. Once in the European club, Spain could begin to benefit from the single market and the unique financial incentives offered to EU farmers under the CAP. Coming in conjunction with a surge in technical and economic efficiency, the new political and trade environment precipitated a massive improvement in the way Spain combined water with other farm inputs to produce high-value food commodities. So it came to pass that the arid south of Spain managed to become a major exporter of food, and very rapidly. Although these premium exports commanded correspondingly premium prices, Spain was able to out-compete other Mediterranean rivals, mainly because of its previously depressed market.

But, of course, what was Spain ultimately exporting?

Its water. So the lunacy of international trade: we pay premium prices for arid areas to 'export' their water virtually.

This virtual trade has an actual cost. The terrible twentieth-century feeding frenzy on irrigated year-round crops has only been achieved as a result of farmers and hoteliers in areas such as southern Spain and California rapaciously raiding their groundwater supplies. Where better to pilfer water from than the invisible stores lurking many metres underfoot? A parched riverbed is a potent symbol of man's water greed, but the drained and abused groundwater reservoirs are less photogenic. Their depletion cannot be so pithily captured. As is always the case in the virtual-water story, the more invisible, the more insidious and dangerous the damage.

154

For every error, an exemplar

Spain is truly the best and worst of all possible water worlds. The errors of the south are worrying. But other regions offer reassuring examples of intelligent, modern and sustainable solutions.

Every country has its internal divisions. Often, identities polarise on a north–south axis. Spain is no exception to this. If the south is crudely stereotyped as the conservative, rural *mañana* culture, then the north, and particularly Catalonia, is vibrant, liberal and urban. Nowhere is this cultural credo more openly expressed than in Spain's second city, Barcelona. Barcelona is at the very heart of the advanced and diverse Catalonian economy, itself one of the major contributors to the national economy.

Being wealthy, Barcelona should, according to one of the underlying theories of our little discussion, have no difficulty securing water for itself, regardless of its local water environment. It is a region more than able to buy piped water. The only doubt is from where. Such have been the parameters of the debate about Barcelona's water supply. Common sense might have suggested water transfers from the neighbouring water-abundant regions of northern Spain. But common sense is a weak force when compared to the potency of water politics. Inter-regional politics in Spain makes a re-allocation from irrigated farming to an urban centre a near impossibility. This might seem no bad thing to you, dear reader. Perhaps if I rephrase it thus, you might see the missed opportunity. Barcelona, as an urban, diversified economy will deliver considerable returns to water. Agriculture, even at the very highest end of the industry, delivers broadly low economic returns to water. Therefore, the inter-regional water politics of Spain are such that water is often not diverted to where it will best benefit the economy. This is the absolute definition of a misallocation of resources.

155

The political difficulties pertaining to transferring water to Barcelona are manifold. There is the little matter of investing financially in a new water infrastructure. This financial cost also bears a political cost. Often in representative democracies, the balance of power is disproportionately held by smaller rural populations. Selling an expensive water-transfer programme to such populations is politically tricky. More so when it is a transfer away from their communities and economics and to a city that is perceived as sometimes aloof and convinced of its cultural superiority. Add into this mix the more immediate political hurdle of disrupting rural livelihoods heavily reliant upon irrigated water and you have a very compelling *realpolitik* argument against diverting water to Barcelona.

With the neighbouring tributary river basins in Catalonia and the north out of the question for political reasons, Barcelona widened its gaze. And it found France. As our image at the start of this section suggests, while geographically very close, France and Spain are worlds (or at least continents) apart when it comes to climate and water resources. Studies suggested that a pipeline from France to Barcelona would be feasible. The idea had growing political and social support. And then something rather lucky happened.

There was drought.

156

Now, it is rare for anyone to assert that a bout of drought is a piece of good luck. It might even seem glib when considering the plight of developing-world farmers. Do not despair. I am intensely aware of the environmental (and financial) horrors facing the poorest farmers in the world. These will be discussed at length in Chapter 5. But the drought that hit Barcelona in the last decade did not result in terrible human suffering. No one died of thirst. The economy did not collapse.

Instead, the local government encouraged families to economise in their water usage. And it worked. Daily individual domestic use fell to below 100 litres per day. Incredibly, it has barely risen post-drought. People became acclimatised to using a little less water. Now, these new lows are the norm. Expensive and economically dubious pipelines from France are off the political menu in Barcelona. No one – except the hydraulic engineers – suffers from this. And there is even a gentle sop to the hydraulic mission. Barcelona built a desalination plant that produces water at roughly €1.50 per cubic metre when on standby. At full capacity, that cost drops to €0.60 per cubic metre. The whole range is highly affordable.

The Barcelona experience demonstrates very clearly that demand management can provide a better, faster and more environmentally friendly solution to a water crisis than the knee-jerk supply-side response. We don't need to be rushing to construct impressive but pricey pipelines. We need to educate people about their water use. Here, a happy model for water wisdom in the industrialised economies.

Going green

Spain has performed a remarkable, and very reassuring, U-turn on water use. In the early days of the EU Water Framework Directive of 2000, Spain was at best an uneasy partner, at worst a dissenter. Spanish worries only strengthened in the face of the even-more-intrusive daughter frameworks stemming from the 2000 directive. But, with the social and political disquiet over the Ebro basin transfer and the cultural and ideological gear-shift of the 2004 election, Spain is now a leading voice on EU water issues.

Of course, this is perhaps a conversion born of suffering. No EU member has water problems comparable to Spain. Its resources issues are so much more challenging than those faced by its northern, continental comrades. No surprise, then, with such high stakes that Spain takes the matter very seriously. Also no surprise that the country should swing so suddenly from opponent to advocate of sustainable water management. Spain might have thought it had everything to lose by the framework directive, but it realises it also has everything to gain.

At the time of writing, Spain is certainly the European leader on clean solar energy. The availability of clean energy is an essential prerequisite of achieving global water security. With the possible exception of Germany, no other EU economy has coped more imaginatively and effectively with the water-energy nexus than Spain. Regionally and globally, it is a beacon of excellence in innovation and behaviour. This has all been achieved rapidly and with very little political pain.

157

Exporting the sunshine

I said earlier that water does what it wants. If we assert that we control it, we do little more than delude ourselves. We can barely store it, can hardly move it and often fail to protect ourselves against it, with tragic results. However, if our mastery of water is almost non-existent, at least we have an ability to persuade and influence it. This is not the case with that other vital life-giving resource: the sun. Of course, we have some excuse, as the sun is beyond our world and outside our reach in every sense.

Although there have been noticeable improvements in the storage of solar energy, the main economic role of the sun remains almost wholly in nature's capricious hands. The agriculture industry, in the words of Paul McCartney, can only 'follow the sun'. This means that water-rich northern Europe, with its long, cold winters, is unfarmable for half the year. Most of the planet outside the tropics is seasonal; our diets are not. The prevailing winds of the culture are such that we expect every object of desire to be available instantly, and affordably, for our consumption. This is the social attitude of the consumer in the industrialised economies of the twenty-first century. It doesn't matter that northern-European economies have presided over a three-fold increase in rain-fed yields for most of their food crops. We demand water-intensive specialist foods on our plates all year round. We don't care whether it is July or December, strawberries have to be on our supermarket shelves permanently, just like any other product.

These rampant consumer demands have, with typical human ingenuity, been met by economies like California and Spain. So it is that Spain 'exports' its scarce water as virtual water embedded within a range of high-value livestock and crop commodities. An arid water environment is dangerously over-exporting its water, virtually, to very water-rich areas. Why? Because truthfully, the water is a proxy for sunshine. The wealthiest parts of the world lack winter sun, so they import it in their food. And the poorer economies, and wealthy thriving agriculture sectors in industrialised economies such as California and Spain, cannot resist meeting this demand.

And this is a process with only one brake at present: the utter over-exploitation and extinction of the exporting economy's water environment. There is no mechanism acting on rich consumers to curb their demand, except perhaps for the very soft influence of the consumer conscience. Similarly, in the exporting economies there exists only the economic imperative to increase production. Trade is absolutely blind to environmental concerns. It cannot be captured in the economic equation. It is an invisible concern. As trade is blind, so too are the traders. This blindness is infectious, and afflicts the end consumers. So it is that parts of the world with some of the weakest and most fragile water environments are over-exporting their water virtually, and pushing their local water resources closer and closer to absolute destruction.

159

These exporters deplete their drought-prone surface waters and their more reliable, but not inexhaustible, groundwater supplies. It is exactly this water-suicide that Spain is pursuing in slow motion. All semi-arid regions, such as Spain and California, have drought as a periodic hazard. One year of drought can be matched by engineering, by dams and reservoirs. More than a year, and the farmers are reaching for the pumps. After two or three years of drought, then the economy is in water crisis. Yet normally the question being asked is not 'What should we do to save our water resources?' but rather 'Where can we get more water from?' Worryingly, virtual-water 'trade' can serve to conceal these existentially challenging water shortages. By doing so, and by deluding farmers, politicians and the public, virtual water stunts the activist politics desperately needed to highlight the environmental consequences of such crazed plundering of scarce water resources.

Water crime does pay

So, by now you are probably thinking that Spain must be in some terrible water crisis. Surely, if what I have just described is accurate, there can barely be a drop left in the entire Iberian peninsula. The surface waters have evaporated, the groundwater has been over-mined into dust, the soil has been turned toxic by irrigation and each and every tap in the country runs dry.

Well, no.

And why not?

160

To use that well-worn catchphrase of President Bill Clinton: it's the economy, stupid.

Between 1997 and 2006, Spain's GDP almost doubled, from €500 billion to nearly €1 trillion. Yet the country is still using roughly the same amount of its own water

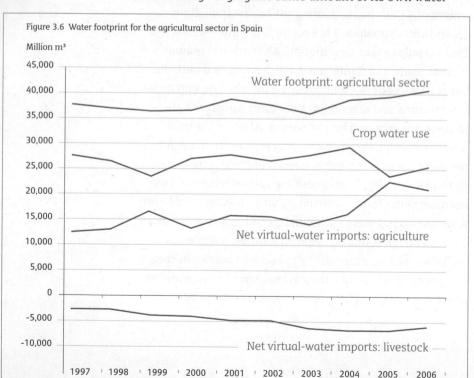

Figure 3.6 Water footprint for the agricultural sector in Spain

Million m³

Water footprint: agricultural sector

Crop water use

Net virtual-water imports: agriculture

Net virtual-water imports: livestock

each year. Although the figure wobbles from year to year, according to the seasonal rainfall, Spain pretty consistently uses about 32 cubic kilometres of blue water and green water each year. However, over the same period of time, the national water footprint has risen by almost 10 per cent. The shortfall, of course, is made up by net virtual-water 'imports', which increased by 25 per cent. The actual quantity of virtual water 'imported' rose by far more, but 'exports' also rose considerably. All of this is a sign of the health of Spain's agriculture industry and its international trade in food. Rather than pillage the local water environment, Spain has chosen to 'import' water virtually. It has the luxury of this option because it is a wealthy, diversified economy. Economic diversification and improved returns

Source (Figures 3.6 and 3.7): A. Garrido, M.R. Llamas, C. Varela-Ortega, P. Novo, R.R. Casado and M.M. Aldaya (2008), *Water Footprint and Virtual Water 'Trade': Policy implications*, Satander: Botín Foundation.

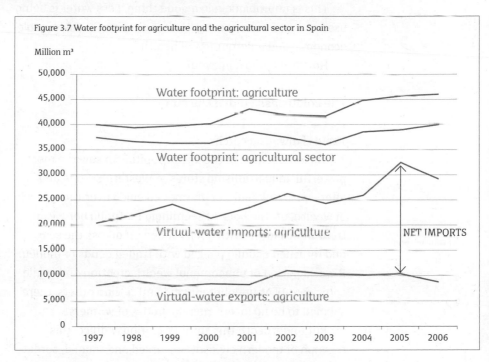

Figure 3.7 Water footprint for agriculture and the agricultural sector in Spain

to water form a virtuous circle. Hence Spain, as California before it, can experience soaring GDP balanced by a more sluggish growth in the economy's water footprint.

Crunching the numbers produces some truly exciting headlines. Over the decade, Spain learned to squeeze 60 per cent more GDP per cubic metre from its water resources. The water footprint of each Euro of Spanish GDP fell by a quarter. If these figures seem a little mismatched, it is because the water footprint includes the virtual-water net 'imports' into the Spanish economy.

162

Because this virtual water enters the economy embedded within products – most commonly in Spain's case as staple grains and other low-value foods – it is more costly, and so the returns on virtual water are noticeably lower than the returns to the same volume of national water. Regardless, the overall economic picture is incredibly rosy, and appears to make good water sense.

This is unambiguously a good thing. Less water is being used to make more money. Here is a recipe for sustainable economic and environmental health.

How is it being achieved?

The colourless gold of the sun

There is always a catch.

The great dawn of the age of capitalism saw the most powerful, industrialising states of Western Europe and – later – post-colonial North America enjoy ever-rising levels of wealth, off the back of seemingly mutually beneficial trade. Ships laden with goods sailed off across the seas and returned equally packed with traded goods or money. It was a period of phenomenal wealth creation and, while some countries undoubtedly did better than others, there seemed to be no losers, merely grades of winners.

But underneath this shining, glorious edifice, this triumph of modern civilisation, lurked one squalid, sordid little word: slavery.

The prize commodity being traded, the fuel that fed the hungry machine of international capitalism, was people.

Trade has no instinctive moral compass. Economics neither. Thus the slave trade endured well beyond the point at which any could make a coherent ethical justification for it. The economic rationale remained sound. So the trade continued.

There was source. There was demand. That is all the economic model required. The agents of the trade remained (deliberately) blind to the unforgivable human and social impacts of the trade. Such things were outside the economic formula. There was no ethical dimension to trade. It is a matter of some debate as to whether there is, even today, much of an ethical dimension to international trade. What is certain is that trade in humans today is the preserve of the criminal elements and the black market. But it was once as respectable as the exploitation of developing economies through international trade asymmetries is today. Some grumbled. Some tried to boycott and lobby and remain outside the system economically benefiting from the cruelty of the trade. They were considered cranks for centuries, harbouring futile and unrealistic expectations The future always makes a fool of the present. So it did with the slave trade, so it shall with today's profoundly unfair system of international trade.

163

The conditions for fair trade are simple. You have a willing seller and a willing buyer. Importantly, both buyer and seller must be equally well informed and equally competent. Such was never the case with the slave trade. Any analysis of it must accept that the trade fell at the first hurdle. The economies that produced the resources – in this case the most basic of human resources – were never willing sellers, but exploited victims. Although the object of the trade has changed, the structure remains the same. All too often, the conditions of fair trade are not met. In sugar, cotton, tea, coffee and chocolate, all but the fringes of trade is conducted with imbalances of power, willingness and competencies between buyer and seller that are both gross and grotesque. Again, as with the early abolitionists, those operating at the fringes of trade have been labelled as fools and innocents. Product boycotts and civic movements for fair-trade goods, supported by internationally recognised codes of practice have, until very recent years, been the preserve of an almost insignificant faction. Even today, though well-established, they form an economically irrelevant minority.

It is vital to observe that the principled shifts towards fairer trade did not originate in the market. The market has no interest in fairness. In fact, worse is true. It has a distinct, vested interest in unfairness. An ill-informed, incompetent and desperate seller is a far better candidate for successful exploitation by a powerful, efficient buyer. Gradually, civil society has improved its own levels of awareness. Interest has grown. Pressure groups developed. Information was disseminated. The casual revolt against well-ingrained, seemingly immutable trade practices gathered sufficient momentum to effect real change. Politicians are ultimately receptive to any civic noise, should it prove loud enough. The adoption of fair-trade practices and creeds by corporations are a sign of global change. But it is only an early sign. The reform of international trade is so piecemeal and slow that it will take another century to remedy the asymmetries that blight the lives of poor farmers and families in developing economies.

How many lives will be ruined and lost in that century of too-slow change?

And how many cheap coffees, chocolate bars and T-shirts will you personally consume?

Beginning the battle

The battle to end trade that is bad for the poor, and often bad for the water resources of the water-scarce regions of the world, has only just begun. It will take many decades. It is we consumers in industrialised economies who suck water from other people's environments all over the world. The destruction this causes is the hidden cost of our inexpensive commodities.

More of this to come in the later chapters.

But, you must surely be calling out now, Spain is not a developing country. It is not being exploited in the same way. It is a willing seller.

The answer is yes and no. Spain is certainly not a developing economy, but it has a deeply water-scarce environment. It is being sucked dry of national water to satisfy the purchasing whims of thoughtless consumers in the EU. The only reason it is a willing seller is because it remains wilfully blind to the dangerous cost to its own water environment. Hence it is indeed another front in this same battle against virtual water's ability to ruin – and then conceal the ruin – of weak water environments.

165

If we do win this battle, between good sense and bad profits, it will only be after this blind, mad over-production and over-consuming has destroyed many aquifers and dried up many rivers. Including in Spain.

A happier final note

Don't pity Spain. It is not in ruin.

Spain has done pretty damned well out of virtual water. I present it here as a success story, albeit one that comes with a caveat.

After a slow start, hampered by its long experiment with fascism, Spain grew rapidly and sustainably in the final decades of the twentieth century. It is a country blessed with a great climate, a large and skilled workforce and some of the best technical resources in the world. Hence it has taken its rightful place at the table of advanced industrial economies. Its performance in sectors other than agriculture has been even more impressive than its innovations in irrigated farming. Since joining the

EU, Spain's transport, industrial and tourist infrastructures have been revolutionised. It is a world destination,
and home to some of the largest and most successful
international corporations. Culturally and creatively,
few economies have enjoyed a late renaissance to match
Spain, and particularly Barcelona. From being the sick
man of Western Europe, it now has a GDP to rival the biggest European economies. At the same time, its population
trajectory has fallen to replacement levels. This is a sure
sign of economic prosperity and social progression.

In agriculture, Spain has intelligently traded its way to
water security. Never could Spain be water-secure using
only its national resources. Virtual water is the only possible solution to the problems posed by its climate. But
Spain has made an economic virtue of a demographic
necessity. For over thirty years, Spain has been mixing
its scarce water resources with its bounty of land and
sunshine, blended with ample virtual-water imports, to
produce high-value livestock and crops. It was a risky
experiment, though Spain was certainly following the
trail blazed by California some years earlier. Amazingly,
Spain has demonstrated that an economy with a poor
water environment can play a globally significant role in
international food trade. And make plenty of money while
doing it. Spain's farmers, businesses and government have
all responded decisively and energetically to the economic
opportunities. Transport, finance and technology have all
been mobilised to support the agricultural sector. In terms
of wealth, and prestige, the experiment has been nothing
but a success.

But is it sustainable?

I fear it is not. Spain has some tough environmental
decisions to face in the immediate future. Spanish society
and its political systems have not proven themselves either
rich enough in knowledge or robust enough in resolve to
steer the country's irrigators and commodity traders to

sustainable practices. And sustainability is not a 'nice to have', to use corporate jargon. It is a definite must have.

The damage is just now coming to light. Coastal wetland environments are drying up, with the subsequent deadly implications for flora and fauna reliant upon them. Groundwater aquifers are vanishing, especially in drought-ridden Andalusia.

The Spanish narrative has been impressive. But the tune must now change. If the water environment is driven this hard for much longer, something will snap, and it won't be possible to put it back together. Spain needs to ease up on water use. This means disappointing the livelihood expectations of the Spanish people, hamstringing a vital component of the economy just as the rest of it is coming apart brutally. Such a course is politically hard to sell. But the implications of no action and no change are even more dire. What politician could survive the day the taps run dry? None.

Spain is not at crisis point yet. But it takes a long time to turn a tanker. The process needs to start now.

167

CHAPTER 4

Big and beautiful: how the BRICS economies could save the planet

No matter if it is a white cat or a black cat; if it can catch mice, it is a good cat.
DENG XIAOPING

It is hard to overstate the importance of the BRICS economies. In many ways, they are the hope for the future. By visiting three industrialised economies, we have seen very clearly that once a nation industrialises fully it installs a suite of physical infrastructure – roads, communication, commodity-storage facilities, dams and reservoirs, institutional infrastructures – an orderly political economy, financial institutions, markets and the regulation of public and private transactions. This structure allows farmers to achieve increases of water productivity in step with population growth. A diversified economy and developed societal, political and financial infrastructures enable successful water management. This is the journey that BRICS have yet to complete.

Brazil, Russia, India and China are four of the largest nations on the planet. They divide into two distinct pairings. China and India have equally large populations. And their economies are growing rapidly. Brazil and Russia have huge water endowments and have substantial potential for increasing their food production and water productivity. That is great news, as India and China (and the rest of the world) are going to need a lot more food by the middle of this century.

In this study, I'm going to take you to China and Brazil. I apologise that we won't be traversing the Himalayas or the Urals. There is much to explore in both India and Russia. Nor shall we peek into South Africa, currently living an inspired water-resource development transition.

First, we shall look at China. This vast and ancient land has the highest population in the world. One in five of us is Chinese. Mercifully, the collective water demands of this vast population and its massive industries are more modest. Though home to one-fifth of humanity, it uses only 14 per cent of our water resources. If I were writing forty years ago, I might be full of grave warnings about the dangers of China. At that time it seemed that China's water footprint would overwhelm the entire global system. Predictions were terrifying. It was thought that there might be a Chinese population of two billion between 2030 and 2050. Instead, Chinese population has levelled at 1.3–1.4 billion. That's a lot of water and food saved. Not to mention energy.

~~~~~ *PART 1* ~~~~~
China: our inscrutable saviour

For a nation culturally dogged by the oft-imposed epithet of its ideology, Communist China is deeply pragmatic. This works to the great benefit of all of us, particularly when it comes to water management.

Size matters
China matters. As Charles de Gaulle famously observed, 'China is a big country, inhabited by a lot of Chinese.' That the statistic is so well known sometimes blinds us to its significance: one in five people live in China. With 1.3 billion thirsty

people, the way China consumes water and water-intensive commodities is more important than the policies of any one other nation. What makes China matter even more is that its almost unique political and civic structure means the leadership quickly converts ideas into action. China gets things done. Fast. And water policy is no exception.

The national diet

The forbidden state

Commonly known for its unknowable nature, China was even more mysterious than usual to observers immediately after the Communist Party seized power in 1949. For three decades under Chairman Mao Zedong, China was closed. The history of those years is defined by the caprices and prejudices of whoever happens to be recounting it. State oppression and violence tinge most accounts of the 'Great Leap Forward' and the 'Cultural Revolution', but it may be many years before an approximation of objective truth is reached. That said, the figures do show us one thing very clearly. Within three decades, the Chinese population increased by almost 80 per cent. Whatever else happened behind the thirty-year veil of secrecy, China certainly developed a weight problem.

171

Slim fast

And so it was that in 1979, the Chinese government told its populace that it must think the unthinkable. They were asked to reduce their family size and make a present, specific, personal sacrifice for a future, abstract, collective good. It was an experiment like no other in human history, and could have proven disastrous. Yet, despite those who argue that human nature cannot be trumped by legislation, China's one-child family policy was a success in terms of adjustment to an otherwise impossible dilemma. As I said earlier, it is the single greatest act of water conservation our planet has ever seen. The population growth avoided would have been enough to repopulate the US (with Canada and Greenland thrown in for good measure). That's a lot of water (and energy) saved. We might do well to remember this incredible contribution to global resource security the next time we criticise China for lacklustre commitments to curbing global warming.

The most remarkable thing about the one-child family policy is that it flies directly in the face of the political norm. For the policy ensures that a future generation reaps the benefit of the current generation's sacrifice. Often in politics, the future is sacrificed for the sake of the moment. Consider, but briefly, current approaches of industrialised countries to climate change. Political action has lagged feebly behind the science. Only once there was a notable groundswell of public, popular opinion could politicians feel sufficiently emboldened to expend precious political capital on even discussing the issue seriously. For many years, the governments in industrialised nations were simply unwilling to address the urgent need to manage energy demand. This unwillingness persisted in the face of a firm understanding of resultant levels of atmospheric pollution. The future was sold to pay for the present. I don't say this to attack the integrity of politicians. They only have a certain, finite amount of political capital, and have to choose wisely how and when to spend it. The future can, politically, be dealt with later. Theirs, the moment.

172

A special case

But let's not pretend that Chinese politics are too similar to those common to Western industrialised nations. In the three decades leading up to 1979, the Chinese state had already demanded radical economic and social reforms from its people. These demands far outstrip any made by the governments of contemporary industrialised nations. Unlike most industrialised nations, the Chinese government is not answerable to its population at the ballot box. Further, there is a cultural acceptance of far greater levels of state involvement in individual lives. The line between the civic and the private life is always arbitrarily drawn; in China, that line sits differently from its equivalent in industrialised economies.

Hence, the Chinese state proved willing to pursue policies with high social costs. With the one-child family policy, it was to be a political gamble worth taking. This colossal, socially intrusive, demographic heave aimed to achieve a suite of unprecedented demographic dividends. The reduction in water consumption was not one of the main anticipated benefits, but Chinese demographic tightening has had a profound and positive global impact with respect to water. The intended targets were housing and energy, and the state was also explicitly concerned with saving in the provision of social and educational services. The consequent reductions in food and water were at best subsidiary aims, at worst happy accidents. I should point out that nowhere in the policy was water-demand management mentioned. Rarely has the unmentioned had such a significant impact. The greatest act of water conservation the world has ever seen was happy happenstance.

173

The diet that worked

As with any dramatic, unprecedented social policy, China's population-control scheme has many critics. Commonly, China was ridiculed for the unconsidered economic and social consequences. It is argued that the young few would be unable to support a top-heavy elderly population. The tragic down side for girl babies has also been identified. Chinese society has certainly paid a social price. Meanwhile China has now overtaken Japan as the world's second-largest economy. The economic fears seem to have been exaggerated just as the global dividend for the rest of the world – reduced water demand – has been ignored.

The social impacts are harder to capture in statistics. One worrying trend has been the social preference for male offspring. Such reproductive misogyny is common across Asia: the one-child policy understandably exacerbates the problem. The Chinese authorities have responded with a blend of compassion and compulsion. Rural families are allowed a second child if the first is a girl; late-term abortions are forbidden to avoid gender selectivity. To our eyes, this is pretty mysterious stuff. Liberal democracies can't quite get their head around legislating on family size. But any political decision depends on two questions: how do you sell it to the populace, and what can they do to you if they don't like what they've been sold? In China, one of the things they can't do is vote you out. If a policy doesn't immediately cause civil unrest, then it will be around for the duration. Ultimately, unlike in democracies, the Chinese can only feasibly reject policies in the short or the long term. In democracies, most things are assessed over a very messy and contentious mid-term. Seemingly, the one-child policy was neither enough to cause instant revolt, nor were its successes too unapparent in the long term for it to cause great public resentment. Hence, it has stayed.

Why?

Broadly, the critics have been proven wrong. Any hydrological and economic analysis of Chinese and global water resources reveals the considerable demographic dividends. Within China, demands for food, water, housing and public services are 25 per cent lower than the forecast prior to the policy's introduction. Rather than hampering the economy, the one-child policy may be an under-appreciated driver of economic growth in China.

But water is what we are interested in. China's population is so great that any change in its size or rate of growth is of international significance. A 25 per cent reduction in food and water demands in China is equivalent to a 5 per cent drop in the global demand for water. Amazingly, China's population grew by only 37 per cent between 1979 and 2009. I say 'only' as it soared by 80 per cent in the previous three decades. Even more importantly, the forecast for the next 30 years is of a mere 9 per cent. This is an heroic story. The virtual-water consumers of the world, primarily the industrialised West and the Middle East states, have been saved by China's one-child policy. It's thanks to demographic management in China that we all can continue to enjoy cheap food imports. By a very simple chain, we can see that our current phase of food security was substantially paid for by Chinese population abstinence.

175

But that's not the whole story...
Not only has China massively reduced its water consumption through strict demographic dieting, but it has pursued considerable improvements in agricultural water efficiency and higher crop yields. As with the UK, China is making much more food with much less water. The outcome of the tragic upheavals culminating in the so-called 'great leap forward' – which among other problems exacerbated famines and food shortages – was a society and economy that could wage war against food insecurity. And this was a war it most certainly won. For example, wheat, maize and rice production all increased by factors of four or five between 1961 and 1991. Although greatly improved transport, communications and market infrastructure helped in this process, much of the growth was due to remarkable leaps forward in water productivity.

Leaky food
Not all foodstuffs are created equal. Poorly developed economies are not as water-efficient in their agriculture as wealthier nations. More water is used to make the same amount of food, as water is wasted along the way. Hence, leaky food. This means that despite consumers in developed countries

munching far more food, the per-capita consumption of water in food is roughly the same in the developing and industrialised worlds. By making food less leaky, the industrialised nations are compensating for their bigger bellies. Productivity pays for the gluttony.

Made in China

176

China's economy continues to weather the severe financial storms of recent years, with GDP growth in rude health. This should be no surprise to any of us in the industrialised world. From computers to clothes, from cars to cat food, China is a successful manufacturer in the international premier league. Relatively cheap mass production of goods in China is one of the central planks of our current consumer binge in the developed economies. We can enjoy our hi-tech luxuries and low-cost daily essentials at a quantity, quality and price that would have been unimaginable only a few decades ago.

But there is a cost.

The reason Chinese manufactured goods, which keep our greedy global economy turning, are so plentiful at such a low price is that the economic machinery of trade is unable to incorporate the value of all the natural resources being used. In economic talk, we might call this a negative externality, meaning that the marginal external cost is not being reflected in the marginal social cost. In plain English, we can say this: the cost of the environmental and resource damage isn't being included in the price.

China is severely testing its resource base. Coal and water consumption are at unsustainable levels. And growing hourly. The story of coal is well known. Shock headlines are never long absent from our media. 'China builds two power stations a week.' It is a familiar tale, and China is often hauled out as a pantomime villain in the vaudeville show of climate-change politics. There is no need to reiterate that point here. What is less frequently commented on is the damage to the water environment. Although industrial water consumption is small compared to the big water used in food production, it is disproportionately dirty. Nothing pollutes like industry. Undoubtedly, severe environmental crimes are being wrought against China's water, but China remains far from transparent and lacks the open society and civic institutions necessary for holding government and business to account.

Yet for us to lecture China from our vantage point of comfort in the West is gross hypocrisy. For whose benefit are these waters sullied? For ours. We who import China's keenly priced goods are doubly advantaged. We enjoy cheap goods and escape the water environment's consequences. One of the many asymmetries of international trade is that unpriced water and energy footprints are borne by exporting nations. For the developing economies, as we shall see in the next chapter, this weight is often economically and socially fatal. The upstart BRICS economies are more robust.

177

A lot of water under the bridge

China 'imports' a lot of virtual water. In 2000 it 'imported' 60 cubic kilometres in food alone. Combined with the water embedded in the imports of industrial goods and services, the total was 74 cubic kilometres for the year. Cast your mind back to the previous chapter, and you might remember that total EU internal virtual-water 'trade' was 69 cubic kilometres. It's a very large amount of water. Yet China is actually a net 'exporter' of virtual water.

If we take a quick look at Table 4.1, we can see how China more than compensates for the virtual-water content of its food imports. Unsurprisingly, the answer lies in the ferocious engine of its industry. In 2000, it 'exported'

55 cubic kilometres of water in manufactured goods. A further 29 cubic kilometres was 'exported' in food.

Table 4.1 Virtual-water 'imports' and 'exports' for China, 2000.
Source: A.K. Chapagain and A.Y. Hoekstra (2003), *Water Footprints of Nations*, Delft: IHE.

178

Virtual-water 'imports'			
Virtual-water volume	CROPS AND LIVESTOCK	INDUSTRIAL	TOTAL
Billion m³/year	60	14	74

Virtual-water 'exports'			
Virtual-water volume	CROPS AND LIVESTOCK	INDUSTRIAL	TOTAL
Billion m³/year	29	55	84

Virtual-water 'net imports'			
Virtual-water volume	CROPS AND LIVESTOCK	INDUSTRIAL	TOTAL
Billion m³/year	31	-41	-10

That's a net 'flow' of 11 billion cubic metres of virtual water being 'exported'. Each drop is a drop that countries trading with China do not have to spend to keep cheap goods in our stores. But the Chinese bear the environmental brunt.

China and Africa

The Chinese dragon lays wonderful golden eggs. These are the low-price consumables bought the world over. But to do so, it must be fed. Its hunger for resources, especially energy, minerals and green water, has taken it to the very same place that the industrialising European nations of the nineteenth century went to sate their resource appetite: Africa.

The tragedy of the African continent is the resource curse. A geography with an abundance of raw materials, land and water, yet caught in a vicious trade trap. The blessing of resource wealth swiftly becomes a curse as these economies tend to fail to diversify and, with the inevitable drop in the market price of their primary-sector exports, they become caught in a futile cycle of having to export ever-greater quantities of their natural resources to maintain the same level of imports. For many African nations, this narrow economic structure and this self-defeating reliance upon asymmetric trade is the bitter legacy of European colonialism.

179

Since 1990, China's public and private companies have turned their gaze towards Africa, and also the resource-rich developing economies of South America. As with its growing power consumption, so with its burgeoning relationships with developing nations there is a consistent media script. This might be fairly summarised thus: China is criticised for pursuing the same aims as nineteenth-century Europe but with few of the immoralities. China is accused of poor domestic human rights and low levels of civic freedom, and is painted as an irresponsible exploiter of developing nations. The most commonly cited examples are those of its close relationships with the media-demonised political regimes of Zimbabwe and Sudan.

International politics is not my field of expertise, but it should be noted that China's track record is that of a comparatively responsible investor and facilitator in infrastructure projects in developing nations. Certainly, communication and relations are often helped by ideological empathy, but China's relationship with Africa is not indicative of any creeping red menace. The days when China gave military support and training to Zimbabwe were days in which President Mugabe was a respected international statesman (and Nelson Mandela languished behind bars).

The past isn't just a foreign country; sometimes, in geo-politics, it's a whole other planet. In 2011, we see a China that offers great economic opportunity to the languishing African continent. Chinese private and public investors are perhaps uniquely suited to helping developing nations because of the very special character of China itself: the world's second-largest economy, with all the concomitant finance and industrial know-how. Yet it is also an economy with more in common with sub-Saharan Africa than the Asian Tigers. Because of its distinct economic make-up, China can handle projects with considerable finance demands and on the very largest of engineering scales. At the same time, China has experience working under poorly developed economic, institutional and political circum-stances. China has a unique suite of capabilities. It can deliver international finance, design structures and has a highly regarded competence in putting these structures in place very quickly.

180

One of China's greatest capacities is in managing complex agricultural and farming enterprises. This has been necessitated by the size of its own farmlands and of its population. Contrast China with the oil-rich Middle Eastern states. They have huge sovereign wealth funds, but all they can do is provide finance. They lack all neces-sary inputs but money. China has the money and the skills and technical expertise. It doesn't need to compete on the world market for consulting or contracting competence. It has invested in its own human resources, and has a diversified economy and a highly skilled labourforce. For the past decade it has had the money too. China's basket of strengths is truly unique in the world.

Given that China is a global leader in agriculture, it follows that it is a global leader in water management.

Remember my golden rule: most water use (and abuse) is in agriculture. Anything China does to improve food production will have a considerable impact on global food and water security.

A harvest for the world...

The world desperately needs an imaginative and sustainable vision for global agriculture. We are close to crisis point. There are simply too many of us, eating too much and using too much water in the process for this to be able to continue. Our approach has to be belt and braces. Farming has to be intensified, but sustainably. This is the belt. Similarly, we need to get more from water and to use it more sparingly. There, the braces. To achieve only part of this would be to court disaster. And it would be the kind of disaster that would lead to starvation, death and civil unrest.

181

This moment in the world's economic history may prove to be a defining one for China. China has deep links with both South America and Africa. Africa certainly and South America possibly will experience a doubling in the demand for food over the first half of this century. The rest of the world will certainly need access to South America's rich water resources. Both also have the potential to increase the productivity of their water resources to meet that demand. China will be instrumental to their success (or failure) to stimulate, and in some cases enhance, that productivity and produce a harvest for the world.

The European and US periods of imperial and post-imperial intervention in Africa laid foundations that have proven to be a poor basis for sustained economic and social development. Now we are in the era of Chinese investment, and sub-Saharan Africa is being offered a new opportunity. China has already made a significant difference. Its unique suite of investment capacity and project-managing skills is compelling. Also significant is that China can invest while imposing fewer conditions than the international agencies of the industrialised economies, or their multilateral cousins. Investment from such bodies comes with capitalist ideological ties, and a hefty dose of self-interest that subordinates the developing world's needs to those of the industrialised world. It is not that China lacks self-interest. Rather, Chinese self-interest has the potential to operate symbiotically with the developing world's own agenda, and not in opposition to it. Already, China has built water-managing and transport infrastructures for governments which have been trying (and failing) to do so for almost half a century. In Sudan, Ethiopia, Tanzania, Mozambique and Angola, some of the world's poorest nations, China is poised to do much more.

182

The question we need to ask is can China help sub-Saharan farmers double their water productivity? Importantly, the answer to that question has to be yes. China has demonstrated that it can manage water resources responsibly. It needs to export that skill and its values of water saving and its growing awareness of resource stewardship. If successful, we will see global agriculture intensify sustainably and significantly. If not, more will starve, and not just in Africa.

You are what you eat (and how much)

So far, I hope I've impressed on those still reading that our attitudes towards food determine our food consumption, and in turn our water footprint. Culturally and nationally, there are great differences in food ideology across the globe. Take my home nation of the UK. To a certain extent, it doesn't matter too much what 66 million people on an island in north-west Europe do or don't eat.

It matters when it comes to 1.3 billion Chinese.

The Chinese people have very firmly held beliefs about food. First, it should be carefully prepared. Mealtimes are the focal points of family and social life. Second, China

should be able to feed itself. This belief has been strengthened by the years of Communist isolation and it underpins
all Chinese decisions about agriculture and trade. And, as
I hope I have by now helped you come to understand, food
self-sufficiency means full water self-sufficiency. Food
self-sufficiency is rare.

In the next chapter, we'll look at Egypt, another ancient
civilisation with the philosophy of self-sufficiency deeply
ingrained in the national psychology. Both economies
are struggling. Both are losing the battle. When we turn
to Egypt, we shall see that the reason for this is a rapidly
rising population. Not so with China, which has, as I have
detailed already, managed its unprecedented demographics. Similarly, China has made great leaps and bounds in
food production, agricultural yields and water productivity. The problem in China is both simpler and harder to
address. The problem is diet.

And when we say diet, we mean our old enemy, the
scourge of responsible and sustainable water use: meat.
China's industrialisation, its rampant GDP growth and
its increasingly deep engagement with global systems
and trade are all contributing to significant shifts in the
national diet. Affluence and meat, for the moment seem
to be bound together. When you consider that China and
India are breaking through into industrialised levels of
national and personal wealth, and with all the cultural
aspirations such wealth brings, and when you view that
fact in the context of their quite enormous populations,
there are some terrifying implications. If China and India
start consuming meat at the same rate per capita as the
US or France, then we will very quickly experience a serious water-management crisis. And dietary changes in the
age of globalisation are fast-moving cultural phenomena.
The diet of a nation can change profoundly very quickly.

If that happens, we might find that we have eaten ourselves into a corner.

183

Currently, traditional dietary austerity remains strong in China. This is the nation responsible for the charming epigram: 'Better three days without food than one without tea.' Judging by its robust response to the recent economic downturn, Chinese affluence seems here to stay. We'll soon get a sense of what this greater wealth will do to Chinese eating habits. We need to hope that tradition, consistency, sustainability and rationality win out against the Big Mac. It's a big hope.

Virtual water for dinner (again)

184

About now, the reader who has been following our story attentively might exclaim, 'Aha, but what about virtual water?'

Virtual-water 'trade' could enable China to impose invisibly and silently a massive water footprint on global resources by importing food commodities. Because virtual-water 'trade' is by its very nature hidden, it allows an economy to appear water- and food-self-sufficient – thereby meeting a psychological need – while also meeting all the physical wants of a thirsty, hungry people.

In the next chapter, we will clearly see that Egypt is enjoying this illusionist's trick that brings water security and at the same time makes it possible to feel that they have water self-sufficiency. Egypt is meeting its water deficit by a progressive, invisible dependence on economically and politically silent virtual-water 'trade'. China is doing something similar, but, due to its huge territorial area, China is also engaged in internal virtual-water 'trade'. This too takes place under the radar of public awareness. For example, the North China Plain, despite being water-scarce, 'exports' virtual water in grain and food commodities to the rest of the country. The farmers in the region are sufficiently skilled that, if given the right price incentives, they can increase production even more to feed those in other areas of China.

But the current endeavours of food producers are not enough. China's virtual-water 'imports' have soared. In the 1990s, China averaged 30 cubic kilometres imported in food. Between 2000 and 2004, the average was 71 cubic kilometres. Most of the virtual water came concealed in soya-bean imports, much of which have been used as animal feed. The increase is exponential. A worrying trend.

Here again is the dark side of virtual water.

The world's biggest plumbing

Water in China

Of course, there is a big issue we have not addressed yet. Just how much water does China actually have? And how is it using it?

China is, overall, fairly water-rich. As you would expect from such a giant nation, the regional variations are so great that national generalisations border on the meaningless. However, China is definitely well endowed with surface and groundwater, as well as with seasonal soil water. It is a mostly rainy country, specifically in the south and east, which experience summer monsoons. Here, the monsoon can be so intense that too much water floods the vast lower Yangtse floodplains. Yet the west and north of China are either semi-arid or arid. Perched in the northwestern corner of the country is the immense Gobi Desert, known in Chinese as the endless sea.

Moving east from the Gobi Desert brings us to the North China Plain, the site of serious water competition over the past few decades. The plain and the irrigated lands of the Yellow River basin comprise the food basket of China, as well as supporting rapidly developing industries and services. However, both areas are now seriously water-scarce. Despite the scarcity, the North China Plain continues to be a major 'exporter' of virtual water in food. We saw such a seeming paradox in the water-scarce US state of California, which – despite its poor water endowment – is both the main supplier of a wide range of food commodities to the US and the economy's leading 'exporter' of virtual water worldwide. Farmers in southern Spain do the same. It seems counter-intuitive, but it is far from uncommon that regions with slight water resources develop into significant virtual-water 'exporters'. It is increasingly the case with the Punjab in north-west India, with Israel and – as the next chapter will show – Egypt.

For all but the most recent decades of China's long and illustrious history, the country has been able easily to cope with its national food and water needs, using only traditional technology. As demand grew, so technological ingenuity responded to the challenge. China has become far better at working its water, and transporting goods around its vast provinces. This has been achieved by a coalition of farmers, engineers and water-resource policy-makers united in an ambition to mobilise new water, and manage and regulate its use. Chinese farmers have, like their British counterparts, become far more water-efficient. Farming and irrigation technology are only part of the picture: transport infrastructure and national institutions have also contributed. It is one thing to improve irrigation and agronomic practices, but without the reciprocal secondary factors of better roads, effective markets and incentivising prices, China would not have achieved a five-fold increase in food production.

186

Both nationally and locally, Chinese governing authorities have been effective – and sometimes highly effective – in stimulating those factors that are beyond both water and the water sector itself and yet serve to transform the capacity of an economy to improve its water productivity. There is more to water than just water; the Chinese administrators understand this. Here is a lesson to learn.

The hydraulic mission – Hong Kong style

But that doesn't mean that China didn't follow its own construction and engineering heavy-hydraulic mission. In fact, it set foot on this journey long before humanity set eyes on the rich lands of California...

Great engineering projects are typified by their long lead times. None more so than the wondrous Grand Canal of China. This 1770-kilometre marvel took a millennium of development. It began its colossal journey in the humid, tropical coastal south-eastern region of Hangzhou, back in the fifth century BCE. It would be added to and extended until the Sui Dynasty, which ruled China from 581–618CE. While the industrialised West was mired in the sword and sackcloth of the Dark Ages, China was building and enjoying the largest man-made waterway in the world.

187

China has a long and rich history of scientific, technological and organisational leadership. But interestingly, the central theoretical and motivational tenets of the Grand Canal project remain pre-eminently relevant today. First, it shows engineers and the state mechanism co-operating in a complex experiment with the environment and the economy to underpin a sequence of civilisations. Second, it clearly demonstrates that trade is an essential element of prosperity. Only by trade are natural resources likely to be used effectively and to the (ever-advancing) edge of their productivity. Only trade allows the exchange of goods and services. When humans trade, a good or service is suddenly benefiting at least twice as many people; the consumer and the producer are now two different people, and each enjoys a separate benefit from the product. So, with food, the producer gains security through having food self-sufficiency, and derives an income from trading the surplus. The consumers in regions lacking natural resources are able to pursue their economic activities, fuelled by a steady supply of traded food. Vitally, it is virtual-water 'trade' that makes possible the existence of cities. Cities in turn drive socio-economic development and the progress of civilisation. (My apologies to any who live in the rural areas, but I hope you accept the broad gnomic truth of my assertion.) The Grand Canal shows this. Although parts of it suffered occasional periods of disuse, the cities along the canal prospered for millennia; China built the canal, and then the canal built China.

Initially, the canal's trading purpose was closely associated with conquest. Brutal as it might sound, conquest is in many ways a primitive form of trade. And undoubtedly, trade (as pursued by the northern-hemisphere-biased WTO) is a modern form of conquest. Originally, the Wu Emperor Fuchai – the man who ordered the first stage of the canal's construction – wanted to be able to supply forces in the north easily from his power base in the south. This ensured that the soldiers in the north did not have to worry about becoming food-self-sufficient during the campaign. Most military conflicts in human history have been decided by one or other side running out of food. Napoleon would have been well advised to learn this lesson during his invasion of Russia. The Grand Canal solved this problem for the Chinese state millennia before it was successfully resolved in Europe. Food and weaponry went up the canal; food and money came back. Until recent centuries, the main function of the Grand Canal remained to bring grain back towards the main city.

188

The canal's highest point is a mere 42 metres. While this implies several helpful qualities in terms of construction, there are also hazards. Not least the fact that the canal traversed several vast lowland areas, including the Yellow River region. All of these were subject to periodic flooding. Nature often disabled the canal. Similarly, defending generals would breach the canal to halt advancing imperial armies, recognising the link between food logistics and military victory. However, while the canal functioned, the Chinese army flourished. In this way, we can see that the hydraulic mission in the ancient societies of China, the Nile, the Tigris-Euphrates and the Indus was a tool to enable the powerful to claim new territory and new subjects.

The Politburo of China: literally building a better future for the People's Republic
Here are the complete graduate credentials of China's Politburo as of 2006. All but one an engineer.
Hu Jintao, 62, President of the People's Republic of China, graduate of Tsinghua University, Beijing, department of water-conservancy engineering.
Huang Ju, 66, graduate of Tsinghua University, department of electrical engineering.
Jia Qinglin, 65, graduate of Hebei Engineering College, department of electric power.
Li Changchun, 61, graduate of Harbin Institute of Technology, department of electric machinery.
Luo Gan, 69, graduate of Freiberg University of Mining and Technology, Germany.
Wen Jiabao, 62, graduate of Beijing Institute of Geology, department of geology and minerals.
Wu Bangguo, 63, graduate of Tsinghua University, department of radio engineering.
Wu Guanzheng, 66, graduate of Tsinghua University, power department
Zeng Qinghong, 65, graduate of Beijing Institute of Technology, automatic control department.
The Politburo is water-savvy. It is especially water-science-savvy. Water issues do not need activists to get them on the agenda. Perhaps we would be globally more water-secure if we had legislatures populated by the technically qualified.

189

The more things change...the more they stay the same
But what is the importance of the hydraulic mission in today's China? The engineering tradition is certainly alive and well. In 2006, the governing Politburo had nine members. All but one of its members were engineers. Hu Jintao, the country's Paramount Leader, graduated as a hydraulic engineer from Tsinghua University's department of water-conservancy engineering. His first job was working on the construction of the Liujiaxia hydropower station. No surprise that China continues to invest heavily in hydraulic works. It was once the top guy's bread and butter.

 190

The Chinese hydraulic mission at the time of writing can be boiled down to three core goals: power generation; flood control; fighting regional water scarcity. Water is being transferred at great cost and expense of energy to the remote arid regions of the west and the North China Plain around Beijing. Further, China's enormous irrigated systems are in the process of being updated.

China has always danced to a different beat from the rest of the world. And if anything, these tempos diverged even further during the twentieth century. The hydraulic mission is no exception. As the century entered its final quarter, industrialised nations grew weary and wary of iconic, expensive hydraulic projects. They had enough over-dammed waterways and were saturated with too many reservoirs, too many canalised rivers, too many over-drained wetlands and too much environmental injustice. As we saw with our study of the US, it was often native peoples who endured the most dislocation. These manic interventions came to an end for two reasons. The first was the successful environmental-activist movement. The second that pretty much everything that could be done had been. The hydraulic mission was more or less complete, particularly in southern California and southern Spain, as we saw in the previous chapter.

So it was that the hydraulic ambitions of the industrialised economies were petering out in the late 1970s. Meanwhile, in China, the communist giant was just awakening to the possibilities. It was at this moment that China embarked on a massive phase of dam, reservoir and hydro-power construction. By the 1990s it had begun work on its two mightiest hydraulic projects: the Three Gorges Dam and the South–North conveyor. They had been on the agenda of the engineering elite since early in the Mao years. So entrenched were they in the national psyche that not to build them would have been politically impossible. It would have been an unacceptable admission of weakness.

191

Not always so wise

For the sake of balance, I should note that China doesn't always get it right when it comes to water. In fact, some features of Chinese water-development policy in the twentieth century are – to put it politely – hard to fathom. Water use in the North China Plain and the Yellow River region is frankly baffling. These water-scarce areas are 'exporting' virtual water to the far wetter south. This is unsustainable unless the 'exporting' becomes associated with high-value crops and not just grain. The Yellow River is relatively small, being approximately the same size as the Nile and having a flow of about 80 cubic kilometres a year. Yet it has been so heavily over-used and had so much water withdrawn for irrigated-crop production that it no longer reaches the sea. Happily, remediation is in train. By way of contrast, the Yangtse River further south is a roaring giant with an annual flow of around 1000 cubic kilometres. Every decade it floods violently, wreaking destruction on cities and communities in its lower reaches. Here I must issue a clear warning. Coping with the uncertainties of the mighty Yangtse will test the capacity of China's top engineering elite. They have already had some success in reversing the destruction of the lower Yellow River. Now they must replicate that success on its larger cousin.

The Three Gorges Dam

Big hydraulic projects don't come much bigger than this, the iconic engineering triumph of Communist China. It has taken over a century to plan, two decades to construct, displaced well over a million people, cost around $26 billion and is alleged to have flooded culturally and anthropologically significant sites and inflicted a heavy toll on people and the environment.

192

But it has also been a prominent national icon, especially since Chairman Mao Zedong wrote a poem, 'Swimming', expressing a vision of 'walls of stone' on the Yangtse River. It would be almost forty years from the moment those words were set down on paper until the National People's Congress voted in favour of the revised plans for the dam in 1992.

There's far more to the Three Gorges Dam than flag-waving demonstrations of national potency. The dam generates a considerable amount of power. At the time of writing, 26 700MW generators are up and running. More are planned. As a pleasant bonus, every drop of hydro-electricity is clean energy. As well as power, the dam's reservoir provides flood protection for cities in the lower half of the basin. It was the devastating floods of 1954 that would inspire Mao's toe-dip into poetry. The lower basin gets an awfully large amount of water. First, there is all the water from the upper basin, with its tributaries in the highlands of Tibet. This accounts for about 45 per cent of the flow. An additional 45 per cent joins the river in the lower basin in the form of rainfall. Combined, the effect is devastating. The seasonal saturation of the monsoon in the lower basin meeting with the flood surge from the upper basin drives the Yangtse to break its banks, with massive loss of life and property. The floods in the summer of 1998 were among the biggest in history, affecting millions and costing tens of billions of dollars. The final 10 per cent is provided by the summer monsoon falling on the delta region in the lower part of the Yangtse as it reaches the sea. The melting glaciers of the Himalayas provide a useful proportion of the water in this mighty system. It's a beautiful and romantic image, the mountains feeding the river. But, in truth, the vast majority of the river flow is added in the lower two-thirds of the basin.

As in all things, there is a trade off. Protection of the population in the lower basin comes at the cost of power generation. The Three Gorges Dam reservoir holds 80 cubic kilometres at capacity. If you're finding the statistic a bit disorientating, it's about thirty million Olympic swimming pools. Huge, but as we shall see in the next chapter, it's still just under half the size of the breath- (and water-) taking Aswan reservoir on the Nile. This African giant holds an astounding 168 cubic kilometres. The size disparity is even stranger when you consider that at the High Aswan Dam the Nile only has a flow of about 16 per cent of the Yangtse's flow at the Three Gorges. (And of only 8 per cent of the often destructive flow in the lower basin of the Yangtse.) Suddenly, thirty million-Olympic-swimming-pools-worth of storage seems trivial when you realise that the Yangtse's annual flow at the Three Gorges is around 400 cubic kilometres. Most years, to function effectively as flood protection, the reservoir has to lower its level to allow for 40 cubic kilometres of floodwater. In other words, it loses a lot of its electricity-generating capacity.

In terms of floods, 40 cubic kilometres should be enough to absorb the surge from most floods, but – to paraphrase the UK Environment Agency's response to a series of floods in 2009 – a once in a millennium flood can come along and make engineers' precautions seem puny. Water can be cruel and unrelenting. When it decides to move *en masse*, there is nothing human endeavour can do to prevent it. However, humanity can only survive (psychologically at least) by planning for the likely rather than the rare yet inevitable event. In the case of the Three

Gorges Dam, the traumatic memory of the 1998 and 1954 floods in the minds of the general public, combined with the emblematic significance of the project in the minds of the ruling elite ensured there was the requisite political will to build the dam and live with the consequences.

The South–North conveyor

A similar cocktail of emotions and inertia lies behind the other major contemporary Chinese hydraulic project. Equally long in gestation and equally blessed by the sainted Chairman Mao, the South–North conveyor project aims to transport 50 cubic kilometres of water per year from the Yangtse basin to the water-scarce north. Here is the wonder of humanity's hydraulic power. This project will take real water from three off-takes of the Yangtse – if all these options are constructed – and transport it to a water-scarce region with a well-developed farming and industrial capacity. Although the Yangtse basin has what an economist might charmingly call a 'surplus' of (blue) water resources (and is what a water scientist might call a 'very lethal river'), its local farming and industry is less intensive than in the North China Plain and it has not developed the necessary physical and marketing infrastructures. I like to think that before encountering the ideas and analysis developed in these chapters, you might have read about the project and said, 'That sounds very sensible, shifting water from where there is too much to where there is too little. It's extremely costly, but presumably makes economic sense because of the farming and industrial demand. And what a great demonstration of our ingenuity and engineering prowess.' Or words to that affect.

Now I hope you will say with me four very simple words: 'What about virtual water?'

Here is the paradox. At great cost, 50 cubic kilometres of real water will be conveyed annually to the north. Yet in 2000, the North China Plain produced crops with a combined virtual-water content of 26 cubic kilometres and conveyed these commodities to other regions of China. This includes the southern regions watered by the Yangtse. Something is not quite right.

Such outcomes result because politics and the insights of water science and water economics do not run in harmony. And politics, not science, is what counts. Politics influence this particular water-allocation policy in several different ways, at several different junctures. First, there is the problem of agreeing what water is available. Second, there are obvious regional and national political forces at play when considering moving water from one area to another. Remember that the political justification lies in the relative lack of water productivity in the water-rich Yangtse basin compared to the advanced and developed farming centres of the North China Plain. The third point to consider is that the notion of the potential of the adaptive capacity of farmers and society to increase water productivity is not yet present in the public discourse. We just don't talk and think in terms of working water harder. This is a strange position to take, given that improving the adaptive capacity to manage water is something that has come naturally to farmers since the birth of human civilisation. Fourth, there are vested interests and political biases that determine which solution gets the resources. Be clear, a gigantic, highly visible hydraulic project is big and sexy. Especially one fixed in the national psyche, as it was blessed by Mao, and particularly in a country led by engineers and hungry for impressive, eye-catching displays of collective strength and prosperity. Fifth, even the moment at which the problem can be revealed to need attention is politicised.

So, what will China do? Currently, it seems to be ploughing ahead with this immense civil project, despite (or perhaps because of) its anticipated cost of $50 billion. A fraction of that money would transform the farming

195

and industry of the Yangtse basin, or buy a huge amount of adaptive capacity to increase water productivity so that the water in the North China Plain is freed up for high-value activities. These measures would negate any need to shift water to the north. Further, not spending $50 billion on the South–North conveyor would mean that a considerable amount of environmental damage simply would not happen. In other words, investing in the south and the north could be far *far* cheaper in terms of financial and environmental costs. I hope that by now the idea of spending such a vast sum of money on shifting inordinate amounts of water 1000 kilometres north seems as questionable to you as it does to me. It is a serious misallocation of resources. Once you grasp the basic idea of virtual water, such hydraulic posturing seems at best a waste of valuable investment resources, at worst ridiculous.

The Chinese authorities are not fools, and they are far from ridiculous. They've held power for sixty years without an election not merely through repression and fear (though there has been some of that) but by understanding their public and the ideas that have been dominant in the discourse for decades. They understand that public opinion is highly susceptible to a bold, bright and highly visible concrete solution like the South–North conveyor, which people have been expecting for many years, even if it is demonstrably more financially and environmentally costly than alternatives. They also understand that their population is blind to the role of virtual water and cannot (or will not) grasp complex ideas such as investing in a region's adaptive capacity. Hence, the wrong solution is politically feasible; the right one politically risky. Though science would choose the right solution, politics chooses the politically feasible. Delusion trumps the underlying fundamentals. Again.

Inside the Forbidden City

China has a long tradition of being closed and impene-
trable. Now, as China becomes more open to the world than
at any time in living memory, it is the future that remains
obscure. China's current rate of economic growth is unlike
anything in history. It is the most populous state in history, and has managed the toughest demographic policy
in history. Undoubtedly, the social, economic and resource
stresses facing China in the future will be immense. But the
leadership has demonstrated repeatedly the tenacity and
temperament to meet these challenges directly.

197

It will be with the same with water.

Currently, Chinese water management is at a cross-
roads between the old established truths of yesterday and
the bright future of improved water awareness. Do not be
mistaken. The grip of the hydraulic mission on the minds
of the public and the governing elite is strong. Naturally, a
ruling class headed by engineers will be enthusiastic for
large projects that generate power, store and withdraw
water for irrigation and transport freshwater to water-
scarce regions. Such policies are intuitive and politically
popular. Better still, they are intuitively consistent with the
national preoccupation of food and water self-sufficiency.

The Chinese leadership has not shirked pushing
through socially and politically stressful policies. Nor is
it blind to important, and occasionally invisible, policies
such as virtual water. It is also environmentally aware.
Although the ruling class has a weakness for the politically
expedient big engineering projects, it is braver than the
political leaderships of the industrialised economies when
it comes to pursuing less obvious (though more sensible)
solutions, including environmentally aware ones. China
is helped in this by the fact that such policies are partly
continuations of earlier Communist initiatives.

Pushing productivity

The first of these policies comprises the series of measures put in place to encourage farmers to increase productivity and water efficiency. Improvements in agro-technology, market management and infrastructure all contribute here. Crop and livestock yields and water productivity need only increase by the smallest amount to have a remarkable effect. Even a 1 per cent improvement each year should do quite nicely. Due to the strict demographic management of the past three decades, China does not need to achieve the massive increases in production which it put on record between 1960 and 1990. Of course we need to add a rather important caveat: this assumes that the Chinese continue to follow a diet with the same levels of embedded water. If China starts consuming meat to the extent of its fellow superpower the US or fellow BRICS economy Brazil, then there could be serious consequences. Therein lies the next great challenge for the Chinese leadership: managing the diet of the Chinese people. Given the clarity and success of China's demographic management, we can allow ourselves some faith in the Chinese authorities' ability to tackle the tricky issue of diet.

Harvesting the rain

The second policy is the national campaign to improve the productivity of soil water, specifically in relation to rain-fed farms. By the late 1990s, soil water was already a significant focus of science research in China. Here, China was definitely ahead of the industrialised nations except Australia. In China, there are national and international conferences devoted to the topic. If you are in Europe or the developing nations of Africa and the Middle East and attempt to start a conversation on soil water and the importance of improving water productivity in rain-fed farming, you meet with blank stares. Soil water is outside the economic model. It cannot be costed. It cannot be quantified in a market economy. Therefore, in theoretical terms, it might as well not exist. But in reality, it is one of the most vital components in keeping humanity fed. Unlike in many nations, Chinese scientists and Chinese departments of state do pay attention to soil water. They get its importance. This is great news for both China and the world.

Dams and trade
China is also acting to shore up food security in two distinct ways. Visibly, China is building big dams and canals for storing and shifting water. Invisibly, it is engaging in virtual-water 'trade'. When pursued in conjunction, both are politically feasible. Eye-catching projects have popular support and can be publicly celebrated. Virtual water remains economically invisible and politically silent. It is not a question of either/or. Both are needed. Yet both are fundamentally different. The grand gestures of the hydraulic project have severe negative environmental impacts; these negative externalities – to use the language of the economist – are not internalised in the commodity price. Plainly, no one covers the cost of the damage. Virtual water, on the other hand, leaves the costs in the 'exporting' economy. Where the hydraulic mission appeals to the emotions, virtual water appeals to rationality, both economically and in enabling us to identify where the environmental costs occur.

199

The virtual-water deal works well for China, and should be morally acceptable to all of us. Remember, China is exporting vast amounts of far more valuable blue water through its manufacturing exports. Cast your mind back to the figures near the opening of the chapter. These exports surely entitle China to import green (and blue) water in food commodities. On balance, despite large imports of food, China is a net 'exporter' of virtual water. Such is the strength and size of its manufacturing export economy. In this context, it would churlish (and wrong-headed) for any to complain about China's water footprint. It's putting in far more than it's taking out.

Virtual water is, at present, restricted to the domain of science literature. But it is well understood by the policy-makers in Beijing.

Number-crunching

All diets come down to number-crunching. I've never been one to indulge in the push-me, pull-me seesaw of guilt and piety that typifies the Western attitude to diet. Calorie-counting, weightlifting, treadmill-timing, waist-measuring, body-mass-index-calculating. The personal diet is a sea of numbers.

The same is broadly true of a national diet. And, as with personal diets, national diets follow trends. There

Figure 4.1 Freshwater withdrawals in the Beijing region 1986-2007. *Sources:* Beijing Statistics Bureau and National Statistics Bureau Beijing Investigation Team (1986–90), *Beijing Almanac*, Beijing: China City Press; Beijing Statistics Bureau and National Statistics Bureau Beijing Investigation Team (1991–2002), *Beijing Statistical Yearbook*, Beijing: China's Statistics Press; Beijing Water Authority (2003–7), *Beijing Water Resources Bulletin*, Beijing: Beijing Water Authority.

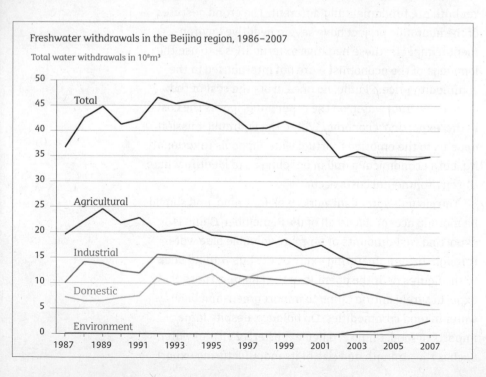

Freshwater withdrawals in the Beijing region, 1986–2007

Total water withdrawals in $10^8 m^3$

is highly encouraging evidence that China is starting to emulate the good qualities exhibited by industrialised economies when it comes to water management. The first is a very simple point: taking less water.

There's nothing too difficult about Figure 4.1. It clearly shows a reduction in water withdrawals in several economic sectors, and a significant drop in water use overall. As we might expect, these data pertain to Beijing, which is technologically and politically advanced to the level of industrialised economies and, hence, emulates their water-use trends.

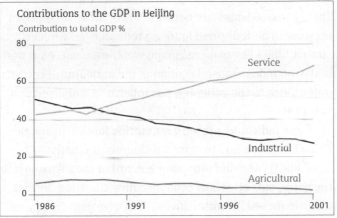

Figure 4.2 Contributions to GDP in Beijing, 1986–2001. *Sources:* Beijing Statistics Bureau and National Statistics Bureau Beijing Investigation Team (1986–90), *Beijing Almanac*, Beijing: China City Press; Beijing Statistics Bureau and National Statistics Bureau Beijing Investigation Team (1991–2002), *Beijing Statistical Yearbook*, Beijing: China's Statistics Press; Beijing Water Authority (2003–7), *Beijing Water Resources Bulletin*, Beijing: Beijing Water Authority.

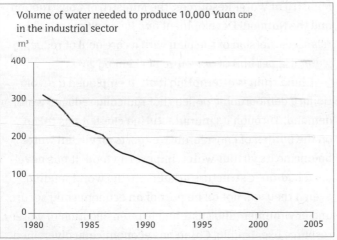

Figure 4.3 Volume of water needed to produce 10,000 Yuan GDP in the industrial sector, 1980–2000. *Source:* S. Jia and S. Zhang (2003), 'Response of industrial water use to water price rising in Beijing', *Journal of Hydraulic Engineering*, vol. 4.

Water, as I have been saying, is all about money. Economic diversification is the secret to enabling an economy to get more money out of less water. This is a trick that every nation has to learn, and there is strong evidence that China is already completely at home in this environment.

Figure 4.2 shows that industrial and service activities have greatly outstripped agriculture in terms of their contribution to China's GDP. This is very important, as both sectors are far more water-efficient than agriculture. The more successful an economy is in growing its GDP beyond that wealth contributed by agriculture, the greater the financial benefit it will be getting from its water resources. The returns to water are better in every other sector than they are in agriculture. Figure 4.3 tells an even simpler story: China's GDP is increasingly water-efficient. As is normal in an industrialised economy, the agricultural sector's importance to the economy has fallen and stabilised at a low level.

202

These indicators are very reassuring for the future. But China is not a nation to rest on its laurels. It is actively moulding its demand management, rather than leaving it to the happy side effects of economic diversification. In 2002, China launched its Water Saving Plan. Five years later, the Ministry of Water Resources, the Ministry of Construction and the National Development and Reform Commission released a version of the plan with a core goal of reducing water use per unit of GDP by 20 per cent by 2013.

China truly is attempting it all. It employed a revolutionary demographic policy that radically reduced water demand. Through its manufacturing clout, it has taken on the burden of considerable 'exports' of virtual water, balancing its virtual-water 'imports' in food. It has developed hydraulic structures that are truly world-leading, even if they will not all be part of an economically secure and environmentally sustainable intensification of water-resource use. Finally, China has economically diversified and is progressively generating its GDP away from water-demanding agriculture.

This is all a work in progress. The signs and early sounds are encouraging. China appears to be following policies that are (mostly) rational and internationally responsible. Those outside China are comfortable lambasting this huge, rapidly growing economy for being too slow to meet our environmental demands and share our prejudices. The Chinese often bat this away as unnecessarily intrusive. This creates the impression that they are being aloof. Far from it. They are being positively polite. Because rather than simply telling us to mind our own business, they could – with justification and more often than they do – point out the hypocrisy of our critique. Chinese policy-makers would like to roll out their water-saving plans even quicker than they currently are. It makes both economic and environmental sense.

203

I don't want to overstate the case. Too often outsiders, especially of the social-democratic leaning, are wowed by the seemingly wondrous social, industrial or political achievements of large monolithic states. Certainly, there is a wide trend of scepticism towards data emanating from the Chinese government machine, particularly that pertaining to the economy. I am not best positioned to judge how appropriate that scepticism is. Is it possible for a nation state in a highly globalised world economy to release the contemporary equivalent of Soviet tractor-production figures? More seasoned China-watchers than I – and there are many – might take issue with some of the detail in this section. China is not my area of expertise. But water is. And it seems to me that a remarkable water-management story is in train in China. By controlling the demographics, by working water harder, by maximising food productivity and by some good engineering, China is making increasingly intelligent use of its own water resources. Better still, it is exporting this expertise through its investments in Africa and elsewhere. Yes, there are downsides, such as the second-best solution provided by the South–North conveyor or the environmental impacts of this and other engineering projects. But on balance, there is much for other nations to learn from the Middle Kingdom. We should watch China's future with interest. I know I shall.

~~~~~~~~~ *PART 2* ~~~~~~~~~
Brazil: a water tower beyond our understanding

204

The first among equals

Brazil sits proudly at the front of the BRICS acronym – a bold, bolshy B kick-starting the whole thing off.

And Brazil has plenty to boast of, particularly when it comes to water. It has a water endowment unmatched by any other BRICS or industrialised nation. Other countries in South America and central Africa have impressive water resources, but there is a significant difference between these economies and Brazil: money. By this I mean the capacity to invest at the massive scale required by such a huge country and economy.

Water doesn't mean much without money. To be water-rich without being just plain rich rich has never helped any country ever. In the next chapter, we will take a look at Ethiopia, the country blessed with the main source of the Nile but always lacking the financial and political capital to use its waters.

Brazil is in a far stronger position. It has been touched by the double-edged magic of economic diversification and industrialisation. It has worked through decades of dysfunctional politics to reveal its global economic potential. Increasingly, it is jostling for a place at the top table in the global economy. In 2008, Brazil even loaned $10 billion to the IMF. An amazing achievement, not least as it started the decade by going cap in hand to the IMF. By most measures, Brazil is one of the top ten economies in the world. Many predict it will be one of the five largest by 2050.

It's not just about the rivers...

With a flow of 8000 cubic kilometres a year, the Amazon is by far the world's largest river. It is an entity of such size, scope and strength that to look upon it is a fearful, awesome and humbling experience. If you have already, you will know what I mean. If you haven't, then go. To look upon the Amazon is to attempt to stare Mother Nature down. You will blink first.

205

Brazil occupies the vast majority of the Amazon basin. The Amazon belongs to Brazil, and it pushes through this enormous country with the insistent force of a high-pressure aorta. Alone, this peerless river and its tributaries would ensure that Brazil was the most water-rich nation on earth. But in addition much of the basin of the Orinoco – the world's second-largest river by flow – also passes through Brazil.

However, as remarkable as it may sound, Brazil's surface waters are barely developed and hardly used, either in consumptive uses, such as irrigated food production, or non-consumptive uses, such as power generation. However, this last is changing, and a number of hydro-power projects are planned, and most will probably go ahead despite public opposition by local peoples and environmental activists. This superabundance of fresh or blue water is mostly inaccessible at present. The mighty Amazon proceeds in its journey, scarcely touched by man. The same is true of the Orinoco.

Amazingly, this doesn't matter too much. Brazil is able to ignore its embarrassment of surface-water riches because of its unrivalled levels of soil water. There is a very good reason why they call it the rainforest: Brazil's green-water resources are what could potentially make the country the water tower of the world.

Energy, fuel, ethanol, diesel: know your bios...
The cultural panic fired up by the wicked problem of trying to stop the planet from overheating while continuing to enjoy all the creature comforts developed in the twentieth century has thrown the terms bioenergy and biofuel out into the public discourse. Probably you are a little unclear about what these words actually mean. Very simply, bioenergy and biofuel are synonymous terms for fuels made from biomass. And biomass is even more simply any biological material from living, or recently living, organisms. Bioenergy and biofuel, then, are broad, generic terms.

Bioethanol and biodiesel are specific biofuels. Both are very relevant for our analysis of Brazil. Bioethanol is an alcohol produced, as alcohol always is, through the fermentation of sugars, starches or cellulose. In Brazil's case, most of the bioethanol is made through the fermentation of sugar cane. Bioethanol can only replace up to 15 per cent of the petrol in regular cars, but hybrids can use a far greater proportion. Biodiesel can be used as a direct replacement for regular diesel, and already is being so used across the world. In California's Disneyland, biodiesel from waste vegetable oil in the resort is used to power the trains that circumnavigate the Magic Kingdom. In Brazil, the story is about bioethanol from biomass raised on green water. Note: economically invisible green water is doing the hard work.

There is plenty of healthy debate on the use (and misuse) of biofuels, and the wisdom (or folly) of dedicating large amounts of land – and water – to their production. I am going to entirely sidestep the former issue regarding how we use biofuels, as it does not pertain to the central topic of our current discussion. I'll touch upon the latter, but remember that I am framing my opinions and judgements through the tight prism of water-resource use.

The lay of the land

Brazil has plenty of water, but it has weak soil. This
is pretty typical of tropical and equatorial countries:
the soil is low in nutrients. It's a problem, but one that
humanity, with its typical obstinate ingenuity, is tackling. Brazilian farmers are using all kinds of agrichemical
approaches to up the fertility of the soil. This is good
science, and Brazil leads in it. The country has plenty of
the one resource we just can't move, contain or control:
rainwater. Therefore it makes sense to add the other
ingredients we need to make industrial farmland as
viable and efficient as possible. The possibilities for food
production are quite incredible.

207

    But Brazil's mind is not just on food. At least, not food
for human consumption. Brazil is also interested in feeding one of our favourite companions on this lonely globe:
the motor vehicle.

    Brazil's farmers and government have given consid-
erable priority to growing sugar cane and corn for the
production of bioethanol. Bioethanol is a relatively clean
source of energy, in terms of carbon footprint. However, it
is extraordinarily water extravagant. Its water footprint is
over seventy times that of oil. Only a country with such a
generous bounty of water as Brazil has could harvest corn
to manufacture bioethanol with a clear conscience. Both
the EU and the US have been experimenting with biofuel
production, but both quickly learnt that they couldn't
afford to lose the land and water from conventional farming without profoundly undermining the availability and
price of strategic food staples. If you are one of those who
believe that oil and fuel determine everything in geopolitics, I have news for you: hunger trumps everything. At
least in the long run. We have not encountered the long
run yet. We are still in the phase of coping with the drama
of energy shocks.

Brazil can pursue biofuel production as – uniquely – it enjoys not just the necessary technical capacity, but also massive water resources. But there's a third factor required: land. And Brazil has vast land resources. Land, water and technology: this trinity enables a country with good governance to fulfil any and all agricultural ambitions. Nowhere has all three in the same magic quantities as Brazil. This is why the US and the EU have shied away from biofuel, whereas Brazil can push forwards. That said, biofuel production is not guaranteed to be a successful industry. Fluctuations in the prices of oil and gas can have a dramatic impact. A sudden drop in their prices can transform a viable biofuel project into a major loss-making white elephant overnight. And oil and gas prices are hardly famed for their stability in the twenty-first century.

But let's not play the pessimist yet. Brazil has plenty to be happy about. The sheer scale of its water and land resources means that it has many strengths and many policy options. Better still, Brazil hasn't even begun to realise the potential of its natural wealth. Unlike the European continent and the US, Brazil hasn't yet cleared all its natural forest cover. There are great swathes of land utterly untouched. Even in the cleared land, there is far more green water to be mobilised than is currently employed. Most probably there is sufficient for Brazil's own needs with enough surplus to meet the extra needs of the rest of the world.

No, we shouldn't be pessimistic at all. In the future, Brazil will increase the productivity of both its green and blue water. There will be further clearing of forest and other woodlands. But Brazil is being reflexive in its land- and water-managing policies. On top of this, we should remember that Brazil is a late developer economically. As such, environmental concerns are more deeply ingrained in its political and economic ethos. The environmental travesties of Europe and the US will not be repeated by the

208

THE GENERATION GAME
First-generation biofuels use crops, such as sugar, grains and oil seeds, as their biomass source. Second-generation biofuels use crop waste, straw and other woody and fibrous biomass. As they are waste products, second-generation biofuels have a far smaller water footprint.

new big economies, provided they are able to get decent prices for sustainably grown and sensibly chosen crops.

First-generation biofuels are a sustainable option for Brazil, at least in the foreseeable future. This model could not be made to work in other economies. The industrialised economies lack the land and the water. They would throw themselves into perilous food insecurity if they attempted anything on a large scale. The developing economies lack the technology and the financing. Of BRICS, only Russia could potentially follow Brazil down this path if it could combine investment, technology and land and water more effectively. Sadly, there is little evidence to date to suggest the Russian bear will be waking from its agricultural hibernation any time soon.

209

Speed the plough

There's plenty of romantic nonsense bound up in the way that we view the farming industry. When it comes to food, we are strangely nostalgic in a way that we would never be about power or water supply. No one harks back wistfully to the days of high-risk coal mining or cholera-infected public wells. But somehow, even the most level-headed of us gets a bit misty-eyed and dull-brained about the image of a noble farmer, tending to the land with only the support of seed, soil and a few rough draught animals.

Of all our rose-tinted dreams of yesterday, this might be the most ridiculous. Don't believe the Luddites. The move to mechanised farming, which took place in the industrialised economies from the 1940s to the 1960s, was one of the greenest innovations in twentieth-century farming. Draught animals used to consume about 20 per cent of crop production. That's a figure so stunning that you might miss its implications on first read. One in five crops were being invested in making more crops. For inefficiency, you can't do much better than that. In North America and Europe, there were tens of millions of draught animals, providing the energy for cultivating, harvesting and transporting crops. When they were replaced by tractors and trucks, this freed up between 10 and 20 per cent of all the land available for crops, most of which was rain-fed.

Here we see another instance of incredible water-savings being enjoyed by wealthy economies. Those states whose farming sectors were able to mechanise were able to use an additional 20 per cent of green water and use it to raise food. Today, China and India are still in the process of moving from a reliance on animal energy to hydrocarbon energy in farming. Unsurprisingly, the developing economies are still shackled to the water-costly animal-traction method of farming. Even today, the energy to run subsistence farms in developing countries is provided by draught animals. These self-same animals upon which their farming model is built are also the single most significant drain on the farm's output. When dealing with the smallest farms, these animals are in direct competition for food and water with the farmer and his or her family.

Interestingly, a new revolution is taking place in how farms are energised. In fact, in some ways, it is a counter-revolution. Brazil is reversing this historic move from water-intensive to water-light farm energy. By producing water-hungry but carbon-friendly biofuels and using these – in place of hydrocarbons – to power the farming industry and Brazil's transport more generally, the Brazilian farming sector is taking vast amounts of land and water resource out of use for food-crop production. No other economy has the natural resources to attempt this. For Brazil though, it might prove a very successful counter-revolution indeed. What Brazil decides to do is globally significant. Will it choose to feed the world or be energy self-sufficient?

A global role for Brazil...

Like China, there is much Brazil can – and will – do for the world. Unlike China, Brazil's options are more numerous and less economically, environmentally and politically constrained. China has to continue learning to do more with less water, and has to export technology and good water-management values to developing economies. The path it should follow was quite narrowly laid out in the preceding pages. Brazil can carve its own way.

But let's now take a closer look...

211

Lucky numbers: Brazilian demographics

Here, an obvious distinction from China. China is a success story, with a draconian demographic policy that has saved the world. Brazil is a country without a demographic problem. Its population is a mere 192 million, making it the fifth-most-populous nation on the planet. At around 8.5 million square kilometres, it is also the fifth-largest nation by area. But the seeming parity of these two positions is misleading.

Whereas one in five of us are Chinese, only one in 40 are Brazilian. Broadly, populations level off as economies industrialise, diversify and increase per-capita GDP. Hence, both China and Brazil have populations predicted to level and then only self-replace by 2050. China has achieved this through strict management. Brazil, through good fortune. Brazil's population for 2050 is estimated at 260 million, and it will probably have dropped to around eighth in the global-population charts. Pakistan, Bangladesh and Nigeria are all expected to overtake it.

At a national level, a levelled population is extremely helpful. It makes managing food and water security far easier. For incredibly large and significant economies such as these two, the stabilisation of population growth is also important globally. By reaching this demographic target, both economies will play their part in protecting sustainable global food and water security. China will not import so much food that it will destabilise the global system. Brazil will be able to export staple-food commodities in quantities large enough to keep many other nations fed and virtually watered. The world will very likely have an additional two billion water-users by 2050. Nearly all of these will come from India, Indonesia, Pakistan, Bangladesh, sub-Saharan Africa and the Middle East. All face water-resource challenges. Brazil's population will have grown by perhaps only seventy or eighty million. Brazil will easily meet its own future water needs. It will need between 80 and 100 cubic kilometres of water per year. Not only will it have enough for these demands, but it will have sufficient for at least two hundred million non-Brazilians as well if it chooses to feed the world and not aim for energy self-sufficiency.

212

Water ways: the many allocative options facing Brazil

The headlines...
Brazil has the world's largest accessible resources of blue and green water. And these resources are pretty evenly distributed. Only the north-east region is water-scarce. This region is less developed and is the focus of major supply-management interventions. The remainder of the country is very healthily watered.

There are worries, though, about the environmental implications of Brazil exploiting its water resources more fully. Not because it might exhaust its reserves. This is absolutely impossible. Rather, the worries focus on what Brazil would have to do to access these resources. At the moment, Brazil's great green-water supplies are supporting equally great natural woodlands and grasslands. Outside Brazil, there are choruses of rumbles in response to suggestions that more vegetation be cleared to provide land and water for the cultivation of crops or the raising of livestock. Most of these rumbles relate to the carbon dioxide associated with such action. Trees are brilliant for many reasons, but the one really vital quality of trees is that they suck carbon dioxide out of the atmosphere and pump oxygen back out. They slow global heating, and they give us all a little something to breathe.

Man-made global heating is the *bête noir* of those in industrialised economies who describe themselves as 'environmentally aware'. Never mind that what they seem to be aware of is simply their own opinions. Nations in Europe and North America who happily cleared their own woodlands with wanton recklessness over the last few centuries now greet any replication of their behaviour by less-developed economies with harsh tuts and sad shakes of the head. Never was their environmental vandalism costed into their economic structures; the strength of these economies owes a massive, collective debt to the world for the environmental harm upon which it is built. Rather than pay this debt, it is passed on in the form of proscriptions to those economies which have not done equivalent environmental harm. The transgressions of the first sinners are truly visited upon the subsequent generation. Because the industrialised world shed its environmental responsibilities to build its economies, BRICS and developing nations are not to do the same. Brazil is exhorted to be responsible in its stewardship of our planet's lungs, yet this duty is only incumbent upon Brazil because the industrialised economies failed to manage their own environments. Brazil's leaders listen, but are understandably impatient with the hypocrisy.

213

The big fat energy elephant

Energy is not a concept that we have discussed in any great detail up to now. But I have a confession to make. It has been the elephant in the room. In fact, it's been sitting there all the time, one giant grey paw planted in the midst of my vegetarian meze, a second resting menacingly on your cheeseburger (shame on you). I've talked about the food–water–trade nexus, but there is a missing corner to our square: that is *energy*.

The reason this elephant has to go on being ignored – despite the potential calamity – is that there is far too much to write and say on the topic of the relationship between water and energy. I have been trying, with forced austerity, to moderate the flow of analysis, for fear of flooding you with many ideas that you may feel you do not need or want. No one likes a bore. Even less a know-it-all. However, one cannot ignore all of the elephant all of the time. In relation to Brazil, it is simply impossible not to touch upon energy.

Brazil's ability to guarantee global food and water security is intimately bound up with decisions about energy. As in so many things, Brazil is spoilt for choice. Its vast land resources and abundant water make biofuels a very viable option. So too are renewables: hydro-power, solar and wind. Non-renewable, but clean, nuclear energy is also possible. Indeed, Brazil has recently chanced to discover reserves of hydrocarbons, so every permutation and combination of energy policies is possible as the country seeks to drive and diversify its economy. But what is important when it comes to the water–food–trade nexus is how great a part of the mix biofuels will play.

You can't use the same drop of water twice. Well, actually that is demonstrably untrue. If there is one truthful statement about water, it's that you can always use the same drop of water over and over again. But you certainly can't use the same drop of water for two different things at the same time. Pertinently, you can't use your water to grow biomass for biofuels while also using the same water (and land) to grow crops or raise livestock. Brazil is already one of the key players in global crop and livestock-commodity trade. What it decides to do with its land and water resources has a direct influence on the global availability of strategic food commodities and virtual water on 'the world market'. Its role can only increase in the coming decades, and with it the significance of its energy-policy decisions.

Let's have a look at Table 4.2.

Virtual-water 'imports'			
Virtual-water volume	CROPS AND LIVESTOCK	INDUSTRIAL	TOTAL
Bn m³/year	15	3	18

Virtual-water 'exports'			
Virtual-water volume	CROPS AND LIVESTOCK	INDUSTRIAL	TOTAL
Bn m³/year	61	2	63

Virtual-water 'net imports'			
Virtual-water volume	CROPS AND LIVESTOCK	INDUSTRIAL	TOTAL
Bn m³/year	46	-1	45

Table 4.2 Virtual-water 'imports' and 'exports' for Brazil, 2000.
Source: A.K. Chapagain and A.Y. Hoekstra (2003), *Water Footprints of Nations*, Delft: IHE.

This table shows the current profile of Brazil's virtual-water 'exports' and 'imports'. What's very clear is that Brazil's 'exports' are huge, and almost entirely in the form of crops and livestock. It is precisely these exports that would be affected by a decision to dedicate a larger proportion of land and water to the cultivation of biomass crops for energy production. By 2050, the question of how Brazil allocates its water resources will be one of the key determinants of global food-commodity prices.

A quick note on food-commodity prices. Or rather, a quick complaint. World prices are not set by supply and demand. Trade is not free, nor is it fair. The playing field is as level as a cliff face. There are two forms of price distortion relevant to our analysis at this point. First, environmental costs are simply not included in the price. As I've mentioned earlier, economists have a lovely term for these: negative externalities. It's one of those tidy phrases, like collateral damage or non-resectable carcinoma, which allows you to forget what it is you are actually talking about by dressing up something quite real and appalling in the anaesthetising language of science or bureaucracy. An example of a negative externality in food production might be washing unmanageable amounts of toxic pesticides and agri-chemicals into a water system incapable of absorbing it. When these negative externalities are not included in the price, because companies and economies are not required to tidy up after themselves, we have what economists like to term a 'market failure'. Or in this case, heavily polluted water and artificially cheap food. Both are very dangerous. Cheap food is doubly dangerous to those who can be encouraged to over-consume. Their ill-health and the environmental ill-health form a pincer movement placing them in serious jeopardy.

The second factor to skew international food prices are the asymmetries in global power. Take the price of sugar or cotton. Internationally, this is not determined by the market, but rather by the US and EU agricultural and trade subsidies on production within their borders. And by determined, I mean dictated. The WTO negotiations are supposed to reconcile and iron out these asymmetries. Rather, the WTO has served to attenuate the reform process intended to erode the strong position of the industrialised economies. These tormenting negotiations have added new chapters to the centuries-long violent and wicked global history of sugar and cotton production and trade. Things are getting fairer. But slowly.

Brazil should not fret. It has history on its side. The global trade hegemony of Europe and the US is the present. But the ascent of the BRICS economies is very much the future.

217

What price water?

With each passing year, our entire world structure is being distilled to function according to one incredibly simple premise: market-determined prices allow equally well-informed willing buyers and sellers to make and take prices that reflect an economically fair outcome. This is the ideology for the post-ideological age. And it suffers the same failing of all ideologies: it only meaningfully exists on paper.

Hidden inputs that remain unincorporated into commodity prices mean that a cost is going unpaid somewhere. Gradually, as we become more wise to the shortcomings of the market system, we push for these negative externalities to be costed into the economics. Culturally, we are seeing considerable success in the costing of carbon-related pollution. The carbon footprint is proving to be a useful way of discussing the roles of consumer behaviour and supply chains. Many think we should adopt the concept of the water footprint, to enable us to understand the true cost of our food. It's a lovely theory. The practice is tough, though. Carbon taxes are relatively easy to conceptualise and calculate. There has been convergence on how to work out the amount of carbon associated with a product. You can fix taxes accordingly. The costs of the outputs of carbon intuitively affect everyone. The atmosphere is the universal sink that we all share. Atmospheric pollution unfairly affects the non-polluter and has often not been paid for by the polluter.

The water footprint is much harder to conceptualise. The way we manage water certainly does cause pollution and other environmental impacts but they are not global in their reach. The damage caused by the mismanagement of water stays within the hydrological system where it is generated. Coming up with a comprehensive concept from which to hang an agreed system of taxation is not yet politically feasible.

218

And before we tackle a task like that, I can immediately think of two improvements that would be easier, swifter and more effective in connecting commodity production and water content. First, we need, at a pace determined by politics, to put an end to the subsidies and protectionist measures deployed in the farming sectors of industrialised economies. And here, I am most specifically talking about EU agricultural policies and US farming subsidies. The second measure is merely the other side of that coin. We need to put in measures to protect subsistence farmers in developing economies.

Our world is built around the pernicious lie that global market forces help economies develop. Global markets can be a very rough way of transforming a primitive economy by introducing a completely new way of valuing goods and services. They don't make the concessions to human suffering and abstract concepts such as fairness that we, as conscious beings, have come to expect in our world. Wise governments – including that of the US in the past and China today – have throughout the present phase of unprecedented globalisation protected themselves from the brutality of the aggressively unfair free market.

In farming, global market forces are not benign. The large, wealthy and well-established crush the subsistence, small-scale and impoverished as an ignorant child might wantonly stamp on ants. The subsidies of the industrialised world mean that their commodity prices are the product of cloud cuckooland. They bear only the tiniest of passing resemblances to the actual cost of the commodity. This asymmetry prevents the farmers of developing economies from being able to push for the same water efficiencies as those seen in the industrialised nations.

As a planet, we need the farmers of Africa, South America and Asia to improve their water productivity vastly. Reason demands that we put in place a system of price incentives to optimise the utilisation of water so that crops and livestock are raised in regions where water is environmentally and economically optimal. Wouldn't that seem the most sensible way to organise our world? Yet we humans are perverse creatures. Just as the best crop and livestock yields are often achieved on second-class land, so the most successful intensification of water in agriculture often takes place where the water resources are much less than agronomically ideal. What would a Martian think, if she (he or it) landed on our planet? Well, after getting over their initial excitement at the superabundant wetness of our planet compared to that on their parched globe, they might begin to wonder why we chose to work water hardest in arid, water-scarce areas such as Southern California or the North China Plain. At this point in history we have an unstoppable propensity to use water as brutally and as intensively as possible in tracts that enjoy temperatures of close to 30 degrees centigrade for most of the year.

219

A new world order

It's the phrase that sends the paranoiac, the fantasist and the very lonesome scuttling off to their search engines hunting conspiracies of global elites, secret cabals and shape-shifting reptiles. The truth, as ever, is more mundane. No one is running the world. Contrary forces and conflicting interests come up against each other. Politics pervades. And despite the friction and the fallout, the planet manages to rotate.

The WTO is the current would-be ringmaster of the global economy. But the industrialised economies own the circus. What they don't know is that BRICS are buying them out. By 2050, there will indeed be a new world order. But it won't be reached through the Machiavellian machinations of shadowy puppet-masters. It will, like all things in human history, come about haphazardly, indirectly and partially accidentally. To attempt predictions is to hold oneself up to be labelled either lucky or foolish – never wise. That said, it's as safe a bet as possible that the BRICS economies will be the main beneficiaries of the changes to come during the next four decades. China, India and Brazil already account for over a third of all food production. The world needs them to increase their food production to at least match the needs of their increased populations. Preferably, there will be at least some small change left over for those in the rest of the world. How important it is then that these BRICS economies pursue sustainable intensification of their water use. Brazil and China have already indicated that they will follow this path. The new world order will give BRICS enormous power as 'exporters' and 'importers' of virtual water. And Brazil will be the main exporter of virtual water embedded in food commodities globally. How big its contribution will be depends on its energy policy.

220

Brazil, then, lies at the centre of the new world order. It will be the food store of the world. Today, Brazil is the leading producer of sugar in the world. One-third of all sugar comes from Brazil. It is also the world's second-largest producer of soya beans. It is the third-largest producer of maize. Its dominance extends to livestock. Brazil is the pre-eminent producer of beef. Its cattle herd is twice that of the world's second-largest beef and cattle economy, the US. While the US has marginally under a hundred million head of cattle, Brazil has a nudge over two hundred million. Yes. That's more cattle than people. This gap between Brazil and the US will only widen in the future. The US has tested nearly to destruction the industrialised systems of intensive grain-fed livestock production. The sector is moving from the sphere of legitimate agribusiness to the world of unbearable science fiction.

Although Brazil has tended to follow this cruel practice, it also produces a large amount of range-fed cattle. The range-fed approach is not merely more humane. It is kinder on the environment, and places a less onerous burden on blue-water resources than grain-fed rearing. In fact, range-fed cattle farming offers a positive contribution to the global aim of improving our mobilisation of water. Most rangeland is unsuitable for crops. Yet the land raises rain-fed natural fodder from green water. Consequently, the only way to access this water resource is for it to be converted – by our unpaid economic collaborator, Mother Nature – into food for grazing animals. By getting animals to eat the grass, we manage to introduce extra green-water resources into our economic system. Without this, the resource could not be incorporated into the economy. It wouldn't be lost, as it would be supporting natural vegetation with all its values and environmental services. But neither would anyone be making any money out of it.

Of course, Brazil is under ever-greater pressure to dedicate cropland to producing animal feed rather than crops directly intended for human consumption Here we start to see the problems associated with the diet of industrialised economies. A diet that is straightforwardly too heavy on the meat.

Brazil faces several choices. It can produce more feed for livestock, and so push further its world-leading beef industry. Or it can devote more resources to biofuel, another agribusiness in which Brazil leads the world. The US faces similar choices, but it does not have the sheer

221

wealth of land and water resources that Brazil has. Less resource means fewer options. What the US has is an absolutely proven track record of competence in farming, and the agricultural sciences and technologies that underpin the industry. Brazil is likewise developing its competence. It may lack the finance and technology of the US, but it also lacks the US's constraints on natural resources. The US is the pivotal food provider at the start of the second decade of the twenty-first century. By the mid-point of the century, it will almost certainly have passed the baton to Brazil. But it will still retain second place. Both these nations have extraordinarily strong natural-resource positions. They are the international guarantors of food security. Although they have large populations, their population-to-resource ratios are fine, and are not expected to worsen significantly. We can continue to rely on them with some confidence, provided their moral compasses point them at responsible international trade with an eye on the water environment.

But Brazil's choices will change what it is that we shall be relying upon them for. Will it be beefburgers, tofu or green fuel for our cars? Most certainly, it will be a mix of all three, and many things more besides. But there are a great many ways in which Brazil might choose to use its resources. Psychologically, Brazil does not share China's terrible fear of starvation. Its people have always had plenty of land and water, and potentially therefore plenty of food. It is demonstrably capable of self-sufficiency, with a surplus great enough to feed hundreds of millions outside the country. Therefore, there is no cultural worry about food security. So it feels comfortable shifting land and water from food production to the production of biofuels.

What's more, there are plenty of improvements to be made. Brazil is very far from realising the proper potential of its water resources, as a cursory glance at Table 4.3 will show.

Average VW content m³/tonne			
COUNTRY	SUGAR CANE	SOYA BEANS	MAIZE
BRAZIL	155	1076	1180
USA	103	1869	469
CHINA	117	2617	801

Table 4.3 Average virtual-water content of sugar, soya beans and maize in Brazil, compared with the US and China.
Source: A.K. Chapagain and A.Y. Hoekstra (2003), *Water Footprints of Nations,* Delft: IHE.

223

Three crops are globally significant: sugar cane, soya beans and maize. Brazil remains far less water-efficient than its main competitors, China and the US, in both sugar cane and maize. Remember, Brazil is no minor player in these crop markets. It leads the market for sugar, is second in soya beans and third in maize. It is producing vast and very globally significant quantities of all three. Clearly, there are margins for improvements in water usage in all three crops. In other words, Brazil could be doing a lot more with a lot less of its water in two of these globally significant crops. It is, from a water perspective, very good to uncover areas where there is a potential for improved productivity. Assuming, that is, that things will be put right.

Being the best

Brazil is poised to become one of the most important economies in the world. It will have the leading role in ensuring that the rest of the world is fed and watered. But how successfully it realises this destiny depends on two factors that lie beyond the water sector: energy policy and economic diversification.

A little shock goes a long way...

We've seen how economies can get shocked into wildly rethinking their farming policies. The devastation and hunger caused by two bouts of industrialised killing led European economies to engage in a phase of unprecedented co-operation in remedying food insecurity during the second half of the twentieth century. The goal was European self-sufficiency, and they pursued it doggedly, both on a national and a continental level. And it was by some measures a success. From the limited perspective of food production, at least. Over the course of four decades, Europe saw a three-fold increase in crop and livestock productivity, while using the same volumes of green water. Mostly, this was achieved through sustainable intensification. Although the environment and its water services were tested, they were not significantly impaired. They were given a hard workout but they weren't crippled.

The only thing is: food self-sufficiency wasn't actually achieved. Rather, the illusion was created through trade and virtual water.

Brazil too had its shock that set it on its current experiment in bioethanol energy security. Brazil's shock was the wild oil-price fluctuations between 1973 and 1979. These jolted and worried the world. Every country outside OPEC and OAPEC began to think profoundly about their energy addiction to predominantly Middle Eastern oil. But no economy bar Brazil could feasibly consider achieving energy self-sufficiency by growing crops for biofuel. Achievement was rapid and significant. By 1977, Brazil was capable of producing 50 million tonnes of alcohol from its bioethanol plants. This level surged by 1985 to 150 million tonnes and might well have grown considerably, if not for a sudden and sustained drop in oil prices. Just as the crises of the previous decade had forced countries to look towards viable alternatives and energy security, so did (relatively) cheap oil mean that Brazil's interest in biofuel evaporated.

224

OPEC AND OAPEC NEED NOT BE OPAQUE...
The Organisation of Petroleum Exporting Countries (OPEC) comprises 12 countries: Algeria, Angola, Ecuador, Iran, Iraq, Kuwait, Libya, Nigeria, Qatar, Saudi Arabia, the United Arab Emirates and Venezuela. The Organisation of Arab Petroleum Exporting Countries (OAPEC) comprises 11 countries: Algeria, Bahrain, Egypt, Iraq, Kuwait, Libya, Qatar, Saudi Arabia, Syria, Tunisia and the United Arab Emirates.

The things you can make with sugar and water

Why is this book on virtual water seemingly diverting into the fascinating but not apparently relevant subject of energy security and biofuels? Because Brazilian bioethanol is made mainly from one crop: sugar. This is Brazil's biggest crop, and Brazil, as mentioned, is the largest producer of sugar in the world. When Brazil decides to devote half its sugar crop to the production of bioethanol instead of exporting it onto the global markets, that's quite a big deal. That is one-sixth of the world's sugar vanishing in an instant. And such a seismic shift in global crop production comes with major implications for water use. The amount of water required to grow the half of Brazilian sugar cane diverted to bioethanol production is roughly 43 cubic kilometres a year. As we will see in the next chapter, that is greater than the amount of virtual water imported by Egypt each year to give it the illusion of water sufficiency.

225

Biofuel production is thirsty work. No country other than Brazil can truly afford to do it. The depth of its green-water resources means it is the country that took the lead and stayed in the game. Aside from Brazil, only the US participates in the industry in any meaningful way. Together, the two countries dedicate about 100 cubic kilometres of water a year to biofuel production. That figure is equivalent to 6 per cent of the virtual water embedded in international trade. The US continues to engage in biofuel production not because it makes economic sense – it doesn't – or because it is environmentally sound – it most certainly isn't. Rather, the US is interested in understanding the potential of the technology. For this interest, the US will subsidise farmers and the industry, in particular subsidising the production of maize, which is the main crop source for US biofuel.

Table 4.4 shows the average water footprint for different types of energy in cubic metres per gigajoule. Yes, I know what you are thinking. 'We're only just getting our brains

Table 4.4 Average water
footprint associated with
different types of energy.
Source: P.W. Gerbens-
Leenes, A.Y. Hoekstra and
T.H. Van der Meer (2008),
*Water Footprint of Bio-
energy and Other Primary
Energy Carriers*, Delft: IHE.

226

PRIMARY ENERGY CARRIERS	AVERAGE WATER FOOTPRINT m³/GJ
WIND ENERGY	0.00
NATURAL GAS	0.04
NUCLEAR ENERGY	0.09
COAL	0.16
SOLAR THERMAL ENERGY	0.30
CRUDE OIL	1.06
BIOMASS average the Netherlands, US, Brazil, Zimbabwe	71.54

1 gigajoule (GJ) = 10⁹ joules = 0.948 million BTU = 239 million calories = 278kWh

around the idea of measuring water in cubic metres. Don't
dazzle us with the gigajoule!' Well, the gigajoule is about
278kWh, if you want to compare it to your home energy
bill, or about 239 million calories, if you want to contrast it
with your weightwatcher's diet plan. But you don't really
need to understand the measures to interpret the table.
Clearly, biomass is the most water-intensive energy source
by a phenomenal multiple. If the world does indeed start to
move towards first-generation biofuels in a more serious,
sustained and substantial way, then energy policy will
become a very large factor indeed in the management of
global water.

Mapping the nexus

A chain of implausible and unlikely connections is forming in our minds by now. At one extreme, we have oil and
the complex mass of political, environmental and cultural
issues that affect its production and price. Conflict in
Middle Eastern nations has a direct impact on the cost
of oil. As this wobbles, so does the market for biofuels
wax and wane. As long as the price of oil stays above $30
per barrel, biofuel is an economically viable industry for
Brazil. When you consider that oil prices are the highest
they have ever been, that the Middle East has experienced – even by its own volatile standards – an especially
fractious decade and that oil pointed at $200 per barrel in
the summer of 2008, peaking at $149, it becomes obvious
why there is so much interest and enthusiasm in Brazil for
switching crops from food to energy.

227

The Brazilian government is reacting exactly as one
might expect of the local political machine. It is trying to
read the global oil price and translate this into economically rational energy and farming policy decisions. The
government decides on the proportions of bioethanol and
biodiesel to be sold on the Brazilian market or on global
markets. Further, it prices both biofuels to incentivise their
use by motorists and the transport industry. All these
actions have an impact on the amount of sugar, maize and
soya beans being produced by Brazil. The more biofuel
produced, the less food. The equation is simple. The less
of these staple foods, the higher the international prices
are pushed. So it is that civil or international conflict in the
Middle East can inflate the price of sugar on the other side
of the world.

'Only connect,' British novelist E.M. Forster famously
urged. But all connections are already, intrinsically there.
It is merely incumbent on us to observe them, and through
observing, to understand, and ultimately to exploit our
better-informed position. Many different pairs of eyes are

upon this complex nexus of commodity prices and government policies: major corporations, national governments and bilateral agencies all try and observe and understand. They analyse the implications for energy security and – because they are all so interdependent – they have to relate these to economic security, environmental security and food security. It is all too much, especially for bureaucracies that are not sufficiently joined up. And within food security, of course, lies water security. We should all be aware of this connection by now. But there are billions of food consumers out there who do not know it and cannot possibly intuit it.

228

At the very core of everything sits the question of the water footprint and the magical, invisible power of virtual-water 'trade' silently to keep the world fed, watered and – partially at least – moving. Yet have the concepts of virtual water or the water footprint gained a place in the energy debate? Not at all. Foolish, when we can so plainly identify the extreme water cost of Brazilian biofuel.

Oil and water

Two simple liquids. Both vitally underpin the activities of society and its capacities to transport and trade.

The oil embargo of late 1973 rocked the world, denting even the confidence of the US. The Arab nations, enraged by US supply support for Israel during the 'Yom Kippur war', and also suffering financially from the depreciation of the dollar, raised oil prices by 70 per cent and announced a staged reduction in oil output. The embargo precipitated a fierce stock-market crash in the industrialised economies, which persisted throughout 1974. The embargo was short-lived, but the repercussions are felt to this day. Psychologically, the US and the non-OPEC countries had been deeply scarred by empty gas-station forecourts and doleful signs admitting to 'no gasoline'. States suddenly felt the need to be energy-secure and no longer victim to the political whims of other nations.

> But it was not to be. *Lightning persisted in its well-docu-mented habit. In 1979, the world was hit with a second crisis. The Shah of Iran's regime had been deposed in an Islamic Revolution, and the new republic was in such chaos that oil exports collapsed. The causes of this second crisis were very different from the first. Yet the result was the same. Queues at the gas pumps, panic on the financial markets, a desper-ate sense of impotence. Barely five years after 'never again', it was a question of 'yet again'.*

Brazil's biofuel story

229

Leading the world

Unquestionably, Brazilian scientists, technologists and engineers lead the world in the development and operation of bioethanol production. This is the Brazilians' industry. Like China, Brazil has ploughed a considerable propor-tion of its annual investment into science and technology. BRICS rightly see technology as the fastest and most sustainable route to economic strength. All have estab-lished leading positions in areas of science that promote their competitiveness. They are leading players in space science, hydro-power generation, nuclear energy, some areas of information technology and, especially in Brazil's case, in bioenergy. All except South Africa have such huge national budgets that if they choose to devote resources to a particular national goal they could not help but succeed It makes no difference whether that goal is space science or bioenergy. The BRICS economies have the potential to develop globally significant capacities, which will always be at worst internationally competitive and at best abso-lutely pre-eminent.

And Brazil stands on the threshold of a new pre-eminence. In the past four decades, the country has followed an ambitious programme of research into crop and livestock production. Its research into sugar-cane and soya-bean crops is unrivalled. Brazilian agri-scientists are among the most respected in the world. Without doubt, Brazil has gained a position of primacy in hydro-power and bioethanol technologies. How did it achieve this and so rapidly?

Left is right

230

Actual achievement requires political vision. I might have given the impression throughout this discussion that I am less than enamoured of politicians. Nothing could be further from the truth. I am in awe of their juggling, of their receptiveness to public opinion and their versatility. Us scientists are not versatile. We doggedly march after an objective truth. The politician can dance with a hundred subjective truths, and feel no shame at the infidelity. As a class, I admire them. As individuals, less so.

One honourable exception I am happy to make is Brazil's President Lula. Leaving aside his humble origins, his ambitions for improving the lives of the Brazilian poor or his left-of-centre orientation – all of which instinctively and rationally appeal to me – Lula has been instrumental in pushing for a sustainable intensification of Brazil's water use. The Bolsa Familia programme may have made the international headlines, but Bolsa Aqua is what interests us here!

Lula came to power in late 2002 on a promise to change the world, and to pull Brazil out of the doldrums. At the same time, he had to balance this ambition with commitments to honouring international contracts, paying down the national debt, complying with the conventions of the IMF and observing the rules of the market. His strong left-wing credentials meant that international observers and Brazilian businessmen were anxious about potential land-redistribution and the possible adverse affect on the agricultural sector. The fear proved unfounded. An early, influential briefing by the Minister of Agriculture persuaded the President that Brazil's position as one of the two leading global crop and livestock producers should not be jeopardised for purely ideological reasons. Importantly, the President and his minister both realised the significance of the sugar crop to Brazil's energy security. The last seven years in Brazil has seen an actively and wisely engaged government, with clear political vision, working in a successful partnership with the private sector to push sustainable water-use intensification for strategic biofuel production and food exporting. Agri-science, public investment in infrastructure and the capital of large corporations are operating in a happy unison in Brazil, and producing quite remarkable results.

231

No fairytales in politics

And around now you were expecting the caveat, surely? My favourable appraisal has been precisely that: one-sided. Brazil's vast lands have not everywhere been touched by good science, enlightened resource development and responsible farming. Why should Brazil somehow prove exempt from the failings and frailties of human nature? In Brazil, it is not only nature's bounty that is excessive; abuses are of the same magnitude. Big water, big land, big mistakes. These are most often a matter of well-established record. The excessive clearing of tropical vegetation cover has terrible consequences for global warming. Our best defence against increasing carbon-dioxide levels in the atmosphere are the rainforests of South America. These are unrivalled machines for transforming carbon dioxide into oxygen. There is a certain madness in destroying these and labelling the biofuels produced on the land clean or green energy. In its own way, the biofuel experiment is proving as calamitous for our environment as our fossil-fuel addiction. Here, the wicked problem of tomorrow, no doubt.

Brazil's story really is defined by the letter B. And the other negative factor is beef. Destroying rainforest and replacing it with methane-producing beef cattle is a double crime against the planet. Yes, I do balance that with the positive fact that by doing so a wealth of green water is made accessible. There are no simple answers. And if Brazil's mistakes are many and well known, then I hope that in this section we have had an opportunity to peek at how Brazil might form an integral part of the solution. A Brazil that uses its world-leading land and green-water supplies wisely will do a great amount of good in managing our global water resources and guaranteeing that people around the world do not die of starvation.

232

A *safe pair of hands...*

China worries many. Often unduly. Russia, still high on the intoxicating fumes of its Soviet superpower strength, is disposed to flex its oil and gas muscles. The threat of turning the taps off in Europe has been mooted too many times; the European scramble for energy security will leave Russia poorer and with less geopolitical influence. Such is the story for those who cry wolf...

But Brazil is politically stable. It has the modesty of South Africa on the international stage, but with greater civic structures. It has the technological savvy of China, but lacks its alienating inscrutability and wilful independence from the global consensus. It can *do* the hydraulic mission as well as any industrialised nation, but may well do so with a twenty-first-century set of environmental ethics. It has proven that it can work in partnership with neighbouring states to build economy-changing hydraulic structures on transboundary rivers. By way of contrast, the US hydraulic mission from 1930 to 1980 was a crazed half century of manic, costly and ill-considered activity. This madding blur of water-resource development in the US's western states inspired Marc Reisner's wonderful and tragic aphorism of 'water flowing uphill to money and power'. 'Economics were fantasy; politics, real.' Brazil's interventions to date have been considerate and what sociologists might describe as relatively reflexive. It will not over-dam as the US did. We shall not see the sorry spectacle of dam demolitions, a rash of which have been observed in the US since 1980.

By halfway through this century, Brazil will be the most important participant in global food trade. My central argument is that food-commodity trade is what ensures global water security. It prevents water wars, starvation and death. It promotes healthy economies, international co-operation and has the potential to maximise the efficiency of our planet's water resources. Brazil is key to all of this. We need to be able to trust Brazil's water management. The country has marshalled its water resources to improve its national economic security. Improvements in Brazilian water efficiency makes the country more energy-secure. This is the motivation. But such national self-interest brings an international benefit. The water tower of the world is becoming ever more productive.

233

There is much to be done. Road and rail infrastructure lags behind the industrialised world. There is much upgrading and building required to speed commodities to food-processing centres and ports. Communications equally need investment. The technology, the finances and the political will are all there. Brazil will almost certainly take these important steps. It almost certainly will answer its calling to become the fountainhead of the world. Its water resources are unique in scale. There is so much more water to be accessed. There is so much room for improvement in productivity. There is so much potential for environmentally sustainable water management. We need it to come to pass.

I said China saved the world by its imagination and bravery in demographic policy. It did. It bought us time.

CHAPTER 5

Keeping their heads above the water: differing experiences in developing economies

Nothing in the world is more flexible and yielding than water. Yet when it attacks the firm and the strong, none can withstand it, because they have no way to change it.
LAOZI

The last among unequals

The developing economies are subject to many and frequent abuses. One of the more insidious – though less actually harmful – is the tendency to group together this majority of world nations as if they displayed any meaningful commonality. Developing economies account for about 165 of the world's 210 economies. Pop stars of the industrialised world may have sung 'We Are the World', but in truth it is the developing economies that are the world. These 165 nations are diverse in population, geography, culture and political structure. Some are fledgling democracies, others monarchies. Some are barely disguised dictatorships, others are collapsed states where anarchy rules. The feature they all share is simple and saddening: many of their people live in poverty.

Strong civic institutions, a functioning representative democracy, an impartial judiciary, guaranteed personal liberties and a diversified economy are the pillars of successful, healthy nations. They remain always a work in progress, constantly threatened by the demands of *realpolitik* in an uncertain world. Those states that enjoy these vital ornaments have built them up over centuries, and cemented them through legislation, reform and – not infrequently – bloody revolution. Underpinning everything is adaptive capacity that is expressed in wealth and well-being. These conditions may be material and financial or perhaps social, and they include access to intangibles such as security and rights.

236

The ancient Chinese philosopher and father of Taoism is right. The firm and strong are powerless to resist the assault of water. How much worse then is the plight of the poor and the weak in the face of a hostile and mean water environment?

The demon in the demographics

Throughout this book, I have dropped sudden, shocking statistics, hard stones thrown into the still waters of your mind. I do it to create a positive effect. Those ripples and aftershocks hopefully hold the key to your own participation in managing our global water resources. Remember, we are starting a conversation here, with the modest ambition of achieving global water security by changing minds. What minds *collectively* decide can bring water security.

Here, then, is another thought to jolt.

Currently, two out of five people live in the developing world. If this figure more than doubles, the global system might not be able to meet their water needs, especially if these developing economies do not begin to catch up with the water-productivity levels in agriculture of the industrialised countries.

Although the one in five people who live in industrialised economies severely over-consume water, predominantly through their meat- and dairy-rich diets, they form a global minority. Better still, the populations of industrialised economies are levelling off. Some are even reducing. Socially and culturally, large families have fallen out of vogue. Economics reinforce the trend towards smaller families. While this might raise concerns about the economy-wide sustainability of a greying population, it is certainly good news in water terms. Stable populations mean that the industrialised world will not generate increased demands for water. Not only that, but there is considerable potential for reducing the water requirements of industrialised nations, mainly by encouraging changes in diet, reducing waste and reusing water.

237

As was seen in the previous chapter, the story of the BRICS economies is rather more mixed. China has a unique demographic record. The one-child policy has had a spectacular, positive impact on global-resource consumption. The demographic dividends China is currently enjoying are normally unheard of outside instances of war or natural disasters and plagues. And possibly the jewel in the crown of these (mostly unexpected) dividends is the reduction in China's big-water needs. Contrast this with India. Here, population growth tends not to temperance but to profligacy. A 60 per cent increase in population is possible in India by 2050. India is a ticking timebomb of water demand. If the cultural tendency for vegetarianism is reversed as a consequence of increasing national and individual affluence, then the world might face a very serious wake-up call within a generation.

And so we turn to the developing economies. Many of their populations will double in size. The 40 sub-Saharan economies will see their populations double by the second half of this century. The world has enough water to meet the consequent increase in demand. But what is lacking from the sub-Saharan economies is the sound governance to manage their water supplies, which could meet this demand. In this chapter, we shall look at three very different developing economies: Egypt, Vietnam and Ethiopia. Tellingly, it will be Ethiopia – the final stop on our whistle-stop global tour and the only sub-Saharan nation visited – that tells the gravest tale. While Egypt and Vietnam are achieving ever-higher returns to water in livestock and crop productivity, Ethiopia has been languishing. The reason is, again, investment and good governance. Or rather, the things that money brings and which, in turn, bring more money.

238

The farmers of Ethiopia – and every other developing economy – need the infrastructures, markets, affordable inputs and predictable prices that enable secure livelihoods and recurring investment. They need what benefited the industrialised nations in the nineteenth century and BRICS in the twentieth.

Remember, farmers are the *de facto* water managers of the world. They manage the big water, the invisible 80–90 per cent of all water used in the global economy, employed for the production of food. Of the eight nation states we will examine in this book, seven have seen significant improvements in their returns to water in farming. We have indeed uncovered a golden rule: the development and diversification of economies is always associated with massive increases in the productivity of water, and these increases are delivered by farmers using big water. That is the big volumes of water integral to food production. Sadly, the converse is also true. Developing economies that falter or face nearly insurmountable financial problems see little or no improvement in their water productivity. Indeed, they even regress. Those impoverished farmers of the developing economies lack the necessary tools to manage water efficiently. As a result, people die. Incumbent upon the global community is the moral obligation to provide these tools – or at least to facilitate their development.

The countries examined in this chapter

As explained, the developing economies are highly diverse,
and appear on three wildly differing continents: Asia,
Africa and South America. However, this study is limited
by necessity. There is neither space enough nor time to
digest a vast exhaustive compendium of facts on global
water, food and trade. Nor would there be sufficient years
left to me to compile it. In choosing only three from 165
developing economies, I have had to be rigorous and cour-
ageous in my selection. Given that water scarcity is one of
the key concerns of this book, I have chosen not to focus on
any economies in South America, where water is in undeni-
able abundance in relation to population and demand in
most of the economies. That is not to say that there are not
lessons to learnt from the developing economies of South
America. Optimistically, I hope that those lessons await us
and that they will show how the South American economies are managing to harness the untapped productivity
of their great wealth in water to the benefit of all humanity.

239

Here I will turn your attention to Egypt, Vietnam and
Ethiopia. Their stories are distinct, illuminating and full of
promise and warning in equal measure.

─────────── PART 1 ───────────
Egypt: apocalypse never

Why there hasn't been death on the Nile

War torments many. Not merely those caught in its mad
dance. Historians, social scientists and politicians all
study wars past and present. The term water wars is nicely
alliterative and gets a reader's attention. It chimes with
our natural paranoia that if a society runs out of such a
basic necessity then violence could easily follow.

A meditation on war is not the main pastime of the water scientist. But the topic began to intrude in my own work. My torment was not so much in observing tendencies to violent conflict over water between states, but in not observing. By the 1980s I was becoming puzzled and eventually seriously frustrated by the absence of violent conflict where it was – according to the thinking of the age – very predictable. There was cause enough. Water scarcity was palpable in the Middle East region, where I mainly researched. In this frustration lay the seed of a powerful – unexpected – explanation.

240

Of all the world economies, Egypt has perhaps the most varied and strongest claims to be the birth nation of virtual water. This most ancient of civilisations may well have been 'trading' virtual water for several millennia; the Biblical figure of Joseph is arguably history's first virtual-water 'trader', using Egypt's grain bounty in a time of famine to insure those living in Egypt against water scarcity by storing food – that is virtual water – in years of plenty. The practice reinforced the state's hegemony and its capacity to project power in the region. However, I have a more personal reason for suggesting that Egypt is the spiritual home of virtual water: its recent water management – both agricultural and political – were inspirational and instrumental in my identification of virtual water.

So it was that in the late 1980s I was grappling with the question of why Egypt hadn't gone to war over water. Everyone's hypothesis at the time was that to ensure water security, Egypt would if necessary engage in military conflict with its Nile-basin neighbours. Egypt's intransigent unwillingness to wage war for water security confused me. How was this water-impoverished nation creating the illusion of water self-sufficiency in the face of a steeply rising population and a series of disappointingly low Nile flows? The answer was lying hidden in data in Egypt's ministries recording wheat and flour imports. Had I not seen that data, I might not have discovered the concept of virtual water for another decade.

How to lose friends and alienate people (in Egyptian water politics)

A little qualification...
It is important to note that I have had the very great privilege of three decades of intimacy with Egyptian water-users, media and the policy-makers and officials responsible for the allocation of water resources. It would be no exaggeration to say that I have come to love and respect the country and its people. But like all important relationships it has been tempestuous at times.

241

Without Egypt, I would never have made progress in identifying and understanding virtual water. For that, if nothing else, I will forever be indebted to this proud and complex nation, caught in the cultural crossfire of Africa, Asia and the West. But it has not been all joy and a meeting of minds.

Science and politics
Like oil and water, these have a natural inclination to separate. Former British premier Tony Blair famously remarked, 'Power without principle is barren, but principle without power is futile.' This is as true for scientists as for politicians. Effective water management requires two things: good science and political nous. If political nous without good science is barren, then I can certainly confirm that good science without political nous is painfully futile. I owe Egypt thanks not only for my discoveries in virtual water but also for my education in practical politics. The learning curve was steep to the point of verticality; the education was tough, and though not always bitter, it was certainly at times rather tart.

What Foucault can teach the water scientist

Michel Foucault – eminent French philosopher, psychologist, social historian and literary theorist – posited the indivisibility of knowledge and power, calling the composite entity power/knowledge. The point is perhaps simpler than the terminology suggests: by knowing, we control; by controlling, we know.

242

For a scientist speaking for many years against the orthodoxy of constructed knowledge, this theory is deeply appealing. Constructed knowledge is always reassuring: to reassure is its *raison d'etre*. It is not as simple as asserting that the politicians feed us lies. Rather, we and they together embark on the construction of pleasing delusions, and then feel mutually reassured when this closed loop feeds back on itself, seeming to confirm its own veracity. Power lies where society agrees the currently constructed version of the 'truth' is located. To speak against this 'truth' is to be – at least until truth is relocated – outside power, to be disempowered. Science is based on observation, constructed truth is the result of political and social processes. There was a time when I believed that to establish the scientific truth was sufficient. Once unearthed, this truth would spread because of its intrinsic qualities and all would bow down to it as dominoes inevitably fall in sequence. Not so. My experience has taught me that the truths are only as significant as their advocates can make them. Their spread is not inevitable. Dissemination falters, regardless of the rigour of the truth's scientific proof. 'The abstract always overwhelms the concrete,' as Marx so well observed.

Dominoes fall slowly…and then only when pushed

The constructed knowledge does not yield without the application of pressure. This is the most important lesson in politics that life has taught me. This was not taught in the lecture rooms or the corridors of research libraries. There, truth is complete once verified by scientific observation. So I was left to learn this lesson the hard way, by encountering heavily defended delusions in the outside world, where proof is nothing and power established by constructed knowledge is everything.

Therefore, after the shocks and disappointments of failed engagements with the political process, an older, wiser scientist emerged. It was this wiser scientist who, upon discovering the concept of virtual water, soberly said to himself that it would take a quarter of a century for it to be widely adopted conceptually. Operationalising the concept in water policy in the tough politics of real-world water allocation and management would take decades. I realised that the first half of that period would be consumed by establishing the idea in the diverse water-science community. Constructed knowledge is not the sole preserve of the political world: the water-science community – comprising engineers, economists, development economists, political economists, social theorists, political scientists, water lawyers and specialists in international relations – is not immune to preferring the comfort of the professional silo. Once the concept had taken firm theoretical root in the water-science discourse, I believed it would take another decade or more of engagement with policy-makers before it would be deployed operationally. At the time of writing, we seem to be on schedule. Eighteen years after launching the concept, with its second name of 'virtual water', I feel that we are more than halfway through this second phase of practical adoption of virtual water.

243

Shoot the messenger

My first significant foray into Egyptian politics was in the early 1990s. At a public meeting in London, I challenged a former Egyptian Prime Minister. Egypt was then the inspiration of my theorising on water security. Remember, it was data about Egyptian imports that had enabled me to identify the notion of virtual water. I was excited about the insight, and thought others would be too. Enthusiastically, I suggested to this former Prime Minister that Egypt was (ingeniously) solving its water-resource crisis by importing food. The response I received was not warm. Vehemently, he rebutted my most basic observation, emphatically stating that Egypt was not short of water.

But this was surely nonsense, I thought to myself. Here was Egypt, in the middle of the Middle East and North Africa region, the most water-scarce region in the world; its population growing; its water supply weakening. How could a former Prime Minister be so blithely echoing the UK's own former premier Jim Callaghan, asking 'Crisis, what crisis?' However, the convenor of this particular meeting, a retired Egyptian elder statesman who had been living in London since the mid-1970s, was taken with my idea. He saw my assertion of the food–water link reflected in his own personal experience. He thought (rightly) that I was onto something and so it was that, despite the disagreement with the former Prime Minister, I found myself invited to a meeting on water security in Cairo.

It is quite flattering to be invited somewhere. For people to think your opinion worth an airfare, hotel rates and – the most valuable resource of the powerful – time, is reassuring. We feel on the right track. We feel validated. Recognised. I was particularly gratified as I believed I had an important and fresh idea to share and that the Egyptian audience would be exactly the people who would most benefit from hearing it. So it was that I boarded a flight bound for Cairo. Discussions and details on the meeting were few. I envisaged a workshop of some fifteen or thirty people. I hoped there might be some policy-makers present, be they high-ranking civil servants or even a junior water minister. As my flight touched down at Cairo airport, I was hopeful that the meeting would prove a small but productive step in bringing the idea of virtual water onto the political landscape of the Middle East and

North Africa. This little trip was an unexpected bonus. A gift that could bring only good things. I was mistaken.

I have never been a sufferer from that common anxiety dream where the dreamer attends a meeting – most often in a school classroom or boardroom – only to discover that they are fundamentally ill-equipped. Perhaps they have been supernaturally stripped of the ability to speak, perhaps they are uncontrollably and hysterically late. Often, the poor dreamer has been rendered naked by his or her turbulent unconscious. Such fears have never particularly struck me, either waking or dreaming. A shame. Those fears might have prepared me for the meeting that awaited.

245

I was taken from my hotel and escorted to the imposing Egyptian Ministry of Agriculture. Inside, with no further explanation, I was hurried through a door that seemed too large for the small, informal gathering I was anticipating. On the other side was a large conference hall where at least three hundred people were gathered, including fifty delegates from across the Middle East. Three ministers of state were scheduled to address the keynote session. The only thought that went through my head was 'This is not the place to launch a complex idea.'

I felt uncertain and yet at the same time assured. Sadly, my comfort was short-lived. The Minister of Agriculture stood up. He talked briefly and warmly. His positive message was clear and irrefutable: there was no water shortage in Egypt. I looked forward to helping change his mind, and to hearing what his colleagues had to say. The Minister of Planning rose. His address was, if anything, briefer still. Warmth had given way to heat, but the tune remained the same: there was no water shortage in Egypt. By the time the Minister of Water Resources and Irrigation rose, heat had cooled to resolution. There was more in the speech that time has erased, but all I remember hearing was the reiteration of that unshakeable article of faith: there was no water shortage in Egypt.

There is a wonderful, anxious moment in Shakespeare's *Antony and Cleopatra* when a poor messenger, with grave news for Mark Antony, pauses full of trepidation at the possible ire his words might provoke. Urged on by Antony, he laconically observes, 'The nature of bad news infects the teller.'

I feared infection. My presentation would be redundant.

What they didn't want to hear

In a world of rising national populations, Egypt is a front runner, and the most populous nation in the Middle East. It entered the twentieth century with a perfectly sustainable ten million souls. Today, its population is over eighty million. There is no way that a population can increase by a factor of eight in just one century and remain water and food self-sufficient. Technology and improvements in crop yields just do not run at that pace. The heavily industrialised and wealthy economy of the UK managed a ten-fold increase in yields over two centuries, but even that required the extra boost of UK and EU farm subsidies. When you throw in predictions that suggest Egypt's population will only start to level off at 120 million, you are forced to accept that water and food security must be achieved by trade. There is only enough water in Egypt to support the needs of fifty million people; for the last thirty years, the country has been in severe water deficit, yet water self-sufficiency is the national mantra.

Here is the dark side of virtual water in play. Egypt entered this wholesale trade dependency in absolute ignorance. This transition required several unrelated factors to coincide during the brief but nationally pivotal period of the 1970s. First, the population passed the forty-million mark, pushing the national water provision to the very limits. Second, President Nasser died in 1970. He was succeeded by Anwar Sadat, who did much to rehabilitate

Egypt in the eyes of the industrialised world, not least
by abandoning Soviet patronage, pushing through economic reforms, further secularising politics, and by
signing a peace treaty with Israel. Globally, staple foods
were plentiful, reliable and available at half cost, thanks
predominantly to US and EU subsidies. Every condition
had quietly slipped into place: an unfeedable population; a
cheap and cheerful world food market; improved international relations for Egypt; greater national wealth. Egypt
silently and sharply accelerated its 'imports' of virtual
water. It has never been food and water insecure since.

This is the message I wanted to deliver in Cairo. These
are the ideas that fell on ears finely tuned to absolute
deafness by the unassailable 'truth' of five millennia of
water security.

247

Introducing...the world's longest river

While the Amazon is definitely the world's largest river in
terms of water flow, the Nile most often wins the title of
longest river. The Amazon is a display of awesome natural
force and fertility, with a hundred times the flow of the
Nile; a potent barrage of water vibrantly pumping through
the wet, green South American landscape. By contrast,
the Nile is a sphinxian riddle. It is an implausible, shifting serpent of a river. It glitters impossibly as it uncoils
its delicate waters through the punishing Sahara. What it
lacks in raw energy, it makes up for in magic, mystery and
potent promise.

Its size is not the Nile's fault. No great river runs on
a north–south axis, but rather on an east–west one. The
reason is simple: rainfall. Those rivers in humid zones –
that flow east to west or west to east in the tropics and in
the temperate latitudes – benefit from rainfall and tributaries throughout their entire length. Hence, the great
rivers – the Yangtse in China, the Ganges in India, the

248

Congo in Africa – all run on an east–west axis. All three have flows ten times the gentle Nile. The Nile is born in the south and runs northward to the Mediterranean across a desert, progressively losing water along the way. Deserts do not provide rainfall to increase the flow. Evaporation and drought are constant blights. However, these rivers following a north–south axis traverse major climactic regions. They bring water from humid regions to deserts. They are disproportionately significant for the economies in their basins, as they take water from regions with high rainfall to those with little or none. This is the story of the Nile's journey through Africa, and also the story of Egypt's amazing good fortune.

The Nile has two major tributaries: the Blue Nile and the White Nile. The latter, because it starts the furthest from the delta, is often considered the source of the Nile. The White Nile originates from high in the forests of the tiny plateau state of Rwanda. From there it travels through Lake Victoria, Uganda and north into Sudan before joining the Blue Nile at the capital, Khartoum. If the White Nile has the prestige, the Blue Nile – as the name suggests – has the water. The Blue Nile springs from Lake Tana in the Ethiopian highlands and provides nearly 60 per cent of the Nile's water. Ethiopia, through the mighty Blue Nile and a cluster of other smaller tributaries, provides 90 per cent of the total Nile water and 96 per cent of the transported sediment, the very thing that has made the Egyptian floodplains such fertile land. In this respect, it would be fair to note that Egypt – with nature as co-conspirator – has been draining Ethiopia for millennia.

For five thousand years, the Nile has provided Egypt with a bounteous supply of blue water. This reliable source of water and – through the yearly flooding of the Nile – food was the making of ancient Egyptian society. Since the opening chapters of recorded history, Egypt has had the good fortune of food and water security, despite being in the middle of the desert. Nature always has the capacity to surprise. Five millennia is a long time. The impact on the collective, national psyche is naturally great. No wonder then that a mere half century of unseen water shortage proved insufficient to encourage the country to face facts about its profound water insecurity. No one wants to believe that the truth of time immemorial can be reversed in a few decades.

No wonder also that the Nile is a resource that nations could easily go to war over. The Nile runs through ten nations: Rwanda; Burundi; Tanzania; Kenya; Uganda; Ethiopia; Eritrea; the Democratic Republic of Congo; Sudan; Egypt. Yet only the last two see the economic benefit of it (see box text). This is no small bone of contention among these East African nations, particularly for drought-ravaged Ethiopia, which provides so much of the Nile's nourishment.

249

One dam thing after another

The Egyptians may be wary of talking about water inse-curity, but they are historically very happy to talk about water management. The last century saw several remark-able water-management initiatives, starting with the Low Dam at Aswan in 1902. The pinnacle of Egypt's infrastruc-tural achievements is the largest water-storage reservoir in the world: the High Dam at Aswan. Completed in 1970, the reservoir – named Lake Nasser in Egypt and Lake Nubia where it enters Sudan – holds a colossal 168 cubic kilometres of water when full. We've discussed statisti-cal blindness before. You are, most probably, grappling with this number and trying to view it in terms of water quantities you can understand. Perhaps this will help. A hundred and sixty-eight cubic kilometres is exactly 67.2 million Olympic swimming pools. This is twice the storage capacity of the Three Gorges reservoir on China's Yangtse

River, one of the world's mighty rivers with ten or more times the flow of the Nile.

The High Dam at Aswan tops another poll. Not only is it the largest man-made water store, it also evaporates more water than any other structure in the world. In a single year, the reservoir can lose up to three metres of depth through evaporation. That comes out as 13 cubic kilometres per year. That's about 5.2 million Olympic pools. In Nile terms, it's roughly 15 per cent of the river's average assumed flow of 84 cubic kilometres. In human terms, 13 cubic kilometres is sufficient water to meet the total water-consumption needs of ten million people. Here is the headline: enough water for one in eight Egyptians evaporates from Lake Nasser/Nubia each year.

250

WELCOME TO RIPARIA
The word riparian comes from the Latin 'ripa', meaning 'river bank'. Riparian is literally a reference to the land next to any stream. However, in this analysis of Egypt and the Nile, I use riparian to denote its specific meaning under English common law: the right of landowners to use water that runs through their land. The riparian water rights associated with the Nile are a contentious topic to say the least: Riparia is not an unambiguously happy land. Welcome!

Carving up the waters

The Persian King Xerxes, according to Herodotus, stood at the Hellespont and demanded the disobedient waters receive 300 lashes with the whip. If Britannia genuinely believed herself to rule the waves, then she was foolishly mistaken. No one rules water.

But owning water is an increasingly important idea.

Green water currently resists incorporation into economic models and modes of thought, causing economists (unwisely) to ignore it. Blue water, however, can be captured, pumped and even valued, especially if the water is used for irrigation and other productive purposes. Where whips and royal commands failed, power succeeds. Britannia may or may not have ruled the waves, but thanks to two international agreements, Egypt and Sudan pretty much believe they own the Nile. They certainly captured it for half a century and are currently struggling fiercely to retain ownership.

These agreements were the 1929 Nile Water Agreement and the highly controversial 1959 Agreement for the Full Utilisation of the Nile. I say highly controversial as the 1959 agreement essentially divided ownership of the Nile between

Egypt and Sudan. Egypt got a whopping 75 per cent of the notional water rights, Sudan a more meagre 25 per cent. However, the remaining seven, now eight – as a consequence of Eritrea splitting from Ethiopia in 1993 – nation states through which the Nile and its tributaries run got precisely nothing.

The Egyptian and water

A very long history

When you have five thousand years of experience doing something, it is very hard to accept that the world has changed and what you have done for five millennia might have become a mistake. Although such a long history of successfully managing the seasonal flow of the Nile has undoubtedly given Egyptian officials and scientists considerable insight, it has also lulled the nation into a fatal false sense of water security. The annual natural cycle of the summer flood and recession make the environment more resilient than most. The soils on the banks of the Egyptian Nile are historically rich and deep, fattened annually by the seasonal flooding, full of Ethiopian silt until the 1960s. This suite of meteorological and hydrological factors makes the Egyptian Nile a hydrological and agricultural phenomenon of unique resilience.

251

Egypt is also a unique test case for us in our ongoing encounter with new ideas on water resources. Its river-drainage system is almost entirely dependent on blue surface water coming from outside its national boundaries. This makes it quite easy to conceptualise and analyse. The majority of economies have a blend of blue surface and groundwaters complemented by green water, better known to you and I as rainfall. In such situations, it is more difficult to track the water-managing performance of farmers using irrigation, as the amount of blue water they require each year is dependent on two variables:

their water-use efficiency and the amount of green water helpfully falling from the sky. In Egypt, the green-water variable is removed. It is far easier than is usual, therefore, to see the efficiency of the farmer's water management of blue water.

Ninety-five per cent of Egyptian farmers only manage blue water. In Chapter 3, we saw how 95 per cent of UK farmers only manage green water. With the UK, we talked about a remarkable ten-fold increase in returns on water since 1800. That's quite an impressive yardstick, but Egyptian farmers have been far from shabby in their own efforts to improve water productivity. In just fifty years since 1960, there has been a significant increase in Egyptian returns on blue water. Wheat yields have increased three-fold. As with the UK, the Egyptians were coming from an already-productive starting point. Historically, Egypt has enjoyed high crop and livestock yields.

252

The irrigated farms of Egypt are impressive. The visitor from Europe, unfamiliar with intensively irrigated farmland, cannot fail to be amazed by the absence of waste and the ingenuity of thrift on display. A very high proportion of land is cultivated all year round, in a way that is unimaginable in a European climate. Vegetation and crops are grown throughout the mild Egyptian winters and, water allowing, they prosper in the high, 30-plus-degree-centigrade summers. Our European winters are cruel enough to stop even the grass from growing. Imagine a field of wheat in wintry France! North European farmers manage only a single crop each year. Further, in Egypt, every hectare of farmland has not only fields of crops but also supports livestock at the edges of every field. Each hectare supports two or more cows or buffalo, or up to four sheep or goats. In Europe pasture land only supports the livestock and does not grow field crops beyond the hay used for animal feed. Worse, the livestock often requires supplementary feed from elsewhere. In the UK, we import feed for much of the livestock reared. Consider the environmental nonsense and wastefulness of that approach for a moment. Clearly, the Egyptian farmer is a bastion of water-management virtue, producing two crops and simultaneously achieving levels of livestock management similar to the average northern European farmer.

So, what is taking place?

Let's dig deeper and choose a clear example for our purposes: Egyptian wheat yields. These have increased steadily over the past fifty years, from 2 tonnes per hectare in 1960 to 3 in 1975 and through to the current figure of 6. If there were a world tournament for the efficient use of water in raising wheat, the Egyptian national team

253

	CROP WATER REQUIREMENTS mm/crop period	WHEAT YIELD tonnes/ha	VIRTUAL-WATER CONTENT m³/tonne
ARGENTINA green water	179	2.4	738
AUSTRALIA green water	309	1.9	1588
CANADA green water	339	2.3	1491
EGYPT blue water	570	6.1	930
FRANCE green water	630	7.0	895
TURKEY green water	319	2.1	1531
US mainly green	237	2.8	849
GLOBAL AVERAGE		2.7	1334

Table 5.1 Wheat and water productivity in Egypt and its major trade partners, 1997–2001.
Source: A.K. Chapagain and A.Y. Hoekstra (2003), *Water Footprints of Nations*, Delft: IHE.

would be continual champions. And wheat is globally very important, perhaps even pre-eminent. By tonnage, it is the leading internationally traded crop. For Egypt, wheat is particularly important. The Egyptians consume more wheat per capita than any other nation on earth. That explains why Egypt is both a significant wheat producer and a major global importer.

But we can't make any real progress without some numbers: the wheat in the belly of science. My old friends and modellers Chapagain and Hoekstra have compiled some very interesting comparative data on water management and wheat production.

254

Table 5.1 clearly shows that Egyptian wheat yields are high, and very similar to northern European yields. And that is despite the fact that Egyptian farmers harvest a second crop in the summer and support livestock on each hectare. Similarly, the quantity of virtual water embedded in the wheat is reasonably low, and similar to levels in Europe. Hence, despite incredible water scarcity – or possibly because of it – Egypt's farmers are performing as well as, and in some cases better than, their counterparts in Europe. Moreover, it is very possible that the climate, soil and water-resource conditions in Egypt could respond to further improvements in agronomic practices. Many consider that there is plenty of potential for increases in wheat yields.

Economists are keen to point out that no matter how great the increases in wheat yield, producing wheat is not a sensible use of a scarce resource. But do not imagine these economists are concerned about the environmental impact. Rather, they observe that even if the yields were to increase to 12 tonnes per hectare Egyptian farmers would not be getting nearly as much profit as they would if they turned their attention to higher-value crops for export to foreign markets. The economists argue that it makes far more sense – from an economic perspective – to import cheap wheat and to use the Nile water to grow expensive crops that cannot be grown throughout the year in most parts of the world.

But this argument, like my gambit with the former Egyptian Prime Minister many years ago, fundamentally misunderstands the psyche of the political leadership of Egypt, which can be summarised as: the Egyptian *perception* of food security is paramount. Note I use the word 'perception'. Guaranteeing food security through trade does less to create the national perception of food security than the conspicuous irrigated farmlands with their costly technology and ever-increasing wheat yields. Economically, and perhaps environmentally, this is folly. But politically it is vital. The question remains: for how much longer will this continue? Soon the balance might shift between this show of food security and a national demand for greater economic returns to water.

255

The politics of virtual water

Wheat and the Cold War

It seems that there is no escaping the word 'politics' in this discussion we are having. Wherever there is water, you can be sure to find politicised issues and politicians.

Egypt is already very effectively making up for its water scarcity through virtual-water 'trade'. Currently, it saves about 33 cubic kilometres a year through imports of crops and livestock products. It saves 7 cubic kilometres per year through wheat imports alone. The country's industrial imports probably account for a further 10 cubic kilometres saved. In total, that is 43 cubic kilometres, or enough water for thirty-three million people each year. Given that the current population of Egypt is around eighty million, we can see that virtual water is vital to the country's survival. Without it, the starvation would begin tomorrow.

Do not underestimate the hunger imperative. Deny a man food for three days and he will be reduced to the

DOUBLE-CROPPING
Not an especially short haircut for young men pursuing a career in the army, professional football or simple butchness, but rather a form of multiple cropping in arable farming.

state of a beast: there is nothing he won't do to get food. Possibly the most important priority of every government in every country throughout history has been to fend off starvation and the accompanying anarchy and unrest that follow in its wake. It should come as no surprise, then, that considerations of food security sufficed to reverse a central plank of Egyptian foreign policy.

The post-war partitioning that began in Berlin and spread through Germany and across Europe soon engulfed the world. By the early 1950s, most countries were aligned, to a greater or lesser extent, with either the US or the

256

USSR. Egypt became firmly orientated towards the East after rough treatment from Western European and US governments in the second half of the 1950s. All this changed when Soviet farmers proved incapable of providing the volumes of wheat (and of virtual water) that Egypt wanted to secure through preferential trade. The US and Europe was offering subsidised wheat at half cost. To a hungry nation, this would prove irresistible. Interestingly, there was a brief period when the Soviet Union actually purchased US wheat and delivered it to Alexandria. It was not lost on officials in the Egyptian Ministry of Supply that US wheat bought by its Soviet ally for Egyptian consumption was hardly a secure long-term option.

The inevitable happened and, in the depths of a food deficit in the early 1970s, Egypt swung from East to West. Since that time, Egypt has – after Israel – been the US's closest friend in the MENA region. No single factor determines elemental shifts in foreign policy. It was not food security alone that turned Egypt towards the West. But food security and invisible virtual-water 'trade' were key contributing factors in re-orienting Egypt's foreign policy after 1970. And yet this is rarely noted in water-science or political history.

The unnameable

Making food policy in Egypt is tormenting. The politicians
are trapped in the sanctioned discourse, built up over five
millennia. Egypt is not short of water. This 'truth' is jointly
owned by consumers, producers and the government, and
is helpfully fuelled by a bullish media. This 'knowledge' is
'power' in the Foucaultian sense. The politicians know this
and therefore cannot contradict it. They are caught between
the demands of reality and subservience to the constructed
truth. Hence sensible, level-headed ministers continue to
stand up and declare that Egypt is not short of water.

And this is why virtual water has been so vital to the
Egyptian state and its ruling class. Virtual water is, as I have
repeated many times now, invisible and silent. Both economically and politically, it cannot be seen or heard unless
you are looking or listening out for it. It is perhaps the only
trade and resource policy that can be followed without even
needing to discuss it publicly. It is so covert that although
existing since the earliest days of human civilisation, it only
acquired a name in 1991. For the Egyptian policy-makers,
the invisible actuality of virtual-water 'trade' provided an
invaluable *breathing space* in their potentially explosive
and emotionally unpredictable water sector.

Economies need such breathing space in political
processes in order to perform the miracle of modern
civilisation: transforming from an underdeveloped to a
diversified economy and, in the process, lifting the majority of the population out of poverty. Consider the plight of
the politician. He or she faces demands from society and
the economy that are too numerous and yet often reasonable. The painful allocative call of the politician faced
with insufficient resources to meet all these demands is
always a tough decision that will displease more than it
will please. Small wonder that politicians seek to bluff,
defer and obfuscate. They need breathing spaces in which
to operate and survive. With political smoke and mirrors,

257

they must distract us from the bad news, as the nurse distracts the small child when giving them a vaccine jab. When it comes to water resources, the politicians are forced to turn a blind eye towards the over-abstraction of local, renewable blue water. In Egypt's case, that means the Nile. Most nations have had to endure several decades of punishing the local water environment to buy sufficient time to diversify the economy and urbanise the populace. The displaced rural population can no longer farm; they migrate to the cities and, it is to be hoped, a diversifying urban economy which provides jobs for them. This

258

is the path trodden by the industrialised nations during the nineteenth century. Today, many other countries are walking this path, albeit in a much more water-stressed planet. And virtual water provides the cover, in the narrow context of water resources, that allows the developmental transition to occur without the population ever knowing how reckless they are being with their water, how close they are to starving and, most important of all, without the beleaguered politicians having to expend any vital political capital on explaining any of this to their citizens.

Outside this complicity stands the environmentalist. Principled, moral and honest, this weasely use of invisible virtual water is anathema. The environmentalist is a guardian angel in an industrialised economy, highlighting our errors and trying to pull us back from the brink of seriously foolhardy behaviour (often succeeding). But in the developing world, the environmentalist's rigid moral framework is an unaffordable luxury. Environmentalists do not want to recognise the toxic water politics in non-diversified economies.

There are things that the politician of a developing economy cannot even contemplate. Population control is one such. Though it makes pure environmental sense, how can a politician sell such a concept to communities that rely on large families as the cornerstone of their immediate economy? Similarly, what politician can ask irrigating farmers to stop pumping and diverting water for environmental reasons when to do so would mean death for their families? Politicians do not avoid these policies out of compassion, but out of calculated fear. If they demand that the farmers cease to pump the water, then they will be blamed for the consequent death and disaster. But experience shows that if politicians allow their populations to continue on a path to ecological catastrophe, the political fallout is less than if they had attempted to avert it. People accept the exhaustion of a water resource. They do not blame the politicians. Most often, they blame the capricious gods. The gods are the oldest scapegoats of failing ruling elites.

259

The virtual-water addiction

It is often said that the 1970s was where it all went wrong. Certainly, the oil-price shocks and the subsequent spike in the price of wheat and other commodities unbalanced several global economies, including that of Egypt. Costly and potentially risky initiatives, such as a plan to synergise Sudanese land and water with Egyptian labour and technology, were abandoned in favour of the quick fix of US-donated and low-cost PL 480 grain. Only ten years later would this expedient dependency on cheap wheat imports begin to trouble the Egyptian government. In the 1980s, an assault was launched on the ascendant importance of wheat imports in the national diet. The formerly regulated economy established under the pro-Soviet regime of President Nasser was giving way to the international tide of pro-market reform. The global cotton market was heavily distorted and, with the local market price rising, wheat became an attractive option for farmers. They responded enthusiastically and, with government encouragement, expanded the areas for wheat crops and drove up yields and returns to water.

GIVE FOOD A CHANCE
In 1954, US President Eisenhower signed Public Law 480 into law. Often abbreviated as PL 480, and referred to by President Kennedy as 'food for peace', the law provides a funding stream for international food aid. Hence PL 480 grain.

There was no subsequent decline in Egyptian wheat imports, but this was due to the rapid demographic expansion of the period. That imports have frequently levelled off is a testament to the great advances made by farmers in wheat productivity. Since the early 1990s, virtual-water 'imports' in wheat have remained level. Conversely, there has been a considerable growth in virtual water embedded in grain imports of maize and soya – used for animal feed – and in highly water-intensive livestock imports.

Three things you can say, and one you can't

As long as the Nile flows steadily and there is bread on the table, there is nothing you can do to convince people that Egypt has run out of water. Any politician who questioned these two certainties would be committing an act of political suicide. When you think of political correctness, you don't often think of water. That, however, is the great unmentionable in Egyptian politics. But what can be said in the current political climate?

There are three clear measures that Egypt takes in terms of water and food management, and these are very openly up for discussion and debate. The first is the issue of Nile water flows. Egypt guards its share of the flow with the tenacity of a beast in a very tight corner. The country has dominated Nile transboundary international relations with the other nine riparians, as well as having strong links with global institutions, including the World Bank. Historically, Egypt has been very effective in dictating the pace of co-operation with, and investment in, water infrastructure in upstream Nile states. Unsurprisingly, this has been with the objective of maintaining its disproportionate share of the flow. In the past decade, this apparently eternal asymmetry has weakened. The second measure is Egypt's phenomenal increases in crop productivity and returns to water. The third is the government's adoption of low-cost food and fuel policies. These enable impoverished families to survive periods of painful inflation.

Here is the sanctioned discourse: Nile water flows, higher yields and low consumer prices. But the elephant in the room is virtual water. This is the fourth measure that, like the imaginary fourth wall at the front of the stage in a theatre, cannot be seen, yet is the most important in the whole edifice. Without virtual-water 'imports', Egypt would have collapsed into food and water insecurity. Instead, virtual water keeps food on the table with its trademark immaculate invisibility.

How easy it is for us on the outside to accept this reality. How hard for those within. The political classes know that solutions to the problem of water security will, in future, come from outside their own water sector. This is not something of which they can easily persuade the population. Most politicians also understand that it will be a long and bumpy political journey to the point at which it is possible to express such ideas in the official discourse. The truth is that Egypt's national contribution to its own water and food security lies not in diplomatic bullying over control of the Nile flows, nor in the impressive hydraulic and agricultural achievements of the high-yield irrigated farmlands. Rather, it will prove to be a diverse and strong national economy that will ensure, through trade, that Egypt remains water- and food-secure. That is a very difficult idea for a politician to sell to a population. Meanwhile, it is best to keep quiet and let virtual water do all the work. In the background, the process is in train. The proof of its success is in the survival of Egypt's political economy despite its limited resource endowments and awkward demography.

261

The future for the pharaohs

The headline figures are unarguable. Egypt has enough water for fifty million people. At the time of writing, its population is eighty million and is expected to reach one hundred and twenty million. Since the late 1960s, the country has been increasingly dependent on virtual-water 'imports' to make up the difference. Currently, about 40 per cent of its water needs are met through virtual-water 'trade'.

What we know for sure

Egypt suffers from a water-demand gap that results from demographics. Simply, there are too many people in relation to water, and that number is going up not down. We can be absolutely certain of the current population size, and we can be reasonably certain about future growth. Another relatively certain trend is the diversification of the Egyptian economy. Egypt's economy will continue to diversify in the future, not as rapidly as the East Asian economies, but it will not suffer the stagnant pace of sub-Saharan African nations either. This diversification holds the key to Egypt's water and food security.

But, unfortunately, that doesn't sit easily with the Egyptian national self-image. Egypt wants its food and water security to come through the macho, literal route of producing enough internally. Such an endeavour, if it were possible, would involve phenomenal leveraging of technology, capital and natural resources. Even then, it would fail in the long term. There is something highly appealing about awe-inspiring irrigated fields and technology-driven hydraulic achievements. But they are, to labour the point, a waste of good resources. The solution will be economic. Currently, the Egyptian psyche is not quite ready to be proud that Egyptian collective human resources will provide their food and water security. But the day is not so far away.

And what we don't

If those are the knowns, what are the unknowns?
First, we do not know what the future holds in terms of
improvements in Egyptian water productivity. Crop yields
are already high and have risen very usefully in the past
half century, but there is certainly room for improvement.
My prediction? Expect to see crop yields rise by 20 per cent
in terms of volume, and much more in terms of economic
value. These yield increases will be matched by proportionate improvements in water productivity. I wouldn't
be surprised if there was the potential for Egyptian water
productivity to increase by 50 per cent by volume. If so,
it would give Egypt the farming potential to feed at least
seventy million people. That, I emphasise, would be the
best-case scenario. It would be impressive. But it would
also be insufficient. Water and food security for seventy
million when you have a population of a hundred and
twenty million is not a recipe for success. It is a recipe for
riots in the streets without economic diversification.

263

The price of food

The external factors affecting Egypt's future food and
water security are even harder to make accurate predictions about. Predictions are the pursuit of fools, but I will
not be around in 2050 to be shamed by my estimates, so I
write with the impunity of mortality.

International food prices will be of great importance,
naturally. These will rise, but not as quickly as they
should. Economic and trade distortions, such as the EU CAP
and its successors and US food subsidies, will continue to
keep international food prices artificially low. As a major
importer of wheat, Egypt's economy as a whole would
benefit from higher food-commodity prices. The increased
income from food exports would counterbalance the rise
in food import costs. But global politics dominated by
the industrialised economies will not allow food-price

increases. The Egyptian leadership has been very nimble in ensuring that Egypt has kept abreast of and participated fully in the WTO deliberations over the past two decades. Egyptian officials have occupied, and continue to occupy, key positions in the WTO. Egyptians are tenacious in their diplomacy, and often successful at getting their way.

The future of Riparia

264

Nowhere is this more apparent than in the negotiations over Nile basin hydropolitics. As mentioned, Egypt has dominated the Nile throughout history. Since the start of the twentieth century, this dominance has been formalised in Nile water agreements. Egypt inherited its Nile hegemony from the British colonial presence; it has not deviated since it became master of its regional destiny. The country's asymmetric relationship with Ethiopia is a marvel of geography and politics. Everything is asymmetrically arranged: blue-water resources, socio-economic development and levels of global engagement. All are skewed in favour of Egypt. Eighty per cent of the water in Egypt comes from Ethiopian tributaries. Ethiopia only uses a few per cent of the Nile flow.

Most significant, though, is the asymmetry in socio-economic development. Egypt is not an advanced industrialised nation, but it is a mighty powerhouse when compared to Ethiopia. In only one area is the advantage on Ethiopia's side: green water. Egypt has almost none. Ethiopia probably has access to in excess of 80 cubic kilometres of green water annually. It's a considerable amount, and about equal to the amount of blue water it naturally loses down the Blue Nile to Sudan and Egypt. I will stop there. I don't want to pre-empt my analysis of Ethiopia further, and we'll return to it very soon.

The relationship between Egypt and Sudan has greater parity, and therefore greater potential for political friction.

Sudan is the only country apart from Egypt to have endorsed the 1959 Nile water agreement. Small wonder. It is also the only other country to have benefited from the agreement. But Sudan is far from pleased with its 25 per cent of the Nile flow. Egypt is resolute. In Nile Framework Agreement meetings, it refuses to compromise its water security. In other words, the Nile belongs to Egypt, and Egypt is going to do everything politically possible to keep it that way. Fifty years on, the 1959 agreement is still not up for debate.

A word of warning: the past is never capable of predicting the future. We cannot use past experience to predict the future of Nile hydropolitics. Yet, we can be reasonably certain that the war for which I searched will not materialise. Virtual water delivered an armistice for the water wars without a single shot being fired, or anyone even noticing. That said, Egypt cannot continue to monopolise the Nile indefinitely. The upstream Nile states will manage to negotiate a share of the flow, though I imagine it will be quite meagre compared to Egypt's current 75 per cent. Sudan has already chipped away at Egypt's share of the flow by commissioning a series of dams and reservoirs that probably lose at least 2 cubic kilometres each year through evaporation. The politics of water, like water itself, are rarely still.

265

The Nile flow

The fallibility and folly of forecasts is amply illustrated by the story of the Nile flows. The High Aswan Dam construction was underpinned by a calculation of the average annual flow. Since 1988, the flow has been consistently higher. This might at first glance seem to be an unambiguously good thing. Certainly, after some shocking low flows in the early 1980s, the increased flow has done wonders for Egyptian concerns over Nile water security. But currently much of that water is lost. Water doesn't sit still while we frantically try and work out what to do with it. Turn your back and it is off. In this case, the western edge of Lake Nasser/Nubia has been subject to flooding across the Toshka spillways and into the desert. At least 5 cubic kilometres on average are lost in this way each year. That is two million Olympic swimming pools.

Eagerly, the Egyptian government has been planning for expanded irrigated farmland, to utilise all this bonus water evidenced by the high flows. Egyptian water engineers have more realistic expectations. Five cubic kilometres is enough to meet the water needs of at least four million people each year. With effective reuse in irrigation and improved water productivity, that amount could be stretched out to water and feed perhaps five million. But Egypt is already 'importing' more than 30 cubic kilometres of virtual water each year. More worrying, it will need perhaps 60 cubic kilometres each year by 2050. Demographics will push this figure up; water-productivity improvements will push it down. The fact of the matter is that Egypt will be expending an unsustainably large amount of international political capital, not to mention hard financial capital, on securing the extra flow and utilising it in irrigation. Such a policy programme for the future cannot fail to generate stressful political situations with the other riparians and the international community as a whole. And even then, the country will potentially be about 40 cubic kilometres short of water self-sufficiency.

266

The hydraulic solution alone is for Egypt insupportable, unjustifiable and doomed to failure. The virtual-water solution has more promise, as it has proved to be suitably flexible and responsive. Rather than scrabbling for ever-greater, unreasonable dominance of the Nile flow, Egypt should be pouring its energy into economic diversification. By doing so, the demographic problem becomes a demographic solution. Egypt will have sufficient human resources to develop exportable goods and services, preferably of high value. In exchange, it will be able to 'import' virtual water. This will not only be cheaper and easier. It will also lead to far better diplomatic relations with the other riparian states, and should prove environmentally kinder. The only true barrier to this is the national preoccupation with the chimera of water and food self-sufficiency.

Climate change

Egypt is lucky. It barely has any rainfall to lose. Certainly, green water is of very minor economic or agricultural significance. Less certain is the potential harm that higher temperatures will do to crop yields through increased evaporation and evapo-transpiration. We cannot model future Nile flows with any precision, but evidence suggests that the Nile annual flow could be reduced by a figure in the region of 10 cubic kilometres. This is a volume of significance but not of strategic significance. Possibly this decline in Nile flows will give Egypt the impetus to turn from the dead-end of attempting to meet its water needs through freshwater resources and to embrace the virtual water solution. Meanwhile, most climate models predict that Egypt will continue to enjoy the enhanced Nile flows experienced since the late 1980s. Consensus is rare in the world: science is no exception.

267

A tale of two conferences

How far have we travelled since I stood up and delivered a speech no one wanted to hear in a large conference hall in Egypt over fifteen years ago?

Very far, in fact.

Allow me to provide a highly illustrative example.

In 2006, I found myself standing in a very different conference from my Cairo experience many years earlier, and in a very different part of the world. I was attending the

World Water Forum in Mexico City. This event is very significant in the water professional's calendar. It is a bubbling soup of different ideas and approaches. We go to speak, but also to listen. Idea-sharing and communication, even in the supposedly rarefied atmospheres of science and international politics, are not as developed as one might wish. We have not come as far as we think from the days of balding apes jealously guarding their hunter-gatherer techniques from the prying eyes of other tribes. The regressive ethos of competition too often dogs and hinders human advancement. At this conference, my failed talk in Cairo all those years ago was very much in the forefront of my mind, as I had been invited on arrival in Mexico City to be on a panel organised by the Egyptian Minister of Water and his senior colleagues. The topic surprised me.

Sometimes a smile starts with the mouth. Other times, it begins in a deeper place. The gut or the mind.

What was the topic of this session being organised by the Egyptian minister? It was 'virtual water' in Egypt and the Middle East region. Progress. This was discursive politics in action – slow and unpredictable.

~~~~~~ *PART 2* ~~~~~~
Vietnam: apocalypse reversed

'Nothing makes the crops grow like peace.'

A world of veterans

We've all been to Vietnam. After the Second World War, the bout of mechanised killing known variously as the Vietnam War or Second Indochina War must be the most frequently cinematically depicted conflict of all time. Unlike the so-called Second War World, the conflict is never shown as positive. Cultural history has recorded it as a terrible battle without sense, without purpose and without morals. Even today, nothing sends a greater shudder down the collective spine of the American public than a reminder of the outcome in Vietnam.

Mercifully, our story of Vietnam does not end with the bloody destruction of the 1960s and 1970s, which saw the population literally decimated in a decade. In fact, that is where the story begins. When North and South Vietnam were finally unified on 30 April 1975, 118 years of warfare came to an end. Continuously, for over a century, this unfortunate land had been the seat of fierce conflict between the indigenous people and a sequence of invaders.

269

In the thirty-five years since the end of the Vietnam War, the country has been rehabilitated to such an extent that there is barely any similarity between the increasingly prosperous, well-ordered society of this thriving South-east Asian state and the images of senseless carnage and destruction played out in films such as *Apocalypse Now*, *Platoon* and *Forrest Gump*. And nowhere has Vietnam proven more successful than in agriculture. Here is the headline: from near-collapse agriculturally in 1975, Vietnam entered the twenty-first century as the second-largest exporter of rice globally, accounting for 20 per cent of international trade. Naturally, such an achievement is built upon considerable improvements in water efficiency.

My story of Vietnam, therefore, is a positive, if little-known, one.

But first, the bad news...

The Domino Theory

With the mid-twentieth-century wars at an end, and the uneasy alliance between the capitalist allies and the communist USSR crumbling, there was a massive scramble by the East and West for spheres of influence in the political vacuum created across the world by the collapse of imperial Europe. After the Communist Party comprehensively defeated the Nationalists in the Chinese civil war, global attention turned to the smaller states of South-east Asia. Here was where the Cold War would heat up.

Western, and specifically American, thinking was encapsulated in the domino theory. The fear was that communist China, and communist uprisings in Korea and Vietnam, would tip the whole region into the communist camp, culminating in the collapse of India, much in the same way as a line of dominoes will fall in turn. The theory was that each collapse into communism would make the next collapse swifter and more inevitable. The US, therefore, was resolved to stop any further dominoes from falling. It was this attitude that led to US involvement in what might otherwise have remained internal civil wars first in Korea and then Vietnam. If Korea didn't prove to be a success for the US, it was at least not a failure. Today, the country remains divided, as in 1954, between a communist north and a capitalist south. Vietnam was to be a very different story.

A very brief history of post-war Vietnam

The reason for dwelling on the violent history of South-east Asia until the mid-1970s is because what has happened since has been yet another mega-experiment in the field of water productivity. We have seen how the UK and the EU, as well as the US, experimented with incentives and subsidies to stimulate and protect farmers after the shock of war in the 1940s. The farmers responded with unprecedented achievements in water productivity. China and India worked their own water-productivity miracles in the 1960s and 1970s. Egypt too has had its water-productivity successes. Next we shall see that Vietnam achieved even greater increases in water productivity than any of these remarkable food-production endeavours once it was released from a century of intrusion and violence.

History clearly relates what happened. The US was defeated. South Vietnam turned communist. But the events that followed the end of the war are often forgotten. Rather than driving the uninterrupted domino-effect spread of Chinese communism, Vietnam clashed with China over Cambodia. That is not to say that Vietnam did not remain communist. The nation was resolutely communist, and remained a member of Comecon until it was wound down in the 1990s. However, Vietnam's close communist ally was not China but the Soviet Union. Hence, when the USSR and its European communist satellite states turned west-wards and embraced (to varying extents) capitalism and the market economy, Vietnam was isolated. Rather than orientating towards China, Vietnam looked east for new partners. It liberalised its trading relations, devalued its currency and sought investors. Vibrant and wealthy Japan was only too happy to oblige, needing countries in which it could invest the capital generated by its trade surplus. Other nations, including the US, followed suit.

271

Vietnam's relations with China have improved con-siderably. This probably says more about changes within China than those within Vietnam. China has brought Viet-nam under its influence through economic ambition rather than military might. Trade between the two economies has grown rapidly, and they are currently in partnership to establish the biggest free-trade zone in the world. China excels at playing the long game. Chinese leader Zhou Enlai was not being glib when, in response to being asked his opinion of the French Revolution's impact, he replied, 'It's too early to tell.' China plays politics with a glacial pace and patience. In Vietnam, it allowed three major rivals to exhaust and impoverish themselves in a destructive war that would drain their resources and seriously damage their reputations.

Vietnamese agriculture

Vietnam has transformed its economy and developed strong regional and international relations since the end of the war in 1975. Nowhere, though, has it succeeded with such rapidity and intensity as in agriculture. From the moment Saigon fell to the Viet Minh in 1975, the agricultural sector has expanded impressively. Even while the rest of the economy developed but sluggishly and uncertainly, agriculture roared ahead. Economic diversification, so vital in the case of Egypt, has been tentatively taking place, particularly since the death of Soviet communism in the early 1990s. But in Vietnam, the achievement of improved water productivity has been exceptional.

If you remember from Chapter 3, the farmers of the UK have generated spectacular increases in green-water productivity. Similarly, Egyptian farmers have clearly demonstrated the substantial improvements possible on already high crop yields, with proportional returns on blue water. But Vietnam matches both economies. It has achieved incredible returns to both green and blue water.

Vietnam has plenty of water. In addition to its rich water resources, it has a temperature that is ideal for crops, averaging between 25 and 30 degrees centigrade throughout the year. Crops don't take vacations. If they did, they'd head for Vietnam. For the first three decades after the world war that ended in 1945, this potential bounty was concealed by the local colonial and civil wars and by conflict with the US. No one thrives during war, except the vultures. Warfare is very far from conducive to improvements in farm productivity. Quite the reverse, in fact. But once the horror of war has passed, untapped potential rushes to the fore. It happened in Europe when, encouraged by EEC/EU and other national agricultural subsidies, there was a remarkable post-war surge in productivity. So with Vietnam after 1975.

Nothing allows the crops to grow like peace. Farmers are not dynamic and entrepreneurial, and I mean that as a compliment. They benefit most from secure and stable environments. The more risks that can be eliminated, the stronger and more productive the farming industry will be. Despite its wealth of resources, in 1975 Vietnam was a rice importer, buying 350,000 tonnes annually. Within the short space of 14 years of peace, Vietnam became the third-largest rice exporter in the world. By the end of the century, it ranked second.

How was this achieved? One factor that cannot be ignored is that Vietnam practises its own highly cus-

273

tomised variant of communism. Today, while the nation underwent a series of economic reforms in the 1980s and 1990s, Vietnam remains a one-party state. That party is the Communist Party. The command-and-control economy may have given way to a socialist-orientated market economy, but Vietnam remains a tightly ordered society, the product of blending Asian conformity with egalitarian principles. As our analysis of China has shown, when the need to kowtow to the ballot box is removed, and unity of purpose and action is primary, economic achievements can be great and fast. Personal liberty suffers; much common good comes about.

The lay of the land

Vietnam has nothing in common with Egypt. The latter has perpetual desert, blessed only by the mystical Nile and its majestic delta. There is no other surface drainage to speak of in Egypt. If in Egypt you are never far from the nearest handful of sand, in Vietnam there is nowhere that receives less than a metre of rainfall annually. The hills and mountains can experience 2 metres each year. Additionally, Vietnam has not one but two mighty rivers, as well as countless smaller ones offering opportunities for irrigation and crop production. It is also very rich in green water. Let's meet the Vietnamese rivers. They are less famous than the others we have discussed so far, but they are every bit as significant.

The first is the Mekong. It is a large river, with eight times the flow of the Nile. It takes monsoon waters from the five equally well-watered nations in the Mekong basin: China, Burma, Thailand, Laos and Cambodia. What really gives the Mekong pre-eminence over the Nile is the fact that it gains a considerable amount of its water in the vast lowlands of the basin. Why is that important? Consider

 274

the Nile. After it departs the seasonally humid highlands of East Africa, it flows for 2000 kilometres through desert. That's an awfully long time out in the heat. The result? Much water is lost by evaporation. The Mekong, however, gets stronger and stronger because rainfall more than compensates for the losses to the atmosphere.

The second river is the Red River, so named because of the heavy silt deposits that give it a rusty colouration. However, you would be forgiven for thinking that the name came from the fierce anger of the flow. It's an unpredict-able and capricious river, and floods with considerable violence. Curiously, it has a close association with warfare. It was an important late-nineteenth-century trade route for Europe into China. This strategic importance provoked France into military conflict with Vietnam. It was a conflict that France won, and as a result Vietnam as a coherent entity disappeared from the maps and into bloodshed for nearly a century.

An unfortunate similarity

Vietnam and Egypt do have one thing in common. People. And too many of them. Vietnam is reproducing itself into a demographic crisis. By 1985, the population was twice that of 1960. Bearing in mind that an astounding 10 per cent of all Vietnamese were killed in the war with the US, that's an impressive growth rate. Although the growth rate has slowed, the current population is 86 million. A hundred million Vietnamese is, environmentally, a frightening prospect. A hundred and fifty is unthinkable. That is not to say that Vietnam could not be food self-sufficient even at a hundred and fifty million. It almost certainly could. The problem is the rest of the world is relying on Vietnam's food exports. Right now, Vietnam provides the rice for two hundred million people around the globe. Vietnam's role as rice chef for the world and its rapidly expanding population are on a collision course. If Vietnam stops exporting, others will eventually be rice-scarce.

275

There would also be stark consequences for Vietnam's economy. By 2005, Vietnam was the world's second-largest exporter of rice, shipping out 5 million tonnes each year. That is a big bowl of rice. Financially, that accounts for more than 6 per cent of Vietnam's export earnings. The significance for everyone outside Vietnam is that these exports comprise 20 per cent of the world rice trade. We should all be very interested in anything that compromises Vietnam's ability to export rice.

Very good with water, very quickly

Vietnam's annual exports of 5 million tonnes of rice each year is very impressive. More impressive is the fact that in 2007, the country produced 36 million tonnes. That is more rice than global trade in its entirety.

The question remains: what did Vietnam manage to do to turn itself from a rice importer with a fractured society and economy in 1975 into an agricultural powerhouse only three decades later?

Of course, the answer lies partly in water. And farmers. Both of which Vietnam has in abundance. Farmers are, as I hope I have made increasingly clear, the unsung heroes of

water management. They are modern alchemists, transforming land and water into ever-greater crop yields. Their
magic is vital; pray it continues. Thousands of years ago,
humans diversified their activities. Some made spears.
Others painted the walls of the cave. The farmers kept
everyone watered and fed, and still do.

This book is not the place for a detailed discussion of
the market economic system. During my life, I have heard
the conventional wisdom twist back and forth in favour
of and against the market economy. One decade we are
all Keynesians. The next, followers of Friedman. I am
no economist, and I greatly respect the discipline, while
doubting many of its practitioners. Yet here is something
I can state with reasonable confidence, based on my own
observation of some facts, and on clear evidence from
history. Farming responds well to a command economy
that assumes they are making an important contribution and one that is fundamental to the sustainable
intensification of natural resources. Please don't read
this as a call for Stalinist collectivisation: that version
of communism was even more blind to the environment
than market capitalism. The point I am trying to make
is that farmers operate best in an environment that
guarantees secure prices and a reasonably predictable
demand for their output. They will always find ways of
producing more crops and livestock to meet a demand
which is attractively priced. If they need to do this more
efficiently, and to produce more from less, they will do it.
They don't need the goad of competition. The post-war
experiment in European farming and the breathtaking
improvements in Vietnamese agriculture over the past
three decades are proof enough.

Though farmers wield considerable control over natural resources, their influence in other areas is limited,
to say the least. They have no control over the factors
that determine the prices of their products. Worse, any

276

influence they have on price lessens with the increased globalisation of trade. The marketing and manufacturing of food commodities is the world's largest industry, yet farmers themselves do not have an effective voice at the top-table discussions. Multinational corporations control this process, and do so in a super-league populated by only a few organisations. There is very little room at the top. The market intelligence and finance is kept far from all but the largest farmers. No farmers in Asia or Africa have any influence on the global food market. The prices created on the global market are fickle. Every time they go down some poor farmers of the world suffer. In some cases, they die. Unstable prices are a hazard that farmers cannot control, and one that can destroy their productivity, and crush their livelihoods swiftly and permanently. This is the plight of many of the world's farmers.

277

However, as discussed earlier, the picture is some-what rosier for those farmers within subsidised regimes. Farmers are not complicated beings. Their instinct is to produce food. If prices are favourable, they produce more. If it will bring tangible benefit to themselves and their families, they will ensure that they utilise all their inputs with greater and greater efficiency. In this way, continual improvements in water productivity are hard-wired into farmers. But this is dependent upon a secure environment and economy. All input supplies must be stable, and not just labour. A network for transporting and marketing produce must be in place, and be unchallenged. Internal markets must function, and there must be the export opportunities for any surplus. Finally, farmers need to know that they can do all this production and selling at reliable and reasonable prices. Vietnam in 1975 could supply none of these essentials, but it put them all in place with a speed and enthusiasm that few could have predicted.

Hence Vietnam achieved an almost four-fold increase in rice production. It did this by working water hard. Only 20 per cent of Vietnamese land is flat and suitable for farming, and so double- (and occasionally triple-) cropping has proven essential. During the summer monsoon, the rain-fed crop yields have doubled from 2.5 tonnes per hectare to 5. Even where the yields were high, productivity has improved. There were farms at the end of the war producing a single crop of 3 tonnes per hectare. By the close of the twentieth century, the same farms were producing three rice crops per year with yields of each of them between 6 and 7 tonnes per hectare. Some farmers were getting over 20 tonnes per hectare. Such hotspots have been the main drivers of Vietnam's impressive increase in production.

278

A very nice Vietnamese takeaway

The news from Vietnam today is very positive. I find it strange that more people do not trumpet this intriguing country's journey from war-ravaged wreck to vital contributor to world food supplies. Its neighbour Thailand has made a similar journey over a similar period. In 1975, it exported fewer than a million tonnes. Today, it is the only country that exports more rice than Vietnam, shifting 7.4 million tonnes in 2007. Together, Vietnam and Thailand have met half of the 25-million-tonne-per-annum increase in global demand since 1975.

We should be applauding Vietnam. We should certainly be looking very closely at how it uses its water. We need to ask ourselves how a country ranked sixtieth in the world by national income has managed to improve its water productivity three-fold in three decades. Vietnam's 5 million tonnes of exported rice represents 10 cubic kilometres of virtual water. That's almost enough to meet the total water demands of any country with more than seven million people. The instinct of farmers is, as I say, to produce food. By doing so, farmers 'export' virtual water. So it has been since the earliest days of civilisation. Initially, they exported merely to the towns. When cities grew up, they did so watered by the virtual-water 'exports' of nearby rural farmers. Vietnam demonstrates how farmers are happy to 'provide' virtual water to consumers on the other side of the world, provided the infrastructure and political climate are in place to facilitate such trade.

This is the positive story of virtual water. A country rich in green and blue water is able, through the international food trade, to contribute significantly and invaluably to global stability. The negative side of the coin is that barely anyone even notices.

279

The price of rice

Everyone likes rice. Dieters complain about pasta. The gluten-intolerant steer clear of bread. But no one can fault rice. It is the most staple of the staple crops.

The price of rice periodically grabs the headlines. These price spikes should not be seen as harbingers of a global food crisis. We have encountered many crop-commodity prices that are fixed politically and not by the market. Rice is no exception.

Globally, the market for rice is small compared to other grains and cereals. Roughly 35 million tonnes are traded each year: this accounts for less than 10 per cent of the total annual global grain trade, which was 360 million tonnes in 2007. The prices are also generally far less subject to price distortions than those of rice's crop cousins, wheat, maize and soya.

However, distortions do occur, and the rice world is still reeling from a sudden price shock in 2008. But it was fuelled by speculation and exacerbated by some serious distortions in the way the commodity is produced and traded. Japan is a major rice consumer with a deep preference for its own very costly rice. The country is locked into a long-term contract to accept low-quality rice from the US if it insists on not opening its market to the blast of cheap rice. Japan has been obliged to accept this arrangement, as it unbendingly protects its own rice producers for understandable aesthetic, social and political reasons. Most often, the obligatory imports are held until they are no longer suitable for human consumption and are then fed to livestock. Even at the height of the rice-supply crisis in 2008, Japan didn't divert this un-needed rice onto the global market, where prices were soaring.

The economist hates impediments to trade. Nevertheless, the impediments make political sense to those that install them. Politicians are not economists or scientists, and their criteria for making decisions are different from those of the siloed professionals. When it comes to rice, any price spikes are worsened because they exist in a relatively small global market where there are massive distortions. These distortions are, for example, the hyper-protection of Japanese rice producers and the exacerbation of the consequences of these distortions by the compensating, but un-needed purchases of unpreferred rice from protected US rice producers. To an economist, this is evident madness. To the politicians, this is diplomacy. It is business as usual, and its eccentricities – provided they do not inflame the anger of the electorate – can be dismissed with a shrug of the shoulders.

Many things would not be better if the economists ruled the world. But the price movements of the global rice market would, at least, be a little more straightforward.

~~~~~~~~~~~~~~~~~~~~~~~ *PART 3* ~~~~~~~~~~~~~~~~~~~~~~~
Ethiopia: apocalypse now

The motherland

Lucy comes from the Awash Valley, Ethiopia. She is short, measuring only three feet, eight inches. She is quite light, weighing only 30 kilograms. And she is about 3.2 million years old.

Lucy is the name for the skeletal remains of an *Australopithecus afarensis*. She is one of our prehistoric ancestors and comes from a time, according to analyses of her knee shape and skull size, after humans had decided that living in trees was old hat but before we had got down to any serious thinking.

281

If Egypt is ancient, Ethiopia is prehistoric. All mankind is descended from one common ancestor: the smart money is on that ancestor originating in this large landlocked nation on the Horn of Africa. Unlike most sub-Saharan African nations, Ethiopia has existed as a coherent state for three millennia. It features, in corrupted and misunderstood form, in Greek mythology and the Hebrew scriptures. The royal line claims (dubiously) to descend from King Solomon and the Queen of Sheba. If age were the only determinant, Ethiopia would be the world's most powerful nation.

But age isn't everything.

Ethiopia has been blighted by an extreme case of national bad luck. Despite being the water tower of the Nile, Ethiopia uses only 5 per cent of the Nile flow. Every year it exports over 80 cubic kilometres of very high-quality water downstream to Sudan and Egypt. That is enough water to make Ethiopia's 78 million people food and water self-sufficient overnight. Similarly, if Ethiopian farmers used even half of that quantity of water to grow well-priced food commodities for export, the nation would become instantly wealthy. Instead, it is one of the poorest economies in the world. Per-capita annual income averages around $333. That is less than a dollar a day.

Poverty breeds poverty. The economy remains undiversified, with over 40 per cent of the GDP coming from agriculture. Many rural communities are peasantry pure and simple. They eke out a subsistence existence on small rain-fed plots. Life is short. Starvation and illness are a way of life. The urban populations fare much better, and Ethiopia's economy is actually growing rapidly, but a global order that favours the strong and penalises the weak does much to hold Ethiopia's development in check.

282

Cry me a river...
Egypt received the Nile from Ethiopia in humanity's prehistory, and is demonstrating no inclination to give it back. In fairness to Egypt, a country of which I am very fond, geography was a more than willing accomplice in what Ethiopians see as theft. The Nile naturally removes water from Ethiopia to Egypt. In the absence of accepted international water law, convention and custom rule. Egypt's argument for its continued enjoyment of the bulk of the Nile flow is that first users should not be harmed by later upstream use. Finders keepers, in other words.

Egypt and Sudan allocated all the Nile waters to themselves in the 1959 agreement. None of the other riparians ratified this agreement; at the time they were still under the yoke of colonialism, with the exception of Ethiopia. With independence, each unsurprisingly has come to voice disgruntlement with the 1959 agreement. Kenya and Ethiopia have been most vocal. The latter is currently leading the confrontation with Egypt during a high-profile phase of negotiations on a Nile Framework Agreement that will weaken the fifty-year-old arrangement – or stitch up, depending where you stand.

It's not what you've got, it's the way that you use it

Geography can be unkind to nations. To others, it extends
bounteous generosity. Geography has endowed Ethiopia
with considerable water supplies. But Ethiopia has had
rather a hard time keeping hold of and benefiting from
these gifts. Eighty cubic kilometres of rich, silt-laden water
is lost to downstream Egypt and Sudan each year. So
much for the blue water. However, Ethiopia also receives
at least the same accessible volume of water each year
as green water in its soil profiles. This enables farmers
to raise rain-fed grains and pulses in the humid summer
season. And it is also the case that Ethiopia's vast rain-fed
rangelands are home to one of the largest cattle populations on the continent.

283

We might want to ask why it is that Ethiopia does not
get to enjoy the benefits of the Nile flow within its own
borders. If we turn to other major riparians that source
major rivers, such as China, India and Turkey, we see a
very different situation. All these economies are currently
engaged in capturing their water resources within their
boundaries for non-consumptive uses such as hydro-
power, as well as for the thirsty business of irrigated
cropping. All three are exploiting this natural resource and
transforming it into clear economic benefit.

The archetypal example is the US. As we found in
Chapter 3, the US hydraulic mission gave the country
(temporary) mastery over water. An impressive network of
dams and pumps has brought world-leading farming to the
Californian desert and generated considerable quantities of
electricity. We can see the distinction clearly. Geography
is not the key determinant: political capacity and a diversified economy are. The higher the national wealth and the
more developed the economy, the more water resources
can be exploited. This, simply, is why an Egypt always
prevails over an Ethiopia. Egypt has far greater political

clout and a more advanced economy. Therefore, it is able to bargain and negotiate better internationally, especially over scarce water resources that are being augmented invisibly and silently in the domain of international trade. Its economic strength and political profile give it advantages over other nations. It also has powerful allies, and all the influence such networks bring.

Egypt and Vietnam have managed, at present, to ensure that water and food provisions keep pace with population size. They have done this in the context of hazardous demographic surges. How? First, they squeezed greater and greater efficiency out of water, increasing crop yields by significant multiples. Second, they have 'imported' virtual water embedded in food – especially in Egypt. Both these approaches required economic diversification and effective engagement with both regional and global economies. Ethiopia has not achieved either of these things.

The global economy is structured in such a way that, once a loser, you almost certainly, irrevocably remain on a losing streak. Ethiopia has been losing for decades. The global food marketeers have no, or at least very little, compunction about kicking an economy when it is down. They don't even register their abuses. The powerful never do. They may not have made the unfair terms of trade, but they certainly enjoy their benefits. The powerful do because they can. The weak exhaust themselves getting the best they can out of their resources. They have no energy to engage in battles that are already lost.

International trade operates without a moral compass. Industrialised economies dump low-cost international grain staples on developing nations. The exporters cannot resist the opportunity. The importers cannot resist a chance to feed their too-numerous urban poor. They have hungry populations to feed. But when the effects of this imported grain stretch out into the rural areas, they fatally wound small-scale farming communities. As the

rich get richer, the poor get poorer. Globally, most economies and industries have grown steadily over the past
twenty-five years. Ethiopia's farming sector has in some
measures contracted. Unable to get sustainable prices
for their products, farmers have been forced into self-
destructive short-termism, selling their draught animals
to survive, but then being forced to return to farming with
hand tools to cultivate and weed crops.

Much of the world is marching forward under the banner of globalisation; a significant minority is not simply
being left behind but tangibly slipping backwards. In such
a context, it is unreasonable to expect significant increases
in crop yields or water productivity. Rain-fed grain yields
in Ethiopia languish between 1 and 2 tonnes per hectare.
These are among the lowest in the world. In the final
chapter it will be argued that one of the world's highest priorities is the nurturing and supporting of poor farmers in
sub-Saharan Africa. These are people who achieve the lowest water productivity in the world. Such farmers need to
double and treble their crop and livestock yields to improve
their own lot. The rest of the world also needs them to do
it so that they play a part in bringing about global water
security for the eight to nine billion souls who will be on the
planet in the second half of this century.

I would like to make an important distinction. International trade has a malign effect on many developing
economies; it is not in and of itself malign. When I say it
lacks a moral compass, it is distinctly amoral rather than
immoral. If the conditions are correct, international trade
can help developing nations. Low food-commodity prices
have benefited better-developed economies, of which
Egypt is an example. Remember, Egypt has been importing virtual water in cheap wheat to make up (and conceal)
national water shortages. In parallel, it has improved
domestic grain yields and dedicated land and water to
the raising of premium crops. Exports of these premium

285

crops deliver considerable economic returns to water. The economy strengthens, both in terms of wealth and international significance.

So, what distinguishes the winners from the losers?

A drowning nation

The enemy within

What is Ethiopia's problem? It's a blunt question but one that needs asking. It has plenty of water, yet suffers food and water shortages, while others nations with no water or agriculture enjoy plentiful and secure supplies. This demonstrates one of the most important points I wish to raise in our discussion: water riches do not guarantee prosperity any more than water poverty ensures poverty. Water has always been subordinate to money and politics. Always.

Ethiopia started the twentieth century ahead of every other African nation. It was the only African country free of colonial control, with the exception of the US's purpose-built tiny coastal state of Liberia. Apart from a brief occupation by Mussolini's Italy, Ethiopia remained free throughout the century.

But the state had more than its fair share of strife and conflict in the twentieth century – this most bloody of centuries. Despite its lengthy existence as a national entity, Ethiopia is afflicted by that ubiquitous and deadly African malaise: fractious ethnic heterogeneity. European colonialism worsened ancient tribal tensions by drawing arbitrary national boundaries on maps. Ethiopia escaped this fate, but its history can be seen as a power struggle between different ethnic communities played out over hundreds of years. The country comprises almost eighty different tribal identities, the largest being the Oromo and Amhara, accounting for 35 and 30 per cent of the population respectively.

A communist military government, the Derg, ruled from 1974 until 1991 with a confused mess of ill-ordered social

286

experiments and genocidal purges. The infamous famines of the 1980s and the collapse of the USSR and the Soviet support propping up the regime led to the defeat of the Derg in a long civil war that ended in the early 1990s. From this messy conflict came the modern Ethiopian state. Currently organised along the lines of ethnic federalism, with local power devolved to ethnically based regional authorities, Ethiopia was a clear loser of the twentieth century, ending in a far worse relative position than the one it enjoyed at the century's start. The nation is held together by an uneasy, stressful and opaque coalition of authorities, bound by a central regime that is not often described as transparent, accountable or a defender of civil liberties. Such an environment makes economic development and diversification slow and uncertain at best, and impossible at worst.

287

But not all of Ethiopia's economic problems are of its own making. Two external forces have very seriously impaired Ethiopia's capacity to improve its economy in general and its agricultural industry in particular. Here, we in the industrialised world must accept responsibility.

The enemies without

The first external factor is the suite of restrictions imposed on Ethiopia, preventing it from using its wealth of blue-water resources. Bluntly, the international community has not expressed much interest in the development of Ethiopia. Charity celebrity engagement and telethons aside, the nation has little impact on the industrialised world. Internal and external strife, a heavy flirtation with communism and a paucity of eye-catching natural resources have all conspired to make Ethiopia of slight consequence internationally. Conversely, Egypt – Ethiopia's far stronger nemesis in the battle for control of the Nile – has positioned itself as an important regional player in international politics. It is perceived as a moderate among the Arab states and has curried Western favour – albeit awkwardly – for nearly half a century.

As I keep observing, politics matter. Certainly, politics trumps rational water-management priorities nearly every time. Hence, Ethiopia might have nature's blessing when it comes to the Nile, but Egypt has the tacit support of the international community. For over two decades, the World Bank has been poised to assist Ethiopia in the construction of hydraulic infrastructure to tap its immense hydro-electric potential of the Blue Nile and to redirect some of the flow for vital irrigated farming. But Egypt has aggressively fought off any upstream hydraulic developments and continues, through a tough blend of diplomacy and delaying tactics, to frustrate Ethiopia's ambitions regarding the Nile.

Be clear. Egypt's dominance over the Nile is grounded neither in geography nor even in military might. It is pure politics. It is the most powerful player in the hydropolitics of the eastern Nile basin – the sub-basin with over 80 per cent of the total blue water of the entire basin; Ethiopia is the weakest. The decades of socio-economic development that Egypt's effective – but waning – resistance has cost Ethiopia has been profoundly damaging. It has lost five decades of progressive socio-economic development. Even if the World Bank, Ethiopia and its donors could mobilise projects and investment today, it would take at least fifteen years to plan, build and commission Ethiopia's much-needed hydraulic infrastructure. In terms of economic and social development, standing still is tantamount to slipping backwards. All world economies are in a never-ending developmental race, and Ethiopia is falling behind. Allowing it to use an agreed proportion of its considerable blue-water resources and, more importantly, helping Ethiopian farmers make effective use of their substantial green-water resources would go some way to helping the nation catch up with the rest of the world. This needs to happen, and it needs to happen soon.

288

The second external factor I would like to emphasise is that old bugbear of mine, and every other conscionable human being on the planet: the egregious international trading system. Ethiopia is primarily a rural economy. As are many other African nations. It is an unambiguous fact: dump cheap grain on nations with impoverished rural economies and you cause pain. And plenty of it. I do not mean purely economic pain, in the sense that an over-strong currency might cause 'pain' to an industrialised nation's export economy. I mean actual real pain. Definite, objective, physical pain being caused to living, breathing human beings in their everyday lives.

289

The weak farming economy of Ethiopia is piteously easy to disrupt. The impact of half-cost wheat exports from the industrialised world has been as devastating as any communist terror or murderous drought. I've rehearsed this argument throughout, but I re-present it to you now as we look at an economy on the receiving end of international trade injustice. While discussing the EU and the US, and their policies of subsidising production and eliminating environmental and energy costs from the commodity-pricing mechanism, I was able to maintain a cool, academic detachment, and perhaps my analysis scarcely registered. Let me correct that right now. Hold in your mind an image of developing-world poverty: the ubiquitous starving children of the Ethiopian famines of the 1980s might be most appropriate here. Now consider this truth very carefully: the artificially cheap grain exports of the industrialised world are an important factor in creating the human misery you are currently picturing in your mind's eye. Don't let yourself off the hook, now. The industrialised world is not a shadowy cabal of Rothschilds and Moriarties. It is you and me. It is our democratically elected representatives acting in our economic, national self-interest. It is our agribusinesses. Our wealth. Our gain.

And it is the developing world's loss.

Half-price wheat murders developing economies. Rural economies rely on the high prices that come about during droughts. But when drought strikes the Horn of Africa, no government can resist the readily available cheap US and EU exports. Anywhere in the world, civil unrest is only three days of empty bellies away, but in developing nations, the baseline for the emptiness of bellies is higher than most. Tenuous and fragile governments in developing nations have large populations of urban poor to keep happy. To fail to do so does not result in a beating at the ballot box, but rather beatings in the street. Such governments make the cynical but accurate calculation that it is better to starve the rural poor than the urban poor. The rural poor are disparate, disunited and disorganised. At least in Africa. Chinese emperors long feared the powerful peasant revolts. But in contemporary Africa the rural poor have no collective power, unlike the urban poor, and they have no political strength.

That they are the lifeblood of the nation is not relevant to their governments, hundreds of miles away. Politics only exists in the here and now. Developing countries will accept the cancer of cheap imports to avoid starvation because they are working on this simple metric of the short term: cancer kills tomorrow, whereas starvation kills today.

A future imperfect?

The future for Ethiopia is daunting, even given the country's thorny past. There is no obvious good news in relation to water or economic development. Every decade brings unsustainable population increases. Each birth that is not cancelled by a death means the environment has to provide a further 1000 cubic metres of water each year. With the population predicted to double to a hundred and fifty million by the late twenty-first century, water and food security seem increasingly unlikely to feature in

Ethiopia's future. Though death is more active and ever-present in Ethiopia than in many nations of the world, his scythe cuts slower than the human reproductive urge.

Ethiopia is doubly damned. Of the other economies we have examined, some have used diversified, developed economies to meet their water and food shortfalls through trade. Others have exploited natural water resources to drive economic development. Neither route is plausible for Ethiopia. Trapped in poverty, it cannot diversify its economy. Politically handicapped, it cannot exploit its considerable water resources.

Theoretically, a doubling of the productivity of water in farming could meet the food needs of Ethiopia's growing population. The potential is certainly there untapped. While the area of rain-fed cultivated land has increased significantly over the past thirty years, there have been no increases in yields. Leaving aside the political and financial impediments to Ethiopia utilising its blue-water resources, the country still has considerable (if sporadic) rainfall. Its seasonality is problematic, but the resource is there and could be used to deliver increased livestock and crop yields. The ensuing wealth could act as a driver of economic development.

291

But there remains the all-important stumbling block: the faulty local markets. Like farmers the world over, Ethiopian farmers would respond positively to higher commodity prices and effective local markets. They would achieve higher yields and improved returns to water. The natural and human resources are in place. Strife has abated, if not calmed entirely, with the result that the transport infrastructure is now improving. Every other economy we have examined in this discussion has achieved greater yields and greater water efficiency in the face of the correct incentives and reliable infrastructures. There is no reason to suppose that Ethiopia should be any different.

However, it will not happen until the essential conditions of fair prices and fair markets are available to Ethiopian farmers. And it is outside their control, or even the control of the Ethiopian government, to provide these vital conditions. It is not my desire to paint them as hopeless or helpless. They are not. Farming anywhere in the world would crumble in the face of the insurmountable obstacles faced by the Ethiopian farmer. If UK farmers could not get decent prices for their produce, the industry would descend into a downward spiral of short-termism and despair. UK farmers do give up. But in the UK there are social-security systems. Not in Ethiopia.

292

So Ethiopia is a country with immense challenges. Yet if the correct conditions could be created, Ethiopia could be turned around. Vietnam was transformed in under a generation from a war-ravaged shell to a global leader in rice exports. The untapped potential within Ethiopia is huge. What is needed is a removal of the terrible disincentives of asymmetric global trade, and the construction of a set of favourable conditions, guaranteeing price and purchase in a stable and secure socio-political environment. If this were put in place, we would be able to test one of the central theses of my argument: farmers can be enabled to deliver food and water miracles for their populations.

Ethiopian farmers could deliver a revolution. If they could be incentivised to improve crop and livestock yields to the levels observed in the other economies we have looked at, they would not only be able to feed and water the rapidly increasing national population. They could grow high-value commodities for export, and further the strengthening and diversification of their economy. They could unlock the true wealth of their abundant water supplies. This would not just benefit the Ethiopian economy. It might just help save the whole world.

The thesis that the potential of land and water resources to be transformed by the availability of new inputs to farmers operating in a more peaceful and more favourable market environment may be tested in the coming decade in Ethiopia. There are global forces in train, called inward investment in land by some. And land-grabbing by others. These initiatives are funded by Middle East sovereign wealth funds and private investors. Investors in India are interested, and so are public and private investors in China. There is South Korean interest, and even speculative interest among Western investors. Some have a track record of damaging water resources in their own countries and would be unlikely to be more responsible with Ethiopia's land and water. Others, such a those from China, have the mix of design experience, project management and even the mobilisation of technical skills, as well as a reputation for delivering projects effectively, that could prove the potential of Ethiopia's underdeveloped green-water resources. As well as realise Ethiopia's hydro-power potential.

293

Journey's end

The big truth we have surely discovered is this: a country's water endowment is less relevant to its water security than the strength of its economy. Having water is not what counts: how an economy uses it is the deciding factor. A diversified economy and a peaceful political structure are factors far more likely to guarantee water security than all the rainfall, rivers and underground reservoirs in the world. Ethiopia has 80 cubic kilometres of green water and another 80 of blue water each year, yet its unhappy political past and current political and economic problems mean that most of this quite literally drains away. Conversely, semi-arid California is currently one of the most important and powerful centres of global agriculture.

There are two different ways of looking at water security. We can simplistically and intuitively view water security merely in the context of water-resource endowment. In other words, it's all about how much water you do (or don't) have. This is the crude and literalistic way of thinking about water that was born with prehistoric man and that, for reasons I hope I have demonstrated, has still not come unstuck in our collective psyche. Basically, we try and ensure exclusive control of as much water as we believe we will need for the foreseeable future. This is a perfectly acceptable way to manage water if you are a Neolithic band of agrarians guarding your corner of a river in a mostly unpopulated world. This is the context in which this emotional and naive approach to water control developed. It is not a very sensible approach for a political economy in an increasingly overpopulated and overeating twenty-first-century world.

What is the alternative?

For want of a better term, let me describe my model as the developed-economy version of water security. In this model, water ceases to be a good in and of itself and becomes a defined benefit, be it in the form of electrical power, manufactured products, sanitation and water supply or – most importantly of all – the big water used in food production. Whereas the old model revolves around one essential component – the literal, tangible presence of water – this new model has four essential elements.

The first is the water resource. Virtual water doesn't replace water: it displaces it. Every country, to a greater or lesser extent, has a water endowment. Sometimes it is slight. Other times bounteous. Rarely is it sufficient to meet all the needs of the population.

The second element is the extent to which an individual economy is able to use water efficiently. Nearly all economies are in water deficit, but much still depends on these economies getting the maximum economic benefit from the water they have. The UK and Vietnam, as we have seen, achieve this through phenomenal increases in yields. Other economies, such as Egypt or California, also make shrewd economic judgements about which crops or livestock to raise. Higher-value products generate export revenue: the food gap can always be met by trade.

Third, we have human resources. I have not dealt with this as fully as I would have liked. In a book that is ostensibly about water, I have delved deep and wide into politics and history. For several pages, I have not even mentioned the titular hydrogen and oxygen compound, be it in its virtual or actual form. Truthfully, there is much more to tell about the role of economic diversity and human resources in providing water security for a country. Briefly, let us remember tiny Singapore. At the very outset of our discussion, I mentioned that this economy can only meet 5 per cent of its water needs. Its water endowment just covers part of its small-water needs; the rest is met mainly by virtual-water 'imports' and blue water piped from Malaysia or desalinated. However, Singapore is able to finance the 95 per cent of imports through a very clever economic exploitation of the 5 per cent available to it. Its highly diversified economy is focused on industries with very low water needs. These goods and services offer remarkable financial returns on water. The wealth generated is subsequently used to pay for food imports that provide water security for this waterless nation.

295

The final piece of the puzzle is politics. An economy must function effectively in regional and international politics, forwarding its own national interest. The strong state uses technology, underpinned by hegemonic political pressures, to capture water resources. The weak state fails to mobilise the necessary investment to install hydraulic infrastructure, and lacks the political influence to win water from its neighbours. Here, in miniature, is the terribly unbalanced relationship between strong Egypt and weak Ethiopia.

If we were to rank economies according to their ability to achieve water security, we would find that water-resource endowment was almost irrelevant. Of the four factors, it correlates the least with successful management. Thus dies localised environmental Malthusian determinism. The rich can become incredibly populous and can draw water towards themselves through clever use of water, but mainly by clever use of wealth and politics. Singapore might top our league table of water managers. Clinging to a small island off Malaysia, this city-state demonstrates that absence of water does not doom a nation to water insecurity. Socio-economic development wins out.

296

The flip-side of the argument would explain why water-rich Ethiopia would languish towards the bottom of our ranking. Its weak economy means that it cannot develop the infrastructure to exploit its water. This tends to self-perpetuate. The economy weakens and self-reliance vanishes. The economic weakness translates into political impotence. Ethiopia has found it to be extremely difficult to assert itself in Nile-basin politics. Until 2010 it has had a history of losing out to its northern neighbour, Egypt. Poverty and hunger bring political instability and strife. Civil war brings greater poverty and hunger. The brutal asymmetries of international trade only damage the nation further. It becomes locked in an addiction to cheap food imports, feeding the belly while the arms and legs of the economy wither and atrophy.

Even if we reversed all these problems instantly and Ethiopia was suddenly gifted, upon your finishing this chapter, with sufficient aid and political support to build a mighty hydraulic infrastructure to benefit from the wealth of its blue-water resources, it would still have lost nearly three-quarters of a century of economic development. For Ethiopia and much of Africa, the future passed them by. They have been inheriting only the past.

CHAPTER 6

Watertight: virtual-water 'trade' and whether humanity sinks or swims

Some water for everyone, for ever.
KADER ASMAL, SOUTH AFRICA'S FIRST POST-APARTHEID MINISTER OF WATER

Down from five to two-point-five.
Down from seven to save the heavens.
DIPAK GYWALI, DIRECTOR OF THE NEPAL WATER CONSERVATION FOUNDA-
TION AND RAJENDRA PACHAURI, HEAD OF THE INTER-GOVERNMENTAL PANEL
ON CLIMATE CHANGE (IPCC)

What we eat and what we don't waste will enable us to be globally water-secure.

Mighty invisibles

Before we part, let me reiterate and distil. Draw some con clusions of my own and, more interestingly, provoke some others from you. On the theme of water security.

Our journey has been through a world of mighty invisibles.

First, there is the invisible water in the soil. This is green water. Impossible to capture in economic terms, and very difficult to quantify. Within the soil, it lies unseen. Yet it raises around 70 per cent of all our food. Our trips, within these pages, to eight different nations has shown us that the farmers of the world have to make the best possible use of this blessed bounty of green water. Doing this prevents us from having to use our very valuable potable water to raise food.

Second, there is the invisible virtual water. This is the water used to raise, and therefore embedded within, the 15 per cent of food that gets traded. Traded food allows the water-scarce to have reliable supplies of food. As a side effect, it also allows the wealthy to have a very rich and very diverse choice of food. It is essential to a peaceful world. Without virtual-water 'trade', there would be war. Countries would be forced to take natural resources, land and water to guarantee that their populations did not starve to death. Virtual-water 'trade' also prevents water-scarce economies from placing even more damaging demands on fragile water environments by attempting to raise food at home. Virtual-water 'trade' takes place so instinctively, easily and silently that the consumers and governments that benefit rarely even notice.

298

Third, we have the invisible driving forces of demography. In the past half century, population explosions over much of the world have forced global water demand up by 300 per cent.

Luckily, there has been – fourth – the invisible impact of China's family-planning policies. Thanks to this, there are three hundred million people who have never existed and who have never put an insupportable extra drain on our precious water and food supplies. In people terms, that's a whole shadow North America that never existed, in effect reducing global water demand by 5 per cent.

There are more invisibles. The links between crop and livestock yields and water security are hard to see on first glance. In response to a trebling of population and the proportionate increase in water demands, there has been a doubling of the amount of freshwater used. This increase in use of freshwater – the blue water – has been highly visible. Engineers, planners, politicians and financial donors have all been involved in this hydraulic mission. Such people make quite a lot of noise. They like to talk about what they are doing. If they don't, environmental activists, who hold a very contrary view, often do. Either way, it's hard to keep the hydraulic mission a secret. Dams, reservoirs and irrigation schemes are all pretty easy to spot. The massive dams of the twentieth century and their reservoirs are among the largest of all man-made structures. You could not get much further from invisible. But while freshwater use doubled, food production increased four-fold. Other things besides the hydraulic mission have certainly been going on, and these are the other invisibles. The credit goes to those associated with the visible: the politicians and engineers. But a greater proportion of water management is being done by our invisible benefactors: the farmers of the world. They perform agri-hydro-miracles on their farms. That this is a new idea is perhaps the most important invisible of all.

299

Farmers are the invisible agents. Yes, the visible agents did a lot. And it wasn't just dams. The green revolution of the 1960s and 1970s could not have happened without the co-ordinated efforts of engineers and agri-science – who brought knowledge and technology – international investment banks – who brought capital – and the politicians and bureaucracies – who made the wheels turn. Despite all this, I contend that the farmers have done the heaviest lifting. Water security was a battle won on the front line of agriculture. There, farmers worked intensely with green and blue water, most often wringing more and more productivity from every last drop. In Chapter 5 we showed that where they have not – such as in Ethiopia – the economic and social outcomes are awful.

The farmers are not the only invisible heroes. There are the international food-commodity trading companies. Rarely are they praised in analyses of this sort. But they are praised here – with some qualification. There is a double irony here. Neither the agents of global water security – the farmers and trading companies – nor the beneficiaries – that's us – are aware that our water security is due to improvements in water productivity on farms. Which brings me to my final invisible: the invisible Nobel Prize. What more suitable award could there be to hand to the invisible agents of invisible trade ensuring invisible water security that has prevented violent conflict? Imagine the wonderful invisible acceptance speeches. These farmers and traders have brought hydro-peace and hydro-security. And these two benefits – at once individually precious and globally strategic – are visible. They are visible to the extent that individuals and society can appreciate the absence of pain.

300

An invisible bad apple

If international virtual-water 'trade' is invisible, then so too are the inequities within international trade. These are wicked invisibles, playing the part of malevolent sprites to the helpful elves of virtual-water 'trade'. These have been well documented throughout our discussion: they are the profound trade asymmetries that allow subsidised crops from wealthy industrialised nations to be dumped on the markets of weak, developing economies, themselves denied any such market-distorting support.

So it is that virtual-water 'trade' itself contributes significantly to the difficulties faced by many millions of poor farmers in the world's weakest economies in playing their part in delivering global water security. We hamstring them when we should be helping them, if for no other reason than by helping them we improve their water-using efficiency, which in turns helps us and everyone. The virtual-water 'trade' in subsidised staple foods on world markets has delayed by decades the development of farm economies that could have achieved high returns to water in the poorest third of the developing nations. This is shortsighted. It must change.

Great beyonds

Beyond water

If invisibility didn't make it hard enough, engaging with
the topic of water security is made even more problematic because so much of what is relevant is beyond the
water sector. Nothing daunts any professional more than
stepping outside her or his own sphere of expertise. You
choose your solution when you choose your counsel. The
king seeking advice will find that the knight will say fight,
the priest will say pray and the peasant will plead peace.
To a hydraulic engineer, the solution has always been and
– in many regions – remains the same: build bigger and
better manifestations of the hydraulic mission.

301

    The water professional is therefore usually worried by
virtual water, because it opens up a frightening fact that
borders on an existential threat: some of the most important factors determining individual and collective water
security lie entirely outside the water sector. No one likes
to think that they are not the best person for the job, especially when the job is most certainly theirs. But that's what
I've realised, and that is the core message of this book.
Virtual-water 'trade' – made possible by the purchasing-
power of diversified and strong economies – secures food
and water for the water-scarce. Dams, canals, pumps and
valves are also essential. However, none of these can move
and control water availability on the same scale or with
the same flexibility as trade and economic development.

    Hydraulic projects are big, bold and very very visible,
but actually nothing really manages to control water
totally, especially not green water, the most technically
inaccessible and hard-to-measure of all water types. So
rather than trying to force water to adapt to us, we should
adapt to water and the environmental services of water.
That is what virtual-water 'trade' has been allowing us to
do – invisibly – for millennia.

Beyond profits

Beware. I am not writing in blind praise of the private food corporations. There is another great beyond to consider. The private sector is also daunted by water security, because there is so much of elemental importance which brings water security that lies beyond the market which the food corporations understand. What are the corporations who make and market water-intensive food commodities good at? Well, their financial success is built upon their ability to cultivate consumers' addictions to fat, sugar, salt and carbohydrates. And these corporations have done an amazing job in encouraging these addictions, and meeting the consumers' ever-growing inclinations (to expand their ever-growing waistlines).

302

That has begun to change. In the last decade, food manufacturers and supermarkets have started to talk about the collective consequences of food consumption on water resources. There are several different explanations. I will quickly look at a few. One that I believe has had little or no influence is morality. The corporate structure is so configured to bypass morality in economic decisions. The company exists with all the legal rights and status of an individual but lacking one vital component: the conscience. Similarly, sensible self-interest about the impact of water scarcity on their supply chains has actually also had very little to do with their new-found enthusiasm for the environment. Corporations are not great at taking long-term strategic decisions. The life expectancy of the corporation has deteriorated. Even the most successful and largest corporations often exist for only a few decades. How then could they be expected to consider the long term when their lives are only of medium-term duration? The corporate imperative is for immediate improvements in share price; the turnover of leading executives is too brief to promote healthy, considered stewardship of a company. Make money and move on has been the corporate mantra.

No. The answer to improvements in water management by food manufacturers and retailers can be found
in two of the biggest buzz phrases of the last decade:
climate change and reputational risk. The former needs
scant introduction. Society has steadily woken up to the
problems of climate change and, while there is plenty
of disagreement, the sheer volume and intensity of the
debates is enough to indicate that it is now taken very seriously indeed as a concept, even by those who deny it.

Although corporations are very bad at responding to
ethical imperatives or distant but real environmental
threats, they are remarkably, intuitively responsive to
societal anxieties. Understanding people is absolutely
essential to getting at their cash. As the public has become
increasingly preoccupied with climate change, so have the
corporations. All have rushed to check their carbon and
energy footprints in manufacturing, transporting and marketing food. This is done to make them more attractive to
consumers and to sidestep that terrible corporate poison:
reputational damage. In a marketplace where brand and
perception are sovereign, nothing can harm a company
more than a bad reputation. Every corporation wants to be
seen as the good guy, and they will stop at nothing to have
that appearance. They will even be good. For a reward.

That reward is the esteem of their customers. In order
to win it, and by winning it win more custom, corporations have quite energetically engaged with the concept
of the water footprint. They have tried to analyse their
products and their supply chains using water consumption as a metric of efficiency. Once corporations decide to
do something, they normally pursue it energetically. Their
investments in research into their water footprints have
been impressive. They are grappling with the bottom line,
and with these existential ethical and reputational issues.
So it is that consumer awareness and capacity to connect
consumption to water security are vital. By understanding

303

this connection, and by modifying their consumption patterns accordingly, consumers can change the behaviour of corporations. The public discourse is shifting, and corporations most certainly have to manage their reputations. Reputational risk has a price tag. Most corporations find that potential price far more costly than the actual cost of switching to products and supply-chain processes that are kinder on the water environment. So the right thing is done, if for the wrong sort of reasons.

Beyond politics

304

Politicians are a reasonably fearless bunch. It's an important part of their job description. They mustn't be easily daunted. They are adept at responding to elemental challenges. They live and breathe the language of social and economic priorities. And yet even these experts in handling uncertainty find it hard to engage with water-security issues.

In truth, water crises are never beyond politics. Rather, the reverse is true. Politicians like to keep water crises well hidden and off the public agenda. Every water crisis is subordinated to another crisis and somehow contained. This is not because politicians believe water to be unimportant. It is because they sense how important it is. They are very aware that the political prices to be paid for addressing explicit water crises are far too dangerously high. To persuade the public to change their approach to water use – by which I essentially mean a serious reform of the national diet, with the consequent knock-on effects for the farming sector – would require expending a very large amount of political capital.

All of us – me, you, politicians and farmers – are daunted by water insecurity, should we begin to sense it. There are so many interacting uncertainties. Politics is the one profession that engages daily with contradictory uncertainties that touch deep emotions, which are very poorly understood. Politics is a world of rough-and-ready responses, and the only one yet devised to cope with the wicked problem of water insecurity. Either we address it now, and accept the immediate and unpredictable political stress. Or we defer, handing on much higher levels of political stress to future generations. Like a boil requiring lancing, there is never a positively good time to deal with a wicked problem, only steadily worsening times...

The NIMBY is an increasingly unusual beast, particularly on a more and more integrated and globalised planet. And climate change is the perfect form of pollution for the era of globalisation. It is inherently collective. Although we don't (always) share the energy we are using directly, energy management takes place predominantly on a collective rather than an individual level. There is a collective outcome to society's energy use. The carbon is shifted from vegetation and land into the atmosphere. This becomes a problem on a global scale, albeit a problem that is felt to greater or lesser extents depending on where in the world you are. Broadly, carbon emissions are averaged out across the shared global atmosphere.

305

Like the environmental insecurities associated with global warming, global water insecurity has come about in an era of rapid globalisation. The impacts of these two problems are, however, different. Global warming is caused by rich societies and shared by everyone. Water is different. Water is used intensively in some regions, but the impacts are not shared by everyone. The outcomes of human intervention on freshwater systems are never evened out. Local river basins and groundwater resources are hit according to local levels of abuse. The asymmetrical usage of dirty, non-renewable energy is unfairly evened out across the planet. Indeed, those in developing nations, often responsible for a disproportionately small amount of carbon emissions, suffer a disproportionately large amount of the pain from higher temperatures and rising sea levels. For water, the uneven pollution hits stay where they were made.

Virtual water, though, gets around this, in part at least. When virtual water is 'exported', then the benefit of the water is received in one part of the world while the pollution and environmental cost remains where the water was used. So it is with China. It 'exports' virtual water through its colossal manufacturing trade. The cheap goods are enjoyed abroad; the environmental damage stays in China. At least until China improves the way it treats its industrial effluents to the levels achieved by industrial economies.

306

Doing the wrong thing extremely well

We've talked about wicked problems. They are both urgent and uncertain. Often, they are the direct result of previous (misguided) attempts at dealing with an earlier version of the same problem.

The oil and gas crises of the 1970s were touched on in Chapter 4. The energy problem is a wicked problem indeed. The big-oil/government nexus responded to the crises by hurrying to develop North Sea and Alaskan North Slope oil and gas resources. We humans are truly amazing. We will find ways to achieve what we desire. But if we set ourselves off on the wrong path, then we only exacerbate the problem while believing ourselves to be solving it. The wicked problem then sends us off on the road to doing the wrong thing. But doing the wrong thing extremely well, as Peter Drucker noted.

We like doing what we can do well. Always, the human preference is for the more familiar path. Even if it leads in the wrong direction. Worse, because of the familiarity, we are able to travel with greater speed and confidence. But all the time heading in the wrong direction. So it was with our response to the 1970s energy crises. By freeing up so much new resource, oil prices were kept artificially low for another

three decades. The costly impacts on the atmosphere were
not internalised in the price of energy. This created the very
dangerous illusion that energy was virtually free. It was certainly significantly cheaper by volume than bottled water.
Environmental destruction became inevitable.

The right thing, which we would certainly not have
been able to do as well, would have been to pursue the
nascent renewable technologies of the time, and build
energetically on research into harnessing clean solar
power. Clean renewable technologies mitigate environmental costs. Dirty non-renewable technologies do not.
Because we launched ourselves in the wrong direction,
with great technological efficiency, we lost several decades
in developing clean technologies. And made it more difficult to reverse the trend. As the threat of climate change
has become a more clear and present danger, we are now
forced to turn our attention to these clean, renewable
alternatives. Yet to attempt a switch to them under the
timetable that climate-change science requires has been
made impossible. It would, though, have been achievable
if we had made a wiser decision when facing the problem
of oil-price spikes thirty years ago. We have lost vital time
in our battle with climate change, built our world around
unsustainable levels of energy consumption and worsened
our addiction to fossil fuels. A truly wicked problem.

Are there comparable examples from the history of
human water use? Of course. We have talked several times
now about the wrong-headed excesses of the hydraulic
mission of industrialised nations between the 1920s and
1970s. The surfeit of dams and water transfers during the
era are a tangible monument to mankind doing the wrong
thing very well. Our hydro-engineering skills are phenomenal. But that doesn't make them the best solution to
water-management problems. The industrialised nations'
errors lie in the past. BRICS run the risk of repeating them.
China, India and Brazil are currently engaged in building

307

even bigger water storage and conveyance infrastructures. All this comes with a heavy environmental cost. In particular, India's mobilisation of blue water has already tested groundwater resources to destruction. It is a very dangerous path. The developing economies, especially those in sub-Saharan Africa, have, however, had barely any impact on their freshwater reserves. There is plenty of scope for them to develop hydro-power and water for irrigation, particularly if they adopt the wisdom of the World Commission on Dams, published in 2000.

308

The World Commission on Dams, 2000

For many reasons and in many different ways, the 1970s was a decade of angst for the industrialised economies. They were years of paranoia and government conspiracy. Of financial stagnation and labour disputes. Of oil spikes and the infancy of international terrorism.

This angst pervaded every area of society. Including the discourse around water management. Environmentalists were becoming more voluble. Their message gained such prominence that by 1980 is was practically impossible – politically at least – to build another dam in an industrialised economy. Since then, around five hundred dams have been dismantled or taken out of commission in North America alone.

The 2000 World Commission on Dams was an important stage in this journey. It sat between late 1997 and 2000 and was chaired by the charismatic South African lawyer and Minister of Water Resources Kader Asmal. The commission had 12 members, representing major private hydraulic-engineering interests, environmental-activist organisations, other civil-society organisations more generally and also academia and public-sector bodies.

Given its pluralistic nature, the group was able to engage with the broader concept of governance rather than being restricted to the narrower idea of government. And government knowing best. How do government and governance differ?

Governance comprises the departments of state, the market, and social and environmental movements. Government is only the departments of state. To engage all three – government, market and civil movements – is vitally important. We have seen from our case studies that the state played a dangerous role in the hydraulic missions of the mid-twentieth century. This error was equally made by states on either side of the ideological divide. Neither capitalists nor communists have a monopoly on hydraulic over-indulgence. Here is a simple aphorism for life. Whenever the state, the market or – far worse – a secret alliance of the two dominates decision-making, the outcome will be bad for society and bad for the environment. In a normal world where uncertainty is the norm, that is always a safe bet.

309

By contrast, governance is pluralistic. By comprising different and gently conflicting elements, governance has the capacity for self-scrutiny in ways that a monolithic state or market cannot. In a person, we generally call this self-scrutiny a conscience. Governance has a conscience. The state or the market alone do not. On the stewardship of water resources, as with most issues of principled reform, the initiatives come from outside the state and the market. The World Commission on Dams operated with the conscience provided by NGO members.

The outcome of the commission was mixed. Certainly, it provided a principled agenda for future water-resource management. And the launch of the report enjoyed a very high profile, particularly because of the involvement of Nelson Mandela, who lent his legendary authority on issues of equity and new directions. But sadly, after publication, many of the principles were rejected by the usual suspects. This was perhaps not surprising. More shocking, the major players in global funding failed to endorse the principles, including the World Bank. That said, the principles still have considerable influence, and it's fair to say that all current water-resource plans and water-management practices bear the mark of their influence.

> ### Tails wagging dogs, wrongly
>
> *It is often the tail that wags the dog. The errors in energy policy since the 1970s provide an instructive, if disturbing, example. They highlight the dangers of government and private-sector alliances in pursuit of the wrong object-ive. Democracies and corporates are structured similarly. Political leaders are accountable to voters; executives to shareholders; companies to customers. But the whole para-digm of accountability collapses when voters, shareholders and customers are ill-informed. Very often they can be manipulated to have appetites for types and levels of con-sumption that are essentially lethal for society. So it has been with energy use. But it's a poor long-term way of life for society. Our political economies are wholly owned sub-sidiaries of the environment. When the environment fails, so do the societies and companies that depend upon it. Igno-rance will hardly work as a defence when our past mistakes come to be our present reality.*

The real way to achieve water security, or 'Why a Big Mac is bigger than a billion-dollar dam'

First: farmers and food

Forget about domestic water use and water in industry. I'm not saying that we should not try and avoid waste in these areas. But they just aren't statistically significant when it comes to making decisions about water security. Roughly 80 per cent of humanity's water use is the big water used to produce food. Of this, about 30 per cent is blue water or freshwater and 70 per cent is rainwater. And every last drop is managed by the world's farmers.

What we need is for farmers worldwide to improve the productivity of green and blue water to meet the rising food demands of our rapidly growing global populations. At the same time, we need to reduce society's water footprint by changing our consumption habits.

The engineers and economists will argue that we should mobilise 40 per cent more water. The politicians will be inclined to throw themselves behind these suggestions. Why? Because achieving impossible (or almost impossible) hydraulic-mission goals – by mobilising money and engineering know-how in the construction of more dams, reservoirs and conveyance structures – is political child's play compared to the horror of having to convince members of the public to change their behaviour. Water is stubborn, but perhaps less stubborn than people.

311

The carrot: price incentives

You'll notice I am avoiding the word 'subsidy'. Well-considered price incentives can encourage farmers to provide crops with less water and with practices that are kind to the water environment. Our discussion has shown that many economies – industrialised, BRICS and developing – have achieved remarkable improvements in crop and livestock productivity. Price incentives have a role to play in these strategic processes. But they must be reliable and long term. Importantly, they should also take into account the costs of stewardship of the water environment – for farmers are certainly the stewards of our water resources.

Trading better internationally

Through trade, 150 economies have run out of water yet remained food secure. Only through trade could such a thing be achieved. With the world population doubling every thirty years during the later decades of the last century, international trade in agricultural commodities proved vital to the survival of many, if not most, of the people on this planet.

However, the invisibility of the virtual-water solution has caused problems of its own. The unfair terms of international trade have exerted a terrible toll on the farming sectors of weak economies. In sub-Saharan Africa, agriculture is the main economic sector. African farmers have the lowest water productivity worldwide. Under-priced foreign food imports from Europe and the US reinforce the poverty afflicting African farming families. These developing states are in a double bind. They are addicted to subsidised foreign food in periods of crisis. Without it, their urban populations would starve. But the imports are strangling their own economies, and pushing their rural populations into extreme poverty and malnutrition.

312

A fair international trading regime would secure the livelihoods of poor farmers in Africa. The current regime does the reverse. It punishes. This in turn keeps the farmers' returns to water too low. Thus the vicious circle is complete. For global water security, we need the water productivity of sub-Saharan African farmers to double. Currently, it is falling in many economies. Making international trade fair will have an incredibly positive effect on the world's water security.

The inevitability of demographics
The more of us, the more food we need. The more food we need, the more water we use. Ever-rising population therefore requires ever-better water management, given that we have a finite amount of accessible green and blue water on this planet. However, managing population itself is not considered a viable option. Except in China. How many economies would be willing to implement comparable family-planning legislation? I would hasten a guess at a figure: none.

And perhaps there is no need. There are quite predictable trends to the demography of economies. In the pre-industrial stage – where the developing countries of the world remain at present – there are very high birth rates. These are mitigated, in terms of a society's consumption, mostly by very high infant mortality. The early stages of industrialisation bring improvements in health, and a drop in infant mortality. This is too sudden to change the culturally dictated birth rates. Hence, family size increases and populations surge. With further industrialisation, birth rates and death rates begin to fall. Fewer new people, all living longer. Finally, the population reaches a point of equilibrium and population growth steadies at the level of replacement. The first industrialising countries of Western Europe took a hundred and fifty years to go from very high birth rates to a near-replacement rate of growth. In the European nations that industrialised later, the process took place over only a couple of generations. The changes in population growth rate during the different stages of industrialisation have unrecognised but direct impacts on water demand.

313

Amazingly, the very best of scientists can be ignorant of these demographic trends. Underestimating the pace of demographic transition meant that, until the 1980s, population scientists continually overestimated future population growth. By the early 1990s, most demographers had fixed on three global demographic scenarios for 2050: a relatively low one of eight billion people, a mid-level estimate of ten billion and a high-level estimate of twelve billion. It need hardly be said that a world of twelve billion souls would be significantly different from one of 'merely' eight billion. However, what the demographic scientists agree on is that peak population will be reached some time in the second half of this century.

It's not just size; it's location
While the size of population growth is obviously very important, location effects the impact growth has on our global water management. And the calculations about

impact are not as simple as one might imagine. The differences between countries have been described throughout our discussion. You will remember, no doubt, that the average American water footprint is considerably larger than that of the average Indian or Chinese. But countries are rarely homogeneous. An American in the arid south-west of the US will have a far larger domestic water footprint than one in the urban, rainy east. And the meat-intensive diets will make for a large water footprint as well. However, as Americans mainly eat food produced on farms with high yields and high returns to water, the average American water footprint is not significantly higher than that of someone living on a poor farm in Africa. This only serves to illustrate the tragic water inefficiencies of the very poorest farmers, and that wealthy diversified economies will achieve greater returns on water, further strengthening their already strong economies. Better water use makes a country rich, and being rich has brought better water use.

314

WHAT GOES UP...
...doesn't necessarily have to come down. Something we scientists call peak population will probably be reached by 2050. After this point, population growth will remain at the near-replacement level only. Fingers crossed. We have to live with future uncertainties. That is an unavoidable fact of life. Best to plan for the worst and behave in precautionary ways.

Keeping it sustainable

What do we need?
Each extra mouth on this planet will need on average about 1000 cubic metres of water per year for its food. To achieve this for the population-growth estimates currently accepted we require a 40 per cent increase in the productivity of green and blue water in food production. The million-litre question: can this be done?

The latter half of the twentieth century saw some spectacular figures. Population trebled. Freshwater use doubled. Food production quadrupled. So it was that despite such rapid growth in the global population, only the African continent ended the century with a high proportion of persistently malnourished citizens. At the start of the century, every continent suffered this blight.

Given the productivity improvements over the past fifty years, the target of 40 per cent by 2050 seems very reasonable. But how sustainable are the gains of the twentieth century? Look closer. South Asia may be a major food exporter, but many of its inhabitants are undernourished. India's groundwater resources have been very heavily overdrawn in many regions. This is a country drinking and farming itself to disaster. Also, I have repeatedly drawn your attention to the nonsensical but common phenomenon whereby water-scarce regions export virtual water to water-rich ones. We can see this in India, where the northwest exports to the east. Or in China, where the North China Plain produces food for the water-rich south. Or in California. Or in Andalusia. Again and again, against the dictates of simple reason, water-scarce regions intensify the use of water and 'export' it virtually in food commodities. It is unsustainable. It is a form of water madness.

315

We aren't going to get any more water from anywhere. Except from South America, where vast water resources remain untapped. Water needs to be used more productively and more sustainably everywhere. And who is going to achieve that?

It's the farmers...

Thirteen thousand years ago, humanity embarked on an important journey. We started changing the world. We did this by transforming natural vegetation into cropland. It was the first time that we started mobilising water, both green and blue. The past two centuries have seen a remarkable acceleration in this mobilisation. This extensification and intensification of green- and blue-water use by farmers is not always sustainable.

But mobilising more land and water is only half the picture. Increasing yields is vital. And there have been incredible increases in the past two centuries. It's not very hard to track increases in green-water yields. Just look at the production per hectare. If we get 10 tonnes on north-west Europe's rain-fed farms where we used to get only 1 tonne two hundred years earlier, we can grasp the potential of productivity growth. Blue-water productivity is harder to measure, as most blue water is used to supplement variable rainfall. Because we can never have a precise, comparable figure for the rainfall, we can't know how much blue-water saving is due to better productivity and how much is due to variable rain.

What have we learnt about farmers?

The UK

Looking back at what we've learnt during this brief engagement with water should give us a sense of what the future may hold.

North-west Europe has seen breathtaking increases in wheat yields. These increases were solely due to better productivity: annual rainfall was broadly constant. By 2000, water was being used nine times more effectively in farming. When we can increase water efficiency so dramatically, it seems ridiculous to be setting ourselves volumetric goals for water security. How can we possibly suggest that we need 40 per cent more water by volume over the next half century when we don't yet know the great strides forward we might very well take in working our current water harder?

Remember our headline figure from the UK: a 60 per cent dependence on imported food in 1930 dropped to a 40 per cent dependence in 1990, despite a 15 per cent rise in population. In the 1980s, after a hundred years of importing wheat, the UK became a wheat exporter. And significantly, the composition of UK food imports has changed. It comprises overwhelmingly food commodities grown in the tropics. Commodities impossible to grow in a northern-European climate – at least at present.

The UK also gets many food imports from neighbouring industrialised economies, most of whom are partners in the EU. Most often, the trade in water-intensive food commodities between the UK and these neighbours is pretty balanced. It is done not for reasons of food security but to meet the diversity of choice. Less Welsh lamb, more chorizo.

Vietnam

Similarly, as we saw in the previous chapter, Vietnam has changed unrecognisably. In 1975, it was a rice importer. By the 1980s, it was an exporter. Before the close of the century, it became the second-largest rice exporter in the world. A secure civil environment and useful price incentives meant that the Vietnamese could increase their rate of cropping from one to two, or in some areas three, crops a year. There are no precise figures for the increases in returns to water. Certainly the monsoon-season rice crop, which is dependent only on rainwater, has doubled its yield nationally. It's more problematic calculating the increase in blue-water productivity in the other seasons. But in the firmament of the unknown unknowns of global water security, this represents but a tiny, distant star.

317

Collective success

To repeat, farmers do not consciously address global water security. But collectively they are key to its achievement. It's a straightforward calculation. Every increment of improved yield contributes directly to water security – assuming that it is not due to increased blue-water inputs. Each of these small contributions to local water contributes to global water security. How? Because the productivity increases are fed through into the global system via 'trade' in virtual water.

As I keep saying, this doesn't mean that grand water infrastructures, or the groundbreaking improvements in seeds, fertilisers, pesticides and herbicides are unimportant. They all play important potential roles in squeezing higher returns from scarce water. Whether they succeed depends on how they are combined by farmers. So if we want seriously to address global water security, then there are some very simple, quick and easy ways to achieve this. And they don't involve massive hydraulic construction projects or whiz-bang agricultural innovations.

We can improve water security by respecting farmers and recognising their part in feeding us and minding the environment. I don't mean taking them out to dinner or buying them flowers, though this certainly wouldn't hurt. I mean protecting them from the uncertainties of their often very variable rainfall and the equally vicious uncertainties of inadequate market infrastructures and international trade. The more favourable the rural economy and social infrastructures, the better the efficiency of the farm. And that means improved water security for all of us.

318

ADAPTIVENESS
The human story is one of adaptiveness. Nowhere more so than in farming. We think of it as an evolutionary term, but our social and economic adaptiveness is what defines us now as a species. We are not looking for genetic advantages that allow us to thrive in a natural environment, rather we are seeking out political devices – or regimes – that allow societies to thrive in economic environments.

Everything you ever wanted to know about farming
The farmer – be it a family farmer or a global corporation – can produce high or low returns to water by combining a vast array of endowments and inputs. Soil quality is one such endowment. Climate is another. Some farmer-friendly climates provide the optimum 30 degrees centigrade for so much of the year that multiple cropping is a possibility. Of course, climate can also be an enemy of the farmer. Droughts and floods are extreme examples of these eternal hazards.

Then there is technology. This has been the main driver of the progressive and extraordinary increases in water productivity since the beginning of the industrial revolution. Transport and harvesting equipment, fertilisers, herbicides and pesticides have all transformed and advanced farming. But technology does nothing on its own. It requires the cultivating context of an economic and social framework suited to its potential. While technology empowered the farmer to win his eternal battle with the environment, the industrialisation and diversification of economies evolved markets expressing demands for food at prices that stimulated production and investment. Farmers could accumulate surpluses that enabled assets to be capitalised. In other words, farming went from being something people did to stay alive, to a fully fledged industry.

Finally there are subsidies. The continual bugbear of this author, though not – I stress – because he worships at the shrine of market economics. Subsidies can provide essential support to the weak. They can also wreak havoc on other – poor – agricultural economies. They must be rejigged with one clear objective: to incentivise poor farmers in developing economies to improve their water productivity. Currently, these subsidies perform the environmentally and socially less useful function of incentivising corporations and mega-farms producing corn for biofuel in the US with massive negative impacts on our project to achieve global water security.

319

Respect the farmer on whom you depend

A wish list for the farmers of the world

Farmers are used to the hard life. Throughout history, they have faced life-threatening conditions, privation, hunger and desperation. Today, for many farmers, the situation is little changed. In developing economies, millions of farmers can scarcely feed their own families, and certainly cannot generate surpluses. They can make no collective advances, economically or socially. And they cannot improve water-use efficiency. Suicide rates are unrivalled. Even in the advanced economies of the world, the farmer's life is most often one of stress, anxiety and price pressures. Suicide again is no stranger here.

Can it really be good sense to make a desperate underclass of the very people upon whom we rely for our food and water security?

We need to ensure that rural economies and societies are transformed to nurture farmers and promote efficient water management and productivity. This transformation has been managed with some success in the industrialised nations of the world. The outcome is a difficult blend of corporatisation at one extreme, and developments in the rural family economies at the other. Regardless of whether a farm is a large corporate concern or a simple family business, it must be managed by farmers with integrity. Social and environmental awareness are essential if we are to achieve good stewardship of our water resources and also improve water productivity.

Ancillary institutions must be in place. Farming, like all industries, requires financial services. In the developing economies of the world, farmers need considerable improvements in material infrastructure, such as village electrification, better roads, regular affordable bus services and reliable water supplies. These need to be matched by social infrastructure: education and health.

We can't expect people to save the world if they are imprisoned in intellectual and financial poverty, and left to suffer the severe health inequalities such poverty naturally brings. Further, rural economies need to be integrated into national and international economies. At the moment, much of the farmland of the developing world is being excluded from the global market. We need to get this land and water into our system. But responsibly. We need these water resources, and we need them to work efficiently. We cannot afford to leave such important concerns in the land of the unknown unknowns.

There is also climate change to consider. Undeniably – though many still enjoy denying it – the coming century will see a reshaping of the international farming landscape. Some regions will be winners. Others losers. Some will find crop and livestock production will be far easier. We've heard anecdotal predictions of vineyards in Scotland.

Other areas will find that the increased environmental risks and scarcity of water mean that agriculture will be impeded, and may even decline. I make no predictions, but two things are certain, and should give some hope for the future. First, farmers have already dealt with a water crisis far greater than that which faces us as a result of climate change in the next fifty years. Yes, you have read that correctly. Climate change has penetrated the popular discourse in a way that science – particularly demography or water science – has not been able to previously.

Once something is embedded in the discourse, it gets discussed more and more. It self-perpetuates. In much the same way as a gossip item on the news works. Everyone is talking about an embarrassed celebrity, ergo let's talk about that celebrity and their embarrassing incident. And the reverse is also true. If something gets missed, it fails to be news, and becomes merely history. Such was the case with the demographic explosion of the second half of the twentieth century. Farmers faced increases in demand that far outstripped any future impact on global water resources resulting from climate change. Demographic policy is controversial, politically very risky and willingly kept off the public agenda. Think how hard it must be for a politician to sell demographic policy if they can dwell on the hotly debated issue of global warming. But farmers can handle the future problems resulting from rising temperatures. Next to demography, climate change is a modest challenge. Second, farmers are highly adaptive. They will adjust their capacities and respond to (and meet) the increased demand for food from all the regions of the world, but there are conditions. There need to be the correct economic and social incentives.

What are these?

Reliable demand is vital. Without this, farmers have to spread their risks in case of a commodity-price crash. The greatest yields are invariably achieved by farms

321

concentrating on a tight group of food products. Farmers also need reliable and safe markets. These basics are very important, and often ignored. Good roads from farms to urban markets are needed. Connectivity is essential. The mobile phone has managed to become affordable in developing economies, and we are already seeing farmers benefit from improved access to information about markets, both local and even overseas. Markets have to have facilities that effectively store perishable goods. Food is fragile. Record-breaking yields can easily turn into inedible mush if storage is not rodent-proof or refrigerated. Again, these are problems suffered most acutely and commonly by the already weak developing economies. Amazingly, losses between the farm gate and the market can be as high as 30 per cent when storage facilities are inadequate. Thirty per cent. Remember, we are only talking about a 40 per cent increase in demand at peak population. What would be the cost of mobilising 30 per cent more water in developing economies? It would be an implausibly expensive endeavour requiring unprecedented engineering ingenuity. What would be the cost of improving storage facilities and transportation with well-tried technologies? It would be very much less than mobilising 30 per cent more water. And the environmental impacts would be positive and not negative. But the human mind can't see the cheap and easy solution. I fear that we will hear governments and international agencies talking first about massive water-transfer projects before they realise that stopping food loss is far more achievable than finding new water.

The price of everything and the value of nothing

I am no acolyte of the free market, but markets are very important indeed. I believe that correct food pricing can promote better water efficiency, contributing to local and

global water security. So pricing food is one of the strongest weapons we have in the struggle to ensure we don't
dry up. Pricing is important to farmers – both rich and
poor, to agri-traders, to supermarket corporates and to
consumers. Politicians have to care about them. There
are two key considerations. From the perspective of this
analysis of water security, prices need to enable society to
be water secure. They need to capture the value of water.
Second, farmers need incentives to use water efficiently
by increasing yields in ways that do not impair the water
resources. There also needs to be a margin to protect the
farmer from environmental shocks. However, although
these things need to be done immediately, that is not how
the world works.

323

We need to step away from the world of science, where
a solution – in theory – follows hot on the heels of a problem. Politics has a different pace. Such changes can only
take place at a politically feasible rate. Politicians cannot
leap up and change the fundamentals of the longest, and
in some ways biggest, trade industry in the world.

Unfortunately, the prices of some of the most heavily traded commodities in this global market don't reflect
the costs of even the measurable inputs, let alone the
uncosted environmental value of water. In the middle of
the nineteenth century, Karl Marx highlighted the failure of capitalist markets to capture the cost of labour in
commodity prices. The fallout from this economic short-
coming was the spur to over a century of revolutions all
over the world. Capitalism has been similarly failing over
the environment. Labour had no voice. So the trade unions
and their political-representative parties were formed. The
environment has no voice either. Who speaks up for it? A
growing crew of activists and scientists.

Marx's insight was correct. The market has a fearsome
capacity to mislead consumers very dangerously by failing
to reflect the costs of inputs. It takes fierce efforts to cor-

324

rect this. History has proven this was the case with labour. Getting the environment on the agenda is an ongoing intensely conflictual process, and one that requires just as much effort, energy and passion. The storm is raging at global conferences, in the legislatures of the world and across the media. The market – as it currently functions – will never help us achieve a secure water future. The very opposite in fact. Left to its own devices, the outcome will be terrible. However, if those leading players in managing and regulating markets in both the private and public sectors can focus on developing a mechanism for reflecting properly valued input costs in commodity prices, then there is hope for society and its water environments.

There is another aspect to consider: the wider environment. We need to introduce price incentives that move farmers away from practices that have severe negative impact on our water and our atmosphere. We do not have bottomless credit with the earth. Crop and livestock production must be intensified. But this has to be done sustainably. I say this not because I'm a sandal-wearing nature-phile. I'm not. I live in the centre of one of the largest, densest urbanised areas in the history of humanity. And I like it. But if we intensify food production unsustainably, we are sowing the seeds of our own demise. Water is the limiting resource.

These incentives could be introduced immediately in the advanced economies. The popular discourse makes it politically feasible to 'green' our agricultural sector. The technology is available. The industry is robust enough. A slower pace would be required in developing economies, naturally.

Free for all

Achieving the impossible

Trade. It could be the answer to all our problems. But right now, this hard medicine is stopping us from recovering. If we were to integrate the poor rural economies of the world further into the current global trade structure, we would only be damning them to greater pain and exploitation. If the terms of international trade remain unfair, this would have a negative impact on the livelihoods of poor farmers, and in turn on the productivity of the vast volumes of water being used by them.

Fair trade might seem a trivial, trendy topic for a serious water scientist to be addressing. Is it not the stuff of magazine-format television and Sunday-supplement columns? How could a marketing fad bear any relation to the solid, real geopolitical issue of water security?

The answer is simple and definitive. The unfair terms of international trade constitute one of the major factors – arguably *the* major factor – preventing African farmers from improving their crop and livestock yields. Other economies have managed to double or treble their water productivity. Vast regions of sub-Saharan Africa, however, have been on the slide. Granted, other nations also suffer from pockets of low productivity. But in sub-Saharan Africa, levels are catastrophically low, lingering at around 1 tonne per hectare or even less.

Some counter this argument by blaming unreliable rainfall and poor soil fertility. I do not for a moment pretend these are not challenges. But they are challenges that have been met and conquered in other economies. The agricultural technology is there to combat poor soil. The water-management wisdom exists to mitigate unreliable rainfall. Other parts of the world have solved these issues. But let us delve deeper. FAO agronomists cite the consequences of droughts in Kenya and the southern

325

MIND THE GAP
The yield gap. Simply, this is the difference in productivity between experimental farms and real-life farms that lack the ideal technical, economic and social infrastructure of the experimental farm.

FOR THE ATTENTION OF...
FAO is an abbreviation you see frequently. But here we mean the Food and Agricultural Organisation (FAO) of the UN.

Horn of Africa as evidence that sub-Saharan yields cannot be brought up to the levels achieved in other areas of the world. However, a recent study circulated in the World Bank demonstrated a strong and clear relationship between productivity in rain-fed tracts in sub-Saharan Africa and proximity to an urban area and the availability of transport. The report talks of the considerable untapped potential of sub-Saharan agriculture. Its findings demonstrate that farms within four hours' travel of an urban area with a population greater than a hundred thousand people operated at roughly 45 per cent of their productivity potential. If that sounds a bit dire, then contrast that with farms more than eight hours away from such areas. They were found to be operating at about 5 per cent of potential productivity.

This would seem to support my assertion that what counts is the infrastructure and support: nature plays second fiddle to human ambition. If I am right, there is no reason that sub-Saharan Africa could not mitigate the problems of soil fertility and unreliable rainfall. It could do it, provided it was able to mobilise the necessary investment. Yet such investment will never be possible as long as the barriers to profitable international trade remain so monstrously high. These are human, economic problems, not problems of nature and climate.

Since starting to write this book the world has experienced a global financial crisis, preceded by the 2008 oil-price spike and associated spikes in food-commodity prices. These food-price spikes highlighted the potential for regional food insecurity – particularly in East Asia and the Middle East. The managers of sovereign wealth funds and major private-sector investors in the regions at risk of food insecurity have turned their attention to regions of the world with the potential to produce food and export food securely. Sub-Saharan Africa has become the focus. This region happens to have the highest proportion of

326

SOVEREIGN WEALTH FUNDS (SWFs)
These are the funds held by national governments. These funds are mainly generated from the export of oil and gas. Norway is a member of this privileged club. The others are mainly in the Gulf and elsewhere in the Middle East.

undernourished people in the world. And a poor record in the good governance which is the prerequisite of effective farming. The land-grabbing activities in sub-Saharan Africa that have reached the attention of the global media are very high-risk indeed.

These African economies need rural and farm investment. But such investment needs to be very carefully focused. The combination of new money with land and water and all the other inputs is an uncharted journey, both environmentally and politically. The prospect is very worrying, as a significant proportion of the inward investment is in the hands of public and private bodies that have seriously mismanaged their own land and water resources. Would you trust an enterprise – with speculation in mind – that has failed economically and failed spectacularly in the stewardship of its own precious waters to come and manage your very vulnerable and very limited water resources? That these incomers do not realise that it is water they are grabbing and not just land is from the point of view of this discussion, the most worrying feature of all. They are not interested in the 30 per cent or more of Africa that is deep waterless desert.

327

David and Goliath

Currently, international trade is dominated by the industrialised economies. Take a look at Figure 6.1 and take another look at Figures 2.4 and 2.5 (pp.54-55).

The figures clearly demonstrate that the overwhelming majority of trade in food commodities takes place between the industrialised nations. Virtual-water 'trade' is very much their world, and the developing economies barely get a look in. Even attempting the most reasonable scale I could for this graph, the asymmetry is grotesque.

Consider, I have been arguing that trade is the best means of remedying a nation's water deficit. The East Asian economies, for example, save water by having high

Figure 6.1 International virtual-water 'trade', showing the predominant exporting regions and major importing regions. *Source:* A.K. Chapagain and A.Y. Hoekstra (2003), *Water Footprints of Nations*, Delft: IHE.

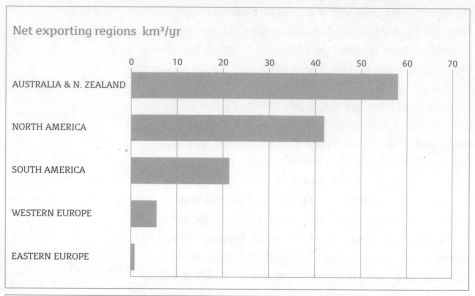

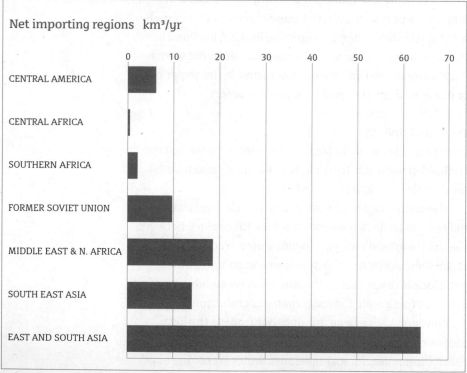

food imports. This frees up precious local water resources that can then be reallocated to higher-value economic activities, particularly the manufacturing sector. And to the environment. Trade makes economies wealthier and more water-secure. But who is playing the game? The industrialised economies run the show, with BRICS elbowing themselves into the action. The developing world is out in the cold. Either they are barely involved, or their economies suffer terribly from the dumping of below-cost food on their local markets.

Hold on there, you might now shout. That's all very well to talk about the suffering caused by the 'dumping' of cheap food on these developing economies, but don't starving bellies rely on these affordable imports? Well, yes. International food trade and emergency food assistance are essential for sub-Saharan Africa. They are also very damaging. Imagine a cancer patient caught between the disease and the chemotherapy treatment that both cures and kills with every dose. For humanitarian reasons, water-intensive food imports are essential during periods of drought. But they are economic poison, and undermine local efforts to improve water productivity. Palliative measures are necessary. But unlike cancer, we know that there is a complete cure for water scarcity, hunger and poverty. It is good national and global governance, socio-economic development – including the wise stewardship and productive use of land and water – and fair trade.

329

Starting to sum up

As we are reaching the moment at which we must conclude, I have little space to persuade you – if indeed unpersuaded you remain. The voices of poor farmers in the poorest economies of the world are easy to ignore: they are as unheard as the squeaks of mice in the hold of the *Titanic*. But they must be heard. Not just because natural justice demands it – it does – but because global water security depends on it too. We have had half a century of the highly productive farmers of the US and Europe – boosted by the best technical, market and social infrastructures in the world – dropping half-price staple grains into world markets. The price of wheat has been falling for a millennium. For the past two hundred years, since the industrial revolution, it has gone into a nose-dive. This has been made possible by the failure to incorporate the energy and water costs into the price.

Make trade fair. And save water.

330

The view from atop a combine harvester

A combine harvester is not the place for quiet reflection. As it booms its way through a Saskatchewan prairie, it is a rocky, restless, roaring sort of location. Yet it afforded me a gentle epiphany.

There I sat, and the landscape and the acres spread out before me with a blunt inevitability. Then it struck me. This inevitability was fathered by impossibility. Canada had no inviolable right to be an agricultural success. The climate and resources are very far from ideal. Indeed, in general, the environment of Canada is perhaps even less amenable to reliable farming than that of sub-Saharan Africa. Those who first ploughed the land a century ago faced an environment just as hostile.

Nor does Canada enjoy the pleasant distortions of farmer-friendly subsidies. It has no equivalent to the EU's CAP or US Department of Agriculture support. It plays the game of free trade fairly. And whenever you play fairly against cheats, you run a very high risk of losing, and losing hard. And yet Canada has not lost hard. In fact, as I sat upon this particular combine harvester, Canada was enjoying a record-breaking harvest.

How was this achieved?

Price. In industrialised nations, farming has evolved from a life of 'non-mechanised poverty and cycles of failure' to a cutting-edge industry able to stare down extreme environmental and economic shocks. And price is the most important device to drive productivity. Canada had exceptionally productive harvests in 2008 and 2009. But this wasn't the result of generosity on Mother Nature's part. The rains were reasonable, but noticeably late in 2009. Rather, the two years were typified by a serious price spike. This spike was the first since 1995, and its cause lay far outside the farming sector: high energy prices. Much was made of the economic havoc wreaked by the sudden, violent rise in fuel costs. But one positive was that it drove up grain prices. High prices promote higher levels of pro-duction, regardless of the environmental realities.

331

Yes, harvests fail. Memorably, the 2002 Canadian harvest was cataclysmic. Indeed, most farmers didn't even take their combine harvesters out into the fields in August and September that year. However, the industry is developed enough to hedge against such environmental disappointments. Canadian farmers can make arrange-ments with banks or – *in extremis* – the government to ensure that both they and the industry as a whole survive a tough period.

So it is that I found myself seated on a combine har-vester, looking out over endless fields of lentils and durum wheat. Those of us who hail from the small nations of Europe – of which the UK is one – can never escape the spatial conditioning of our birth and childhood. I grew up in the countryside of the north-east of England. It was verdant, lush and seemed to roll outwards to infin-ity in every direction. But you could lose the county of Northumberland in Saskatchewan and never find it again. You could easily misplace the entirety of the UK in Canada for quite some time. The Western European concept of space is not appropriate from a global perspective. My work has taken me to truly immense landscapes. For this, I am deeply grateful. My innate parameters for comprehending distance belong to someone raised on a small island. Sitting on the cab of the combine I was an old man. Regardless, the enormity of the Canadian prairies filled me with the excited awe of discovering an unknown place.

Gazing on this infinity of a huge family farm, I had then to imagine the distances that lay beyond the harvest. All these crops were destined for the Mediterranean and the Middle East, many thousands of miles away. Here before me was an implausible mass of land, water and crops, and the harvest was to travel half the world. And this breathtaking achievement, which would have seemed a fanciful impossibility less than a century ago, is now mundanely taken for granted. It is an accepted fact of life. Yet who could have predicted it? It is an impressive example of human organisational skill. The specific commodity needs of distant consumers, suffering extreme water deficits, are met by having their preferred and essential commodities grown on an almost completely depopulated landscape on the other side of the world. In this case, managed by farmers who have adapted to managing vast tracts of land and green water, as well as complex and specialised inputs. Not least they had learnt how to cope with financial risk and to deal with the global players such as the giant agritrader Cargill and the equally powerful seed and fertiliser corporates. Meanwhile the families in the Middle East like to think that their bread and their lentils are raised locally. I have checked.

332

Amazingly, Canadian prairies get very high, and increasing, returns to an annual rainfall of only 500 millimetres. How is it done? Energy is a big part of the answer. These farms are dependent on huge inputs of energy. These inputs are needed to mobilise the people and equipment required. The people are few in number, but are massively capitalised. A century ago, a quarter-section farm would have had the family, some draught animals and some basic cultivation equipment. And not much else. How different things are today. By 2008, the new palace in which the tractors, cultivating, sowing, fertilising and harvesting equipment were garaged and kept safe accounted for about US$3 million for a farm which had grown in the previous decades to about 7000 hectares. All of this is a farming miracle. It is also an energy miracle. The energy inputs make the harvesting, transportation and storage infra-structures very efficient financially. The bottom line is fine. Particularly if you are the farmer. Or – to an extent – the consumer. But the atmosphere worldwide bears the costs. We can't skip on this bill, and at some point – seemingly quite soon – nature is going to come to collect on the debt.

333

Over the past decade, Canadian prairies have seen an increase of 20 per cent in yields. That means the green water is being worked 20 per cent more productively. The biggest contributing factor to these recent yield improvements was the adoption of low-till methods of cultivation and seeding, along with the parallel development of herbi-cide technologies. Low-till methods have been around for over a century, but were mainly employed – and with great success – in the middle of the last century by Aus-tralia. On seeing the fruits of this approach, Canada has more recently followed suit.

DOING THINGS BY HALVES OR QUARTERS
When the US was settled, a section was a square mile, or 640 acres. A quarter section is simply a quarter of this: 160 acres.

Technology and energy unlock the potential of water. Although costly, these routes are cheap compared with trying to relocate physical water resources to the Canadian prairies. Water doesn't like to be moved: it prefers to go its own way. And green water does not object to being used effectively in the service of crop produc-tion provided the principles of water stewardship are not transgressed. The effective stewardship of blue water is much more difficult to achieve than for green water. This is because every year the green-water budget available to the farmer is fixed by nature. The farmer cannot make more rain. When farmers use blue water for irrigation they can pump surface water and groundwater to meet their needs, ignoring the plight of the river or the aquifer. Drought years tend to come in twos and threes. By the third year the blue-water flows and surface and ground-water reservoirs are seriously depleted. Farmers cannot overdraw the soil water. They readily overdraw their blue-water resources. As noted in an earlier chapter, wherever we irrigate we run out of water.

So it was, sitting on a mechanical beast of agri-industry, a speck in an endless plain of wheat, that I saw the reality of sustainable water intensification opening out before me. Tellingly, there was very little water involved at all...That which there was, was very well used.

334

But a little word of warning...

Perhaps I should just mention quietly that agriculture isn't really all that good for the environment. Generally, it impairs the blue-water services of the environment. Irrigation in particular makes whole tracts unusable. Incentivising farmers to raise production through fair and reliable pricing is vital. Ensuring that environmental considerations are all included in the economic equation is equally important. Sustainable intensification must be a two-part deal: we need to do more, but with less, and with less of a toll on the environment.

Low-till or no-till
Farming has its own parables on doing the wrong thing too well. European farmers encountered different environments when the northern European powers colonised the world in the late eighteenth century, and especially in the nineteenth and early twentieth centuries. The colonial powers tried to export as much of their culture and practices as was expedient and compatible with suppressing peoples

and occupying their lands. Often, those colonised absorbed these cultural, social and economic imports. Land, however, is far less pliant than people. Deep ploughing was the norm in northern Europe. This deep intervention was good for weed control, and the cold winters did other good things to the soil structure. In cold Europe.

These practices did not travel well to the colonies. They did not translate, and proved to be very damaging to soil, water and plant ecologies in these new territories. Here there were no cold winters. Weed control needed a different approach. Australian farmers were the first to spot the problem, and introduced equipment that merely scratched the surface and did not kill the valuable nitrogen-fixing – that is naturally fertilising – leguminous plants that co-existed with the main grain crop. These legumes were naturally occurring in some regions of the world. They have since been introduced into others. These low- and no-till approaches to crop production have increased yields, and have reduced energy inputs for cultivation and the costs of equipment. That's the good news. On the downside, they have required additional herbicide and related energy inputs. Every solution seems to have a wicked element to it. Only time can reveal how deep the wickedness runs. Perhaps in the future someone will be writing about some as-yet-undiscovered folly related to low- and no-till approaches.

335

A family business

The story of Cargill is one of those tales that could only be true in America. It is The Godfather, but with grains not guns. It begins, as do all great American legends, with a man. And a dream. William Wallace Cargill leaves his Wisconsin family home and buys a grain warehouse in Iowa, situated on the new-fangled railroad. The year is 1865. W.W. – as he soon becomes known – is an intelligent entrepreneur. His business grows rapidly, and by the end of the century Cargill has a network of grain storage and transportation links stretching through the Mid-West. A union – through marriage – with another great farming family, the MacMillans, strengthens the business further. Steadily, throughout the decades and the generations, Cargill grows and grows until now – after the first decade of the twenty-first century – it has an annual turnover of about $130 billion. And it is still family-owned, while turning over an income that would place it well up the league of national economies. And there are another four or so US family corporates in the same global game.

Cargill is incredibly powerful. No decision about international food trade, and certainly no decision made by the US government in this area, can be taken without its input. Privately owned companies are, by their very nature, private. To the outside world, they are at best opaque and at worst utterly unknowable. Further, when power and wealth accumulate without transparency or accountability, we have a tendency towards suspicion. Even us rather measured water scientists are not above such speculation. Cargill is a very well-run business indeed. Its morality is no more dubious than that of any other multinational corporate. Certainly, its objective is to make money. But it does want to do this by feeding the world, efficiently and as cost-effectively and profitably as possible. Granted, its motivation may be economics not morality, but the two are not mutually exclusive. Cargill was quick to react to the risks to its reputation posed by the concept of energy footprinting. It had to calculate the energy footprint of the company's grain production and the trade with which it is associated. It needed to do this and produce some figures before activists, opponents or rivals did it and spun a negative narrative. Cargill compiled the figures and responsively tweaked its policies. Not because it loves saving energy, but because it loves making money. And poor corporate reputation is a barrier to profits.

But while energy is a vital element in the Cargill supply chain, the company is a global giant when it comes to virtual-water 'trade'. At the time of writing, there is no public evidence that Cargill is at all aware that it handles a massive proportion of international virtual-water 'trade'. The penny, I feel, may just be dropping at Cargill (and other massive agri-businesses). I don't doubt that Cargill will move with lightning speed to capture the idea for its corporate interests. But until very recently the company was just as blind and deaf to the role of virtual water as the rest of us.

Players such as Cargill could be pivotal in the global stewardship of water. Its managers are as experienced in hedging the costs of inputs as the best in Wall Street. If they could be incentivised to be as watchful over the productivity of green and blue water, and especially watchful on the stewardship of water environments, we would all live in a much more water-secure world. Hopefully, the water needs of the world and the self-interest of a small number of very wealthy individuals will flow together. Heaven help us if they run in opposition.

337

Eat for victory

The problem

The figures quoted earlier on increased water-use efficiency were inspiring, were they not? In the last fifty years, our global water demand has trebled as a result of population growth. In the same fifty years, we have grubbed twice as much freshwater and used it as a blue-water (or irrigated) input into farming. We've also seen a four-fold increase in crop and livestock production. A lot of these improvements have been in the increasingly efficient use of economically invisible green water, which handily falls from the sky with great frequency.

Wonderful figures. Except they aren't. Looked at another way, they show a horrifying fact. We are caught in an unholy race to increase food output. What we are not doing is considering whether we should be producing that food in the first place. Here, as ever, we are doing the wrong thing very well, in fact, we are doing it more and more. Now it is time to stop.

It has begun to dawn on various different elements of society that there is something wrong in the way we produce, market and consume food. I am not here to make the arguments for health or animal welfare or climate change. There are serious and important arguments for all three. I am here to argue the case from the point of view of water security.

338

Now, as we conclude, we are back where our journey began. Remember, I caught your interest by asking you to guess the water content of your breakfast. It shocked you, I hope. Perhaps, at the time, it was simply too strange an idea for you to grasp. How, you may have asked yourself, can these things take so much water to produce them? Having circumnavigated the globe with me over these past few hundred pages, I hope you can make more sense of those opening claims. Think of all the places we've visited and all the ways in which we have seen water used – and abused. You might now have a working understanding of the virtual-water 'movements' and water footprint, and how these can enable us to compare the water content and costs of different commodities, corporations, individual consumers and whole economies. As a result, we have a working measure of water costs and a growing awareness of the tragedy that water is not valued according to its cost of delivery, never mind its environmental values.

It is time to start applying this measure practically and rigorously. Doing so should help us to augment our personal and our collective global food policies. If we recalibrate our approach to food, it can support, not under-mine, global water security. It can save not squander water. But it requires sacrifice. It requires belt-tightening. Real actual tightening of belts, as we all genuinely get a little bit slimmer. This diet-led reduction in girth will be very good for water-resource security.

Waist management

I began this chapter with three quotations. The second of these was from Dipak Gywali, a water guru based in Kathmandu, the third was from Rajendra Pachauri, the head of the IPCC. They coined two simple slogans for more environmentally appropriate diets: 'Down from five to two-point-five' and 'Down from seven to save the heavens.'

These mantras on food are easy to chant, but harder to adopt.

339

As 80 per cent of all water consumption goes into food production, nothing at all is as important as our food-consumption habits. Overnight, we could find almost all the extra water we need to meet the requirements of the peak population predicted for 2050. How? By going veg-etarian. That's all it would take. We would have solved the bulk of our water dilemma with four decades to spare. But we do not need to make such drastic changes. We could achieve most of the benefits for the water environment by a more measured transition.

As a keen observer of society and its embedded prefer-ences, I do not expect consumers to change behaviour quickly. A transition to more sensible eating with major impacts on water footprints can be achieved. Not all livestock rearing is bad for the water environment. Much meat production is carried out on rain-fed pastures on land that could not raise crops. On these tracts the soil water has no opportunity value – as the economists would put it – for any other productive use. Raising cattle and sheep – evolved to feed on grass – makes good sense to the farmer as well as to the nutritionist, to the steward of water resources and to the consumer. Note the absence of the agri-corporations and the supermarkets in this list. It is when livestock commodities raised on grass have to compete with meat and dairy products fed on grain, and especially on subsidised grain in intensive feedlots, that things go awry. These animals feed on commodities raised on land and water that could be producing grain and other crops for direct use by people.

If we could return to a system where the livestock products we consume are raised on grass, our water footprints would be benign and our health much improved. Meat would be more expensive, but since those that are over-consuming it should eat less, then pricing meat as a special food – even a luxury-food commodity – would help us to be more healthy. Cheap meat has proved to be very bad for our health. It was noted above that the agricorporations and the supermarkets do not fit the grass-fed livestock rearing model. They live in a world of competition, and drive the race to the bottom of cheap food. They are masters in synergising subsidised feed and industrialised livestock production, and in waging contract wars on the family farmer.

340

Cheap food: solution and problem

> *If you want cheap food, well here's the deal: family farms are brought to heel.*
> 'COUNTRY LIFE', STEVE KNIGHTLY

The food-producing, trading and retailing corporations hold the key to sane and sustainable water use and management. They could operate with a strong environmental-stewardship compass. But they are slow to adopt one. The reasons are obvious. A rapid shift to properly costed meat raised in ways that secure our water resources would require huge sections of the corporate agricultural sector to switch over to different products. It might take decades. Some businesses would be utterly destroyed: abattoirs and slaughterhouses, meat-packing factories, animal husbandry. Others would be altered beyond recognition. But truthfully, humanity has adapted to far larger and more problematic seismic changes. Consider the demands consequent on population increase, urbanisation and industrialisation, Once the changes have occurred, few contemplate the possibility of reversing the step. We have found new futures.

In this is the first of the mantras. The average daily water footprint of a heavy beef-eating human is 5 cubic metres per day. The average for a vegetarian is 2.5. 'Down from five to two-point-five.' Of course, both Gywali and Pachauri are realists. They have to be: they fraternise with politicians constantly. Sometimes in the glare of global press frenzy. In countries where there is a culture of heavy meat consumption, Pachauri urges switching to one meat-free day a week. Thus the second mantra: 'Down from seven to save the heavens.' We are fortunate that India, a very populous country, is predominantly veg-etarian in culture. We are also, cynically, fortunate that the two billion poorest people in the world cannot access cheap meat. It is a great worry, environmentally at least, that the poorest will progressively eat more meat as its price continues to drop in the face of ever-greater supply. Sadly this trend will almost certainly outweigh any of the benefits afforded by the people in the richer economies becoming more careful about their diet, and reversing the recent growths in obesity associated with meat-eating. Poor people in poor countries are more numerous than rich over-consumers in the industrialised world.

There is so much uncertainty. Oddly, perhaps the big-gest question is what will the people of India do? If greater affluence brings greater meat-eating there, as it seems to be doing in China, we are in for a rough ride. We also need to work on convincing the one and a half billion people living in industrialised economies to eat sensibly for them-selves and the planet. By which I mean most of the readers

341

of this book. I'm not going to tell you to stop eating meat. But I am definitely going to ask you to cut back. This is not a binary formula. It is not the case that either we manage our water perfectly or we are in complete chaos. Every little bit helps. An American heard Dipak's mantra for the first time in August 2008 after I had used it in a speech 24 hours after Dipak himself had coined it over dinner the previous evening. This American was walking beside me downstairs on this grand occasion, and asked knowingly, 'Listen Tony, would three-point-five do?' To which I replied, 'Of course.'

But cut back. And cut back now. It really does matter. More than anything else you as an individual can do. These food-consumption patterns affect 10–20 per cent of global water use. That will certainly make the difference between a world that is water-secure and one that is not.

342

Waste management

But it isn't just our diet about which we need to take more care. The way of getting food from producers to plates, and from there to our household waste bins, needs serious consideration. We are highly wasteful, particularly in the industrialised nations. In the advanced economies, we throw away approximately 30 per cent of food purchased. That is a terrible statistic. What a revolting tribute to our feckless, thoughtless selfishness. How can any society expect to survive if it is mindlessly discarding a third of its most precious resource? It perishes in cupboards. It goes off in fridges. It sits on the side of the plate before sliding into the dustbin. The developing economies have their parallel figure. They also lose around 30 per cent of their food, although, as mentioned earlier, this occurs between the farm gate and the market. One loss is the result of affluence; the other of poverty. At least poverty is its own excuse.

Never can waste be reduced to zero, or even near zero. But these current figures are unacceptable. The problems of the developing economies have already been discussed.

Investment and planning can solve these, just as these problems were solved in the rest of the world. The waste by households in the industrialised world is far more pernicious and insidious. It is not a question of fixing a problem by throwing thought and money at it. It requires a cultural shift. This is hard, but never impossible. If food wastage can become as unacceptable socially as drink-driving, beating children or doctors endorsing smoking, then we should be able to halve our waste. I use these examples advisedly. All three were perfectly normal in my youth. This shift then, can occur in under a lifetime. And it could save almost half the water we would need to find to meet the needs of an eight- or nine-billion-strong population.

343

The answer is in the shopping basket

There it sits. The water needs of our peak population future are there in our shopping baskets. It is possible for food consumers, producers and markets to solve the problem of water insecurity. It is within their gift. All this without a jot of greater water efficiency, without a single hydraulic project. Everything could be solved by such personal demand management approaches. What we eat and what we don't waste will enable us to be globally water secure. Switching from meat that is grain-fed will also improve our health, mitigate climate change and mean that we won't be exploiting and butchering so many animals.

The answer is simple. But where is the politician brave enough to champion it? How many more dams and water-transfer projects will be built before someone takes the stage to argue passionately for an international change of diet? I fear I may not be around to discover the answer.

The virtual-water gallery

Some useful numbers: your conversion table

METRIC MEASUREMENT		US IMPERIAL MEASUREMENT
1 litre (l)	→	2.113 pints (pt)
1 cubic metre (m³)	→	244.172 gallons (gal.)
1 giga-litre* (million m³)	→	810.71 acre-feet (ac/ft)
1 cubic kilometre** (km³)	→	810,713 acre-feet (ac/ft)

* 1 giga-litre is the same as a million cubic metres, which can be written as 1 mn m³. And it is also the same as one-tenth of a cubic kilometre, which can be written as 0.1 km³

** 1 cubic kilometre is the same as a billion cubic metres, which can be written as 1 bn m³. And it is also the same as 1 giga-metre, which can be written as 1 gm³.

US IMPERIAL MEASUREMENT		METRIC MEASUREMENT
1 pint (pt)	→	0.473 litres (l)
1 US gallon (gal.)	→	0.003785 cubic meters (m³)
1 acre-foot (ac/ft)	→	1233.5 cubic metres (m³)

COFFEE BEANS
21,000 litres per kg

PORK
4,800 litres per kg

LEATHER
16,600 litres per kg

HORSE
4,100 litres per kg

BEEF
15,500 litres per kg

GOAT
4,000 litres per kg

COTTON
11,000 litres per kg

CHICKEN
3,900 litres per kg

SHEEP
6,100 litres per kg

RICE
3,400 litres per kg

CHEESE
5,000 litres per kg

SOYA BEANS
1,800 litres per kg

MILLET
5,000 litres per kg

SUGAR
1,500 litres per kg

WHEAT
1,300 litres per kg

COFFEE
140 litres per cup

BARLEY
1,300 litres per kg

RED WINE
120 litres per glass

MAIZE
900 litres per kg

BEER
75 litres per glass

T-SHIRT
2,700 litres per T-shirt

APPLE
70 litres per apple

HAMBURGER
2,400 litres

BREAD
40 litres per slice

MILK
1,000 litres per litre of milk

TEA
30 litres per cup

EGG
200 litres per egg

A4 SHEET
10 litres per sheet

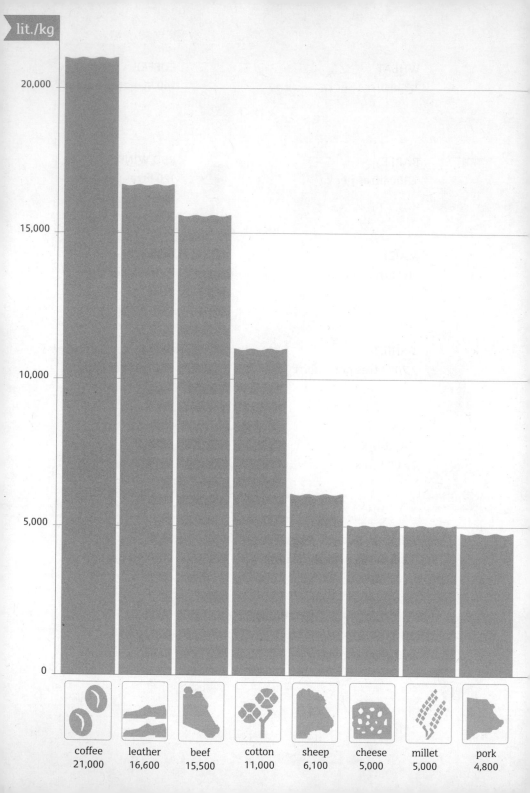

lit./kg

20,000

15,000

10,000

5,000

0

coffee
21,000

leather
16,600

beef
15,500

cotton
11,000

sheep
6,100

cheese
5,000

millet
5,000

pork
4,800

How much water does it take to produce one kilo of...?

Consider the virtual-water cost of beef for instance.

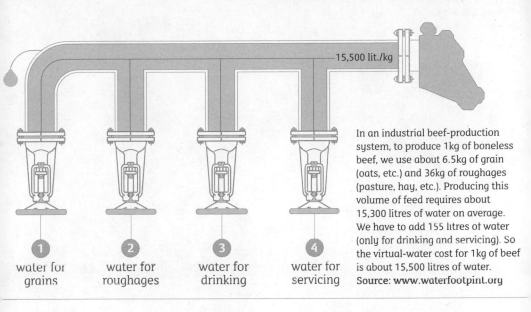

15,500 lit./kg

1. water for grains
2. water for roughages
3. water for drinking
4. water for servicing

In an industrial beef-production system, to produce 1kg of boneless beef, we use about 6.5kg of grain (oats, etc.) and 36kg of roughages (pasture, hay, etc.). Producing this volume of feed requires about 15,300 litres of water on average. We have to add 155 litres of water (only for drinking and servicing). So the virtual-water cost for 1kg of beef is about 15,500 litres of water. **Source: www.waterfootprint.org**

horse	goat	chicken	rice	soya beans	sugar	wheat	barley	maize
4,100	4,000	3,900	3,400	1,800	1,500	1,300	1,300	900

We drink and *eat* a lot of water.

The virtual-water cost of a product accounts for all the water used in producing it. Here you can compare the virtual-water costs for some familiar items of food and drink.

1 litre of milk
1,000 litres

1 egg
200 litres

1 glass of wine
120 litres

1 glass of beer
75 litres

1 slice of bread
40 litres

100

10

0

Area of the drops is proportional to the virtual water embedded in each product.

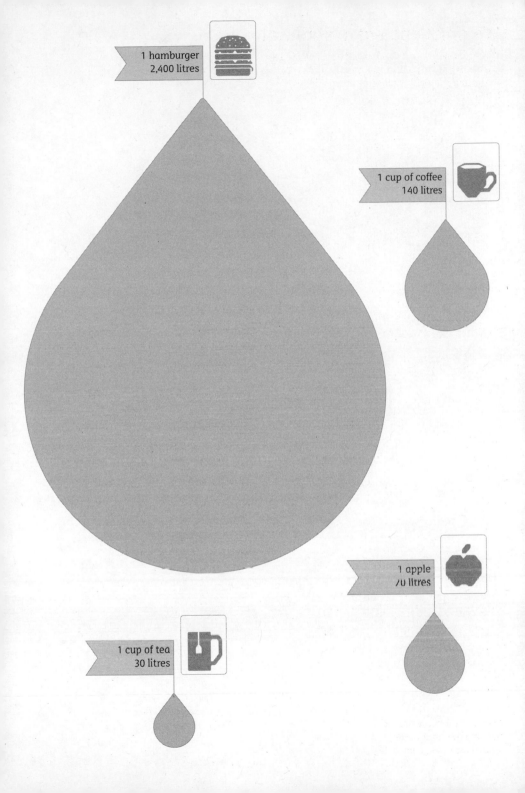

Index

357

359

361

363

365

366

367